SOCIALISM

AND

THE AMERICAN SPIRIT

SOCIALISM

AND

THE AMERICAN SPIRIT

BY

NICHOLAS PAINE GILMAN

Thet 's the old Amerikin idee,
To make a man a Man an' let him be.

The Animosities are mortal, but the Humanities live forever.

 BOOKS FOR LIBRARIES PRESS
FREEPORT, NEW YORK

First Published 1893
Reprinted 1971

INTERNATIONAL STANDARD BOOK NUMBER:
0-8369-5696-6

LIBRARY OF CONGRESS CATALOG CARD NUMBER:
70-150183

PRINTED IN THE UNITED STATES OF AMERICA

TO THE

RT. HON. JAMES BRYCE, M. P.

A SLIGHT SIGN OF THE GRATITUDE FELT BY MANY AMERICANS
TO THE AUTHOR OF

"THE AMERICAN COMMONWEALTH."

They steered by stars the elder shipmen knew,
And laid their courses where the currents draw
Of ancient wisdom channelled deep in law,
The undaunted few
Who changed the Old World for the New,
And more devoutly prized
Than all perfection theorized
The more imperfect that had roots and grew.
They founded deep and well,
Those danger-chosen chiefs of men
Who still believed in Heaven and Hell,
Nor hoped to find a spell,
In some fine flourish of a pen,
To make a better man
Than long-considering Nature will or can,
Secure against his own mistakes,
Content with what life gives or takes,
And acting still on some fore-ordered plan,
A cog of iron in an iron wheel,
Too nicely poised to think or feel,
Dumb motor in a clock-like commonweal.
They wasted not their brain in schemes
Of what man might be in some bubble-sphere,
As if he must be other than he seems
Because he was not what he should be here,
Postponing Time's slow proof to petulant dreams:
Yet herein they were great
Beyond the incredulous lawgivers of yore,
And wiser than the wisdom of the shelf,
That they conceived a deeper-rooted state,
Of hardier growth, alive from rind to core,
By making man sole sponsor of himself.

James Russell Lowell.

PREFACE.

A NOTED author has urged the appointment in some leading university of a "professorship of America." He would like to see there one man whose special business it should be to teach the students "that there is such a reality as American thought, that there are certain principles which belong to the American government, that there are certain feelings which are experienced by none but an American, such customs as American customs, . . . and that there has grown up a social order which is distinctively American." Rev. Dr. Hale repudiates, of course, the notion that science is one thing in Europe and another in the United States. American economics has no more existence than Belgian physics or Spanish chemistry. But the main point is beyond dispute. There is "a social order which is distinctively American." It has been woven on the roaring loom of time by the American spirit. In these days when, as Mr. George Jacob Holyoake has said, the social question "is not only in the air, it fills the air," I have thought that a place is still open in an abundant literature for a discussion of the American answer to socialism.

This volume is not a history or exposition of modern socialism. Many matters that usually go to fill works on the general subject will be found conspicuous for their absence, and much is taken for granted, as already familiar to the reader ordinarily well acquainted with the existing literature. My one object is the treatment of a special aspect of socialism, — its standing and its probable future in the United States. America has much to learn from Europe, but sheer imitation of the Old World by the New is by no means a duty. The American socialist, however, is quick to assume that a governmental telegraph is advisable here because the system is reported to work well in England, and that national railways should be adopted in America because they are found in France and Germany. But the great differences in natural conditions and political institutions forbid such easy conclusions. A nation spread over an enormous area may well pause before copying a governmental telegraph or railway system from comparatively small and compactly settled countries like Great Britain and France. A constitutional republic of federated States may well pause longer before adopting an economic novelty from an empire like Germany. The deeper inquiry is pertinent, whether the spirit of the American people is consonant with such methods, and whether it gives reason to prophesy the spread of socialism as a guiding principle. Such an inquiry as to socialism under American conditions and confronted by the American spirit may be of sufficient interest and consequence to justify the existence of a volume which it is a happiness to be permitted to dedicate to James Bryce.

It has seemed desirable, in the first place, to give a little precision to the much abused terms "individualism" and "socialism." Each of these, strictly taken, denotes an ideal which never has been realized, and in all probability never will be. Conceived more loosely, as permanent tendencies in human nature which vary in the intensity of their expression from time to time, both have their justification. The present drift of many thoughtful minds is plainly toward socialism, in the general sense of an expansion of the powers of government — local, State, and national — beyond the sphere in which they have heretofore operated. The leading topic of this book is the American Spirit as it has been manifested in our history, and is now compact in our institutions, and expressed in the life and literature of the present. I consider the American temper only so far as it bears upon the two social theories, not in the least supposing that I have exhausted the subject.

Such a determination of the American attitude naturally leads to an exposition and criticism of the two forms of socialism attracting the most notice in the United States to-day. The first of these is so largely literary in its origin and its activity that one might well designate it "romantic socialism" rather than by the inappropriate name of "nationalism." In considering Christian Socialism, I have compared it with its English forerunner in 1848, and have tried to answer the fundamental question of the relation of the social teachings of the New Testament to modern civilization. I assume here, as elsewhere, in this work, that the economic unsoundness of scientific socialism has been sufficiently demonstrated by such writers as Professors Böhm-Bawerk, Marshall and Graham, and Mr. Rae.

Gladly turning to more constructive work, I next consider some industrial changes and reforms which would tend to correct the present bias toward individualism. Among these, the closer union of employer and employee still seems to me one of the most important and most feasible. The argument for industrial partnership here given is directed against objections which received little attention in my volume on profit sharing. The considerable progress which the system has made in the last four years is briefly summarized. The comparatively large amount of space devoted to profit sharing should not lead the reader to infer that I consider it a panacea for industrial troubles. This chapter may serve, rather, to counterbalance the necessarily general treatment of other subjects in this work. The social problem yields most surely to the exertions of specialists working on different lines. Legislation is one of these lines, but only one; the governing powers in America need purification to-day, rather than an enlargement of their field; a variety of political reforms should precede much extension of the functions of the State.

A higher individualism and a social spirit are at the heart of our progressive civilization, the meaning of which I endeavor to point out. They make their strongest appeal to those who reject the name of "socialist," since they believe the socialistic ideal a thing as little to be desired as it is to be expected in a world of reality. The way to Utopia we must all, none the less, be traveling; it lies, for no small distance, over the difficult road of moral improvement. Economic science, individual culture and the social spirit, — all have claims upon us. May my readers find here some help toward a practical solution of the apparent opposition of these demands.

N. P. G.

West Newton, Mass.
February 16, 1893.

CONTENTS.

SOCIALISM

AND

THE AMERICAN SPIRIT.

CHAPTER I.

INDIVIDUALISM AND SOCIALISM.

TWENTY years ago a leading matter of debate among thoughtful people in the English-speaking world was "the reconciliation of Science and Religion." Peace between these forces has been practically attained, after much discussion, through the recognition of the simple fact that each holds a rightful place in human nature. Neither can be accepted as representing the entire compass of our being, nor should either be denounced by the other. Religion and Science are still vigorous and intact after the long and eager debate. The one power seriously injured was the dogmatic spirit, exemplified equally in theologians destitute of scientific training or method, and in natural scientists ignorant of philosophy and theology. Now that the dust of this controversy is settled, it should be plain to all that neither Science nor Religion can suffer real harm from the other. It is as plain that no "reconciliation" is needed, if each power will put away dogmatism, and be content to rule supreme over its part of that human nature which includes both, and much more than both, in its

largeness and complexity. The adjustment of knowledge and faith in the creed and the practice of
generations and individuals must be left, where it
belongs, with each generation, with each individual, as
life gives enlightenment.

At the present day, another pair of supposed com-
batants concentrate upon themselves the attention of
civilized mankind in a large degree. The "social
problem" which deeply occupies the mind and heart
of our time is essentially the issue between Individualism and Socialism. Are the two reconcilable, or
must one be preferred to the other by progressive
races? Voices are not wanting to tell us that there
is no half-way house between State Socialism and
Anarchy, — between an enormous extension of the
functions of the State on one hand, and a virtual
abolition of State control on the other. The ears of
them that will listen are filled with the cries of extremists who unite only in denouncing the actual
order, employing a rhetoric and a logic which pay
little heed to reason, and a sentimentality that has
small concern for the laws of economics or the fundamental realities of human nature. When they occasionally give attention to each other, the Socialist has
little difficulty in showing that the Anarchist is a sentimentalist of the future, who dreams of an impossible
race of men needing no constraint, since they have
arrived at perfect virtue and entire reasonableness:
the Anarchist has no more difficulty in demonstrating
that the Socialist is a sentimentalist of the present,
far astray in supposing that the majority of men can
safely be trusted with extreme power over the minority.

Meantime, the man of scientific temper cannot recognize in the ideal picture drawn by the Socialist or by the Anarchist a natural development from existing society. He is altogether unable to perceive why the human race should be given up to exclusive control by the principle of Authority or by the principle of Liberty. These two principles have blended, in various degrees, throughout human history; and if to-day, as ever before, "only law can give us freedom," freedom only can give us law. The meliorist and the optimist must reject with decision the irrational denunciation by Socialist and Anarchist of the present order of things, which they declare incapable of improvement except by revolution. One may easily discover the fundamental pessimism underlying the superficial trust in human nature (in the future) professed by these two classes of extremists, — those who would free mankind from all control by government, and those who would give the majority unlimited power over the minority. If human society is now so evil as to need complete transformation, after thousands of years of life on this planet, where is the just foundation for hope that all will be well under any scheme, since this is to be administered, of necessity, by the same human nature? The scientific spirit, on the other hand, joins with practical philanthropy in declaring a deep faith in the ability of mankind to improve its lot upon earth through the method of evolution. The development may now be conscious to a great degree; reason can accelerate that "unreasoning progress of the world" of which Wordsworth speaks; but, in all probability, the forward movement will be on lines already found to be practicable, toward an ideal the equal of which no theorist has yet conceived.

The word "compromise," which will at once be spoken with profound disdain by many, is seen to be out of place when the philosophic mind perceives the truth that is in Socialism and the truth that is in Individualism, and advocates a course in accordance with impartial insight. No man sees by a "compromise" between his two eyes; no man walks by a "reconciliation" between his two feet; no man works by adjusting a "truce" between right hand and left hand. The two eyes, the two feet, the two hands, are parts of one and the same body: they are under the high direction of one and the same mind. So human society includes the Socialist and the Individualist. It has never been under the complete control of either: it never can be and remain both "society" and "human." It will continue to take from either, in every specific time, good counsel for the day and generation.

The dispute concerning Science and Religion lost most of its bitterness when the contestants came to understand better the nature of both forces; when they at length appreciated the fact that neither can cast out the other from complete human nature, and that the only "reconciliation" needful or advisable is attention to its own sphere on the part of each! The existing controversy between Socialism and Individualism concerns material interests of vast importance, as well as great issues of thought and feeling; yet, however this fact may tend to prolong the discussion, the result can hardly be different from that reached in the more speculative debate between Science and Religion — a better understanding of the rights of each in the totality of human life. The problem in each particular case is to determine the advantage and disadvantage, to individuals and to society, of a proposed measure for industrial, social or political change. Some general considerations at the outset may aid in the just determination of such instances. Let us then, at the risk of commonplace, make clear to ourselves three important meanings of the two words at the head of this chapter: we may thus be able to rule out significations of Individualism and Socialism which are not germane to our discussion and serve only to confuse.

I. The subsistence of each human being as a distinct entity is the primary individualism. It implies physiological, intellectual and moral independence. Existence as a separate person, the life of which must be preserved by means of food and clothing and shelter directly appropriated; which should receive a training of its mental faculties and should have a moral character of its own, — this is the ineradicable nature of *Homo sapiens*. He can never merge himself in another personality, and cease to be an individual of his species. But he may live in contact, more or less close, with the other individuals who comprise, with himself, the entire number of the species living upon this earth. Next in force to the imperious instinct of self-preservation is the instinct which compels the preservation of the kind; and this implies the society of man and woman. Human beings who completely deny the social and the sexual claim, seeking the desert or the forest to live a purely individual life, — so far as this is possible, — have always been a slight and exceptional minority of the race. The mass of men have ever lived in sexual relations; whatever form these might take, they have constituted a social bond of some kind, and rendered complete individualism — life by one's self — impossible.

The position, indeed, that the family, not the individual, is the unit of human society is in harmony with most of the known facts of the social development. The family produces the individual, rears him to the age of self-defense, and, in all but the lowest stages of human life, retains a hold upon him to the end of his days. Complete individualism from the first breath to the last is practicable for no human being. No man has ever desired it in whom human nature had a normal evolution. The social instinct, which Man shares with the other animal species, is deep-rooted in his being, and is reinforced by innumerable motives, of an intellectual and moral order, which the brute can never feel. We are under it, every hour, "the natural law which will have it that the species 'man' cannot subsist and prosper but by association. Whatever else we may be in creation, we are, first and foremost, at the head of the species which are called by instinct and led by necessity to the life of association." The only individualism possible for a man who respects his own nature is within the limits of society. In the broadest sense of the terms, we exemplify, every day, a natural individualism embraced in a necessary socialism.

II. The individual, living in the social state and profiting by it every hour, may make himself the "number one" for which he very carefully provides at all times, or he may recognize his position as one of many members. He may, after the manner of most, practically shape his life by the maxim, "Each for himself," or he may adopt the wiser rule, "Each for all, all for each." The individualism of the former course is stigmatized as "selfishness" by all moral teachers. So common as to be considered by some the root of all wrong, — as when they say that "Self is Sin," — selfishness is often confounded with a due and proper care for one's own welfare, for which, obviously, each person can, on the whole, care best, and for which he is justly held responsible. "Self-hood" — a term of which Dr. Orville Dewey well suggested the revival — marks precisely this natural and fit single existence and activity of each human being: like "boyhood" or "manhood," it denotes a great fact of human life, not to be set down as wrong or right, since it is fundamental, beneath all moral distinctions.

"Selfishness," the exaggeration of "selfhood," is, of course, far more common than "self-neglecting," although the latter is not so rare an offense as moralists generally suppose. Consistent egoism in moral practice is a fallacy as great as "solipsism" in metaphysics, — the doctrine that nothing exists but one's self, — to which in logical science the name "individualism" is, indeed, given. To view one's self as the central reality is a mistake to which all men are exposed in various degrees, so strong has Nature made the self-regarding instinct. Such individualism is the proper theme of the moralist; I advert to it here mainly to point out that we should not carry over into the sphere of economics and politics the moral judgments which are entirely proper in discussing the "individualism" which is equivalent to "egoism" or "selfishness." There is a sociability as well which must not be confounded with benevolence, and deserves no praise, in itself considered, as it is simply a natural craving.

In the world of economics and politics, Individualism has a distinct meaning as a name given to the "theory of government which favors the non-interference of the State in the affairs of individuals." Obviously, this is a principle or doctrine which one may hold consistently with the most hearty desire and effort for the good of others. The common welfare being the object to be reached, the question is of the best means for attaining it. The judgment to be pronounced on any person for holding that individual effort is this best way, is, properly, a purely intellectual matter. One gives no sign of immorality, no indication of selfishness, if he expresses distrust of the fitness of Socialism — in the general sense of a "theory of government which favors the interference of the State in the affairs of individuals " — to promote the general welfare, and prefers the method of Individualism. A belief in Socialism as the most advisable method, on the other hand, is no proof of the moral unselfishness of any person. He may have embraced this opinion from thoughtlessness, from sentimentality, from any one of a hundred varieties of unreason. His personal adhesion can be judged to have moral quality only when acts of self-sacrifice accompany it, and purely on account of these. A very selfish person, of the most pronounced despotic vein, may preach Socialism as the one proper theory of national construction. The most unselfish of men, assiduous for the common welfare, may hold that Socialism is economically impracticable and ethically undesirable. At the start, therefore, we should put away decisively a common assumption of the Socialist, — however often it may be unconscious, — that the Individualist is such because of the selfishness of his character. The only species of individualism which deserves moral condemnation is the practical sort which pays very little regard to the general welfare. Confusion and fallacy must result from passing moral judgments upon Individualism and Socialism when put forth simply as economic and political theories. If the former may serve as a cloak for selfish unconcern for the common good, the latter may likewise be a convenient substitute for personal effort. "Egoism" is an illegitimate connotation of economic and political individualism: "self-forgetfulness" is an equally illegitimate connotation of socialism in the same field.

III. When we attempt a stricter definition of Individualism and Socialism as economic theories, to the carrying out of which certain political institutions are necessary, we find that Socialism is the more easily denoted of the two terms. This probably arises from the circumstance that such Socialism is still chiefly a theory, while the opposite Individualism is largely a fact of the existing order: it is usually easier to define a theory than to describe a condition. This Socialism is a scheme for an ideal industrial state, never yet realized; it is put forward as likely to be a vast improvement on the actual order of civilization, which, in all its varieties, is usually designated in contrast as Individualism. "The economic quintessence of the socialistic programme," according to Dr. Albert Schäffle, who is generally recognized as speaking with authority here, is "a method of production which would introduce a unified (social or 'collective') organization of national labor, on the basis of *collective or common ownership of the means of production* by all the members of the society. This collective method of production would remove the present competitive system, by placing under official administration such departments of production as can be managed collectively (socially or coöperatively), as well as the distribution among all of the common produce of all, according to the amount and social utility of the productive labor of each."[1] Again, he says more briefly: "*The Alpha and Omega of Socialism is the transformation of private and competing capitals into a united, collective capital.*"[2]

In contrast with the precision of these two definitions of Socialism, the definition of Individualism already given from the "Century Dictionary" — "The theory of government which favors the non-interference of the State in the affairs of individuals" — seems vague. We shall do well, therefore, to define the term again, in exact contrast with the words of Dr. Schäffle. Economic Individualism would then be the system of production by means of private capital (held by single persons, firms, corporations or coöperative associations): this method of production demands a free labor-contract, open competition, and distribution to individuals. The Alpha and Omega of individualism is, accordingly, private and competing capitals, with a large measure of individual freedom from State control.

As a matter of fact, however, the complete antithesis of State Socialism is scientific Anarchism, — the doctrine that all interference of the State with the individual is unadvisable, and that the State — in the sense of Government — should be abolished. The actual condition of civilized man in the modern State is, of course, the logical negation of anarchy, and the institution of private capital is everywhere recognized,

---

[1] *The Quintessence of Socialism.* By Dr. A. Schäffle. English edition, p. 4.

[2] *Ibid.* p. 20.

in opposition to Socialism. But each existing government differs from every other in the degree to which it intervenes in the affairs of individuals. Thus, as a practical matter, the doctrine of Individualism professed in any given country has respect much more to specific proposals for enlarging the present degree of State ownership or control, than to a complete denial of the right of government to control at all. The individualist will reject *in toto* the quintessential doctrine of socialism that *all* the means of production should be owned by the community; but he is, practically, known rather by his opposition to specific measures which would extend the functions of government as it is. The declaration, that "Government is a necessary evil," should be a sure indication of the anarchist, contemplating the present state of things, rather than of the individualist; but, in fact, it is a maxim with thinkers like Mr. Herbert Spencer who reject anarchism and profess individualism. "Government is a necessary good" is the natural belief of the socialist, but it can also be professed as a creed by all opponents of anarchism, even by those who would grant to the State but a limited measure of control over the individual: within those limits State control might well be good, and often only good.

If we attend chiefly to the facts of the existing situation in the United States, we should, then, consider Individualism and Socialism as two opposite *tendencies*, moved by either of which an American citizen may advocate or attack a definite and particular measure of legislation. The Utopia of the individualist, if Mr. Herbert Spencer may speak for him, is an approach to anarchy: the Utopia of the Socialist

melts into communism. But neither scheme is proposed for immediate adoption here by sensible advocates. Specific measures tending to enlarge the present field of State action — such as fuller control or
ownership by government of the telegraph and the
railway, or the shortening of the hours of labor by
statute — make up the programme of the socialist of
to-day; he welcomes support of any such measure by
those who are far from accepting or desiring it because it is a step toward the full realization of the
socialistic ideal. He criticises the existing State for
not going far enough in positive legislation for the
general welfare. From principle, he supports every
proposed law which would have the effect of enlarging
the functions of government, and, so far, restricting
the activity of the individual, bent on his own welfare
alone. The socialist feels sure that the result of each
experiment of this kind will be so satisfactory that
further steps in the same direction will follow, one by
one, until the expediency of the complete plan of
State production will at length be conceded by the
great majority. He does not often take into serious
consideration the probability that the extension of
State control which is desirable at any given time is
limited; or the further probability that, at some stage
of the progress toward the ideal, assumed to be necessary, the opposite tendency toward a fuller assertion
of individualism will set in, and give the onward
movement of society quite another direction. If in
these United States, for instance, the National Government should erelong operate the telegraph as it
now does the mail system; if the National Government or the various States should afterwards buy up
all the railways and run them at cost; if, contempo-

raneously, tne cities of the whole country should take
into their hands the manufacture of gas and electric
light, and assume ownership of the street-railways —
it is plain that, if all of these measures were successful, the movement to establish the State as the one
capitalist and producer would acquire far greater
strength than it now has. But it is entirely conceiv-
able that the limit of the profitable extension of the
functions of government might be soon reached, and
that the success of some of the undertakings mentioned would be so moderate as to discourage the
people from proceeding farther in this direction.
That the progress of human society is on one straight
line, under the control of one predominant force, and
that this force is the tendency to State Socialism, is
the fundamental assumption of the Socialist.

The Individualist, on the contrary, in all his degrees, tends to unfavorable criticism, not to high
admiration, of the manner and the results of governmental activity at present. He concedes that a nation
may well tolerate a certain degree of inefficiency on
the part of its officials in executing their present
tasks, this being, on the whole, more endurable than
the evils which would result from putting the same
duties upon private persons. He opposes, however,
any considerable further extension of the sphere of
the State, and looks to education of the individual
mind and conscience and to general progress for relief
from existing evils. The extreme individualist would
not only resist the tendency to socialism, but would
also retrace some steps already taken in that direction, as he would say, such as universal free education. There are very few, to be sure, in America who
hold the creed with such rigor. The practical effort

of those who here accept the name of Individualist is
to maintain the actual status against the strong tendency toward socialism which characterizes the time.
If this can be successfully resisted, they trust to
gradual enlightenment to weaken gradually the power
of the State. The anarchistic ideal, into which extreme individualism blends, is not to be reached by
crying and striving. The individualist trusts in natural law and in the unforced evolution of society: he
exerts himself with more or less energy simply to resist efforts contrary to this law which tend to promote
an artificial development. He does not often concede
the probability that such individualism as is well for
the society of one age may be unfitted to the free
development of the society of a later age. The present tendency toward socialism he would explain as a
reaction toward primitive ideas which have long since,
for the wiser minority, been fully exploded by experience. He stands stubbornly on the defensive against
this tendency, feeling sure that, unchecked, it can
only result in great evil.

Between the apparent fanaticism of the extreme
socialist and the patent Philistinism of the extreme
individualist, there is sufficient standing ground for
the great body of human beings who would not govern their lives by one hard-and-fast theory, but will-
ingly confess that mankind is influenced by many
forces, that progress is a resultant from the diverse
action of these, and that the appeal is always open to
experience, — the teaching of the past and trial in
the present. In the actual situation such a party of
"animated moderation" neither desires nor attempts
a theoretical "reconciliation" between the Anarchist
and the Communist, between the extreme Individual-

ist and the full-fledged Socialist. The reflective
"opportunist" prefers to follow the statesman who
adapts legislation to the needs of the day, rather than
the enthusiast or the Bourbon. He knows that progress is rendered more secure if action is preceded by
the fullest discussion between extremists; this he
accordingly welcomes, but he reserves ample right to
criticise each extreme as irrational in theory and impracticable in fact, unless qualified by the other. He
will calmly bear any amount of reproach from the
typical individualist or the thorough-going socialist,
for being a "trimmer," a "compromiser," or an
"empiric." Such reproaches are the natural portion
of those who strive to form a philosophic idea of
human progress through sincere submission of the
mind to the teachings of history and the counsels of
moderation.

The argument of this volume is that what may be
properly called "the American Spirit" allows to both
Socialism and Individualism their due weight, and
that it has shown a path between the two extremes of
paternalism and "administrative nihilism" which the
American people, at least, may well continue to
follow. It is a spirit, we may say here, at once humane and practical, conservative and progressive,
hospitable to ideas and acute in criticism of their
working in the concrete. Three later chapters will
be devoted to a necessarily imperfect exposition of its
contents, so far as social problems are concerned. I
desire now to emphasize the humaneness of this spirit
in its attitude toward extreme theories of individualism, and, in the next chapter, to make a general estimate of the present tendency to socialism from the
practical standpoint of the same temper. How far

in actual life the American Spirit will go, in the immediate future, toward accepting the proposals of State Socialism, and how far it will rely upon the method of individualism, is the concrete problem toward answering which the remaining pages of this book may afford some instruction not altogether vain.

In the midst of the world-wide agitation of the social problem, the primary disposition of the susceptible, lively and curious American intellect is unmistakable. The American is as alert to hear or tell any new thing as the ancient Athenian. Whatever may be the application of an idea to his own circumstances which he will finally make, his hospitality to the idea itself is generous. His readiness is such as to deceive the foreign-born thinker, who will calculate from the sale of hundreds of thousands of copies of a socialistic romance that there must be a million or two of convinced socialists in the United States. Such arithmetic only amuses the American himself, thus asked to translate simple intellectual curiosity into difficult practice. But he would be quite other than himself did he not largely sympathize with the humane temper which is responsible for much of the socialistic agitation of the time, and desire to understand fully the programme of action put forward. The American means to keep up with the times and the progress of thought.

The most characteristic feature of the intellectual movement of the last few years is its rejection of the individualism of the preceding generation and its attraction to socialism. In one form or in another, Socialism, when roughly defined as the doctrine that the welfare of all deserves first consideration, is commending itself more and more strongly to thoughtful minds of the present generation. Individualism, if loosely held as the doctrine that the welfare of the single human being should be of engrossing importance to himself, is distinctly losing its hold upon the intelligence of civilized mankind. Socialistic movements are prominent in every country where the modern spirit can be said to have penetrated. Imperial Germany, republican France, constitutional England, and democratic America are filled with the discussion, as well as despotic Russia. A spirit of discontent has come to weigh most heavily, indeed, upon the citizens of the countries that secure the largest measure of civil freedom and political rights to all. The prevailing mood of civilized man is one of disillusion. He has waked from dreams of the perfect happiness to be found in every person's doing what he pleases, limited only by the liberty of every other person to do the same, to face the hard realities of a world where utmost freedom is *not* utmost bliss. The old world of status has disappeared before successive onslaughts of the champions of contract, preaching the gospel of free competition as a cure for every ill that social man is heir to. But the generation which has seen the most unlimited competition known to history, and listened, with what satisfaction it might command, to the proclamation of the "struggle for existence" as a sufficient philosophy of human life, has witnessed a popularization of the most demoralizing of ethical doctrines. The pessimism that seems a natural outgrowth of the hot climate and the rank fertility of India which, as De Quincey said, make "man himself a weed," is a strange exotic in the temperate zone, where the manly Teuton blood has been wont to thrill with the joy of combat. That despair of life to which Schopenhauer first gave notable expression in Europe, that deep-seated conviction of the inability of existence to satisfy human desire which underlies Indian religion, has spread a blight over many choice minds of the most virile of civilized races. Apart from pessimistic theory, an intense and general discontent with many realities and some plain tendencies of modern civilization, free and democratic as it is, has begun to find expression in public opinion and in formal legislation, rudely breaking down many of the most sacred privileges of a jealous individualism.

The recent change of attitude toward the State, — from suspicion, and even hostility, to hope and even confidence in its power of help under present evils, — is most marked in England, where numerous statutes have embodied the spirit of "paternal legislation," once the *bête noire* of British economists. If in America there seems to be less of such change, one important reason is that we had already embodied in our institutions a strong social element which easily advances toward more distinct expression, as public opinion tends to remove more and more from practical individualism. The citizen of the United States does not need to be convinced that the State may go very much farther than mere self-preservation, and have as much justification for its course as the individual. Under civilization, men and women are not content with the coarse necessities of animal existence; they will have comfort, beauty, luxury even, for mind and body. "The theory of life which regards a scramble for the means, first, of subsistence, and afterward of luxury, as the proper business of man; the theory of politics which allows

to the State only the task of keeping order among
such high-spirited competitors, — these theories dismay us by confounding the conditions of social with
the conditions of animal growth; for the doctrine of
self-help suffices our animal nature. Hunger, lust
and vanity are strong enough to satisfy themselves,
and the work of trying to do it for them would be
endless; but, with our social perfection, it is otherwise. There mutual assistance, not self-help, is the
law; there we are all members of one another; there
each finds his well-being in the well-being of all."[1]

In such a position we must recognize the spirit of
civilization, of humanity, of Christianity. There is
too common a disposition to treat politics, economics
and ethics according to a pseudo-scientific method,
which learnedly compares the habits of the inferior
animals and seems to reduce man to their level by
omitting the specially human elements of his developed nature. This method will assuredly soon lose
its unreasonable vogue in a rejuvenescence of humanity; and this means a refreshment, in the mind of
civilized man, of such ethics as Paul and Jesus taught.
The humane doctrines of membership in the body
social, and brotherly kindness, which pervade the New
Testament, are infinitely higher, as they are infinitely
truer to the properly human life of man, than the
doctrine of the natural struggle for existence and the
untempered rage of pure competition, falsely supposed
to be the choicest outcome of modern wisdom.[2]

---

[1] *The Limits of Individual Liberty*, by F. C. Montague, p. 176.

[2] Sir S. W. Baker thus writes : "In every direction we see a
struggle for existence; the empty stomach must be filled, therefore one species devours the other. It is a system of terrorism
from the beginning to the end. The fowl destroys the worm,

The order and precedence of things it concerns us deeply to know have been strangely mistaken by many who are called scientists, but who, in respect to the most vital life of man, are more properly esteemed sciolists. The latest knowledge acquired by man, far from being necessarily the most important, is often the most easily dispensable. Knowledge of physical nature, precise enough to deserve the name of science, was a very much later acquisition of mankind than the very considerable knowledge of human life and character which has come down to us from remotest antiquity. Every one is aware of this truism; but only a few seem mindful that this was so because knowledge of man has always been, is now, and, in all probability, will always be, of more weight and consequence to us than the most astonishing developments of natural science. Because of their absolute necessity to society, the fundamental rules of right living were very early discovered and widely acted upon. Acquaintance with the laws that dominate human intercourse preceded by thousands of years the scientific perception of outward nature. Justice was known and appreciated — "more beautiful than the morning or the evening star," Aristotle declared —

the hawk destroys the fowl, the cat destroys the hawk, the dog kills the cat, the leopard kills the dog, the lion kills the leopard, and the lion is slain by man. Man appears upon the scene of general destruction as the greatest of all destroyers, as he alone in creation wars against his own species. We *hear* of love and pity, and Christian charity; we *see* torpedoes and hellish inventions of incredible power to destroy our fellow-creatures. . . . The lover of nature . . . in all his studies will discover one great ruling power of individual self, whether among the brute creation or the vegetable world. Of the civilized world I say nothing." — *Wild Beasts and Their Ways*, pp. 453–455.

when physics was unexplored and chemistry unknown; the law of love saturated a New Testament ignorant of economics and incapable of mental physiology. Justice and kindness — we cannot remember it too often — are more necessary to man than science and luxury. Any theory which goes back of these immemorial duties, to find in the instincts of brute man a justification for the selfishness and greed which still beset us, is, in fact, reactionary, not evolutionary; not an intellectual advance, it is a moral retrogression. Its teachers mistake a progress in perception of facts for an advance in actual morality; in truth, the theory — unformulated, indeed, yet dimly perceived — long preceded in practice the higher morality. Human animals lived for untold years according to the strictest meaning of the struggle-for-existence ethics. They trampled and tore each other, in blind animal rage and lust. Ignorant of systems of evolution-philosophy and political economy, they fought and died, in relentless warfare, in sheer obedience to pure individualism and the rule of *laissez faire.* Stern experience gradually subdued, at what a cruel cost of generations poured out like water on the ground, this savage strain of bestial living; and the ages at length brought a finer moral practice, according to the rudiments of purity, justice and kindness. The true human world was not very old when the Dhammapada and the Sermon on the Mount perfected its moral law to a point hardly yet reached by one in a thousand in halting practice.

For the sake of intellectual clearness, for the unity which it gives to thought, the philosophy of evolution is most welcome; but it is a blunder in thought, as it would be a crime in action, to substitute a system of

ethics which applies to the whole animal world in
place of the higher law for man, perceived ages back,
and as yet fully obeyed by a few elect souls only.
That higher doctrine, in appreciation of which humanity has ebbed and flowed inconstantly, rebukes
our native individualism with its undying assertion
that men are members one of another. It animates
our personal ethics at their noblest; it inspires public
spirit and philanthropy; it has made human society
decent and kept it sweet.   If sometimes unjust to the
individual, ignoring the gain to all that comes from
the finest cultivation of each, its errors have been
more than compensated in times when gross individualism gives rise to the most partial theories of duty.
Do any to-day fear an approaching era of socialistic
effort which shall extirpate personal energy, and make
the individual a mere cog in a vast machine of State?
They should try to appreciate the monstrous development, during the last fifty years, of wealth and the
greed of wealth, and estimate, with some approach to
accuracy, the debasement of the modern mind, as
compared with former times, by the all-prevailing lust
for ease and pleasure.   What is most needed is not a
crusade against socialism in the holy and infallible
name of free competition, but a determined reaction
against the gross individualism too abundant in our
time.

Such a reaction should not be allowed to carry us
to the other extreme. The socialistic movement of
our time is profoundly important; it indicates the
wider range and deeper hold which a true religion of
humanity is destined to have. Yet blind surrender
even to the best of impulses and tendencies is always
unadvisable. Our first duty to all classes of society

is to try to understand their position, entering into
their thoughts and feelings with a hospitality that embraces all sorts and conditions of men, — the rich and
the poor, the well-to-do and the ill-to-do, the respect-
able "bourgeois" element and the "proletariat," if
such there be. Socialism, in every form, should be
held "no longer with the heat of a narrow antipathy,
but with the quiet of a large sympathy." In other
words, it should be rationalized. The true antidote
to a most unsocial socialism is found in constant reference to the other great tendency which is sure to remain, and will certainly avenge every excess of the
unbalanced apostles of a new heavens and a new earth
in which private possessions may not be held and the
individual is severely discouraged from asserting himself. The multitude, apotheosized by the socialist,
has never yet been the home and haunt of pure
reason. "Always vote with the minority," when
great issues are first discussed, is, on the contrary, a
comparatively safe rule. "The remnant" will believe
in a higher doctrine of individualism than the selfish
practice, and in a more rational socialism than sentimentalists applaud. Perpetual discrimination against
cant, new and old; against hardness of heart and
softness of brain; against watchwords and agitations
which set one class in bitter conflict with another;
and against a sour philanthropy which, in behalf of
the poor, reviles the rich, and, to soothe the lot of the
unsuccessful, curses the prosperous, — this is one of
the first of duties for the benevolent who would deserve and retain the respect of the thoughtful.

CHAPTER II.

THE PRESENT TENDENCY TO SOCIALISM.

THE inclination to embrace some form of Socialism is so strong at the present time that a brief examination of its general causes may well precede an inquiry into the compatibility of the developed system with the American Spirit. It is obvious, at once, when we consider the matter, that the extreme interest of the civilized world in social problems is not a token of degeneration. Only in a society that has been rapidly growing in wealth and benevolence would so much time and thought be spent in discussion of the means of making education and comfort universal. As the number of the well-to-do increases, the community at large has more freedom from "looking out for number one:" the milder feelings of human sympathy erect themselves when the struggle for existence loses its bitterness, and the individual career ceases, indeed, with many to be a struggle. There will, always be a sufficient number of imperfectly developed human beings to whom wealth and leisure will mean only persistent self-indulgence and constant search after a novel pleasure. But, with the large multiplication of moderate fortunes, the great body of those who have a competence that allows a measure of freedom from engrossing personal cares will naturally turn somewhat of their attention to the lot of their less fortunate brethren. It is upon hearts made tender by delicate living, upon minds "at leisure from themselves" through the ease of their material conditions, that the "bitter cry" of poverty falls with effect. When the stronger half of mankind is still struggling with nature for an adequate subsistence, it will take little thought "how the other half lives," and will often be slightly concerned whether this half lives a properly human life.

If the contrast between wealth and poverty is greater now than ever before, — and this may well be doubted, — it is not because the poor are poorer, but because the rich are richer. The greatness of the difference in these latter days not only stirs up many of the poor to envy and hatred; it also excites a few, at least, of the wealthy to thoughts on the responsibility of fortune. Much more important is the fact that it concentrates the attention of the great body of men who are neither rich nor poor upon the whole question of the distribution of wealth. The social agitation is proof of an increase of knowledge, as well as a natural result of remarkable material progress. Great sections of mankind, of whose condition the historian and the statesman have usually been ignorant, have been studied with pains as essential members of "the people." It is the whole people whose progress History endeavors to tell and Statesmanship to continue. There has been a practical limit, heretofore, at which the interest of the historian stayed. Now he explores very carefully the condition of every order of society, so far as the evidence will allow, and stops short, not because of a failure of interest, but because of a lack of material. Such material the students of society to-day are accumulating for the future historian in embarrassing abundance. No

class or condition of men subject to the severe necessity of working for daily bread is left neglected by
the curious eye of the student of economic and social
science. The facts he reveals seem to fall with the
force of novelty and surprise upon the minds of those
who, under a deficiency of bread, could easily resort
to cake!

These same facts have been urged with much more
persuasiveness, as regards the general public, by the
men of letters who have used the novel — an instrument of vast power to-day — to picture, with deep
effect, the daily life of the hard-working and suffering poor of great cities. A long line of writers of
fiction, from Charles Dickens to Mr. Walter Besant,
have thus made known to the prosperous the sorrows
and miseries of their weaker brothers and sisters in
the great family of humanity. It is a credit to the
religion and the philanthropy of to-day that such
appeals, made by those who have studied the concrete
problem of poverty, have not fallen upon deaf ears.
Though, beyond a doubt, the astonishing material
development of this century has outstripped the mental and moral evolution needed to balance it, yet the
intellect and the conscience of civilized mankind are
showing themselves steadily responsive to demands
rightly made upon them. Enthusiasm for humanity,
far from dying out of the life of Christian nations,
was never so vigorous before, and we may well be
confident that it will prove adequate to its task. The
increasing direction of religious feeling from the future world upon "the life that now is" furnishes a
motive power for philanthropy such as it has often
lacked, to the discredit of the Church.

The result of many tendencies, deep or superficial,

of our generation, the prevailing social disturbance excites a wide discussion of the political, social and religious creeds of the past. No institution is safe from criticism in this day of restlessness of the human spirit. The rights of the individual are as little exempt as the Family, the State or the Church. A wave of Socialistic reaction against the individualism fashionable a generation ago rolls in with power. A hundred influences assist its coming, and many persons lose their judgment before it. Yet its victorious course will have to respect the law of gravitation, and it must soon find its level. The great vogue of Socialism renders only more imperative the duty of sifting the possible from the impossible in its programme, that long discouragement may not result to all reformers, because of unwise attempts to do too much and go too far.

The great mass of the thorough socialists of our day are far from irresistibly impressing an observer as men who "see life steadily, and see it whole." The cleverest minds among them often reason from narrow premises to conclusions which contradict the widest-reaching lessons of human experience. The violent denunciations of the prevailing order in which they indulge are usually as far removed from truth as from charity. They have not yet convinced any considerable number of disinterested students of politics and economics that the socialistic programme is even feasible, to say nothing of its desirability in comparison with the actual situation in all its promise and potency. Never have there been wanting men amply able to plot out an ingenious scheme for revolutionizing society as it has naturally developed itself. A real cycle of Socialism seems to have been accomplished in the United States since the days of the Come-Outers and other agitators of 1835–45. Impatient of living from hand to mouth, according to the homely method of common-sense, the social reformer would take "a large view," and have all men live according to a few great and simple principles. This generous temper, to which we may not refuse our respect, for it is the true strain of the poet, the prophet and the saint — the eternal children of the world's undying youth — is broken when it comes to inevitable questions of ways and means. Its high simplicity is no match for the extreme complexity of modern civilization: its ideals prove "no thoroughfares" in the actual human world, and its means of cure are soon exhausted. We are obliged to return upon experience and science for help and direction.

A philosophic view will moderate the disappointment which arises in every high mind when it compares its ideal — even if this be realizable, as is by no means always the case — with the halting pace of mankind; it will moderate as well the ardor of expectation from any ideal put into practice. This world is yet in the go-cart, and it should not be reproached as if it were able to choose its own way in perfect freedom. The ideal, too, put into action soon loses half its charm, and ceases to content. Any scheme which promises the full peace and entire satisfaction of mankind condemns itself. These blessings have never been permanently held by any people deserving respect. If philosophy thus dampens our zeal, it causes no lasting discouragement. It promises no attainment of a final Kingdom of Heaven upon earth, but it gives the pledge of continued progress to those who are willing to pay for it in work, not in words alone. Each step of this progress is clear, as the time for it comes, to the scientific mind which studies the facts and tendencies of the day, — without overmastering enthusiasm it may be, but with a clear eye, a cool head and a ready hand. So vast a subject is society, and so innumerable are the actions and reactions produced by any important change, that the prime requisites for the reformer are definiteness of aim and limitation of field. The comprehensiveness of the socialistic programme is enticing to the untrained mind; but the wiser head views with great distrust such proposals of wholesale reconstruction by the hands of those who have had no success in dealing with a small portion, even, of the social fabric. A philosophic review of the whole field will result in a determination to study it carefully, piece by piece, and to cultivate it in sections, after much study has given full enlightenment.

Such a review will lead us to regard the socialistic movement as due to the growing pains of civilization. It is not a sign of decay, but of promise. It indicates not the corruption, but the essential vigor of the social body. It shows that mankind is progressing, but not progressing fast enough to suit our desires. As we advance in civilization we find new benefits and we fall into new evils; but our resources are continually multiplied and the lengthening roll of our successes gives confidence for every fresh encounter with the enemies of human culture, old or new. We should not exaggerate the dimensions of the actual social difficulties in America. The great mass of the literature of socialism is of foreign authorship, and refers for justification to European conditions which obtain in America in a much less degree, or

not at all. We have no East London on our hands
and souls, and but one city that approaches even to
that sad centre, greatly as it has been improved of
late. The land, despite the rhetoric of the single-tax
men, is still open in large measure to all who are
willing to live upon it, as the record of abandoned
farms in New England goes to show, and the experience of manufacturers who have vainly tried to remove their workmen from city to country.

The social problem that confronts practical people
is, in very great degree, the problem of the city.
With all its importance and difficulty, we must remember that even yet only one fourth of the population of the United States is urban. It has fast risen
to this proportion from one thirtieth in 1790 and one
sixth in 1860.[1] In a hundred years the population of
the country has increased sixteen times (in round
numbers), but the urban population has increased one
hundred and sixty times. We shall probably soon
be a nation of whose people "one half lives in towns
of 4,000 inhabitants or upwards."[2] We have not
yet mastered the political problem of city government, and it stands to reason that much more complex industrial and social difficulties of the city should
be still confronting us.

Not only is the social question very largely confined
to the cities: in the cities it is also a difficulty
mainly created by the foreign population, which in
1880 was 27 per cent. of the whole population of the

---

[1] The United States Census which gives these figures defines
the city as a population of 8,000 or more, under one local government.

[2] Prof. A. B. Hart, in the *Quarterly Journal of Economics* for
January, 1890.

cities and towns of 4,000 people and upward. "In other words, the cities and towns, which have but a fourth of the population, have more than half the foreigners." In the large cities of 200,000 persons and upward, 32 per cent. of the population was foreign born. "New York in 1880 had 40 per cent., a proportion since somewhat increased. . . . In Holyoke and Fall River, the foreigners had increased to 50 per cent. in 1885, and are probably increasing. Chicago is popularly supposed to be more than half foreign." [1]

The word "foreigner" has never yet been synonymous with "barbarian" in these United States; all our population, except the Indian, is, in fact, descended from men foreign-born. But the much lower level of recent immigration has properly excited alarm among sober-minded Americans as to the capacity of the country to assimilate the very raw material of citizens which is now arriving in superabundance. The burden was great while fertile land was to be had almost for the asking in the unsettled West, and labor was everywhere in great demand. Now that the best available land has been occupied, and labor difficulties have arisen and multiplied, the congestion of our great cities with multitudes of Hungarians, Poles and Italians calls for restrictive measures which shall throw upon the nations of Europe the rightful care of the ignorance, poverty and incapacity of their own citizens. With immigration regulated in accordance with the first principles of international justice, America can still absorb a large foreign element, as she has done in the past, and out of the most unpromising material continue to make tolerable citizens.

[1] Professor Hart, *Ibid.*

Meanwhile the first duty of every immigrant, Americanized or not, is to keep the peace; if he does not observe the established order of the Republic, the law will know how to deal with him, when, for instance, he commits murder in the name of socialism, anarchism or any other theory, good or bad. When the foreigner casts his lot in a land won and subdued by men of English blood, and freely enjoys all the benefits which their long toil has acquired, he makes but a small return if he spends a few years in acquiring a practical knowledge of American institutions: he displays but little wisdom if he immediately sets up his ignorance of American freedom against the knowledge of those who have lived their lives under it, and inherited all its traditions. Systematic Socialism in America counts its great body of adherents among these foreign-born who have arrived but recently, and with whom it is the only feasible method of being "agin the government," — their life-long habit at home, where the government was an alien power. The absurdity of such a position in a land where government is "of the people, by the people, and for the people" will but slowly penetrate the brain of the ignorant Pole. Until it does so penetrate, men of American sense, who know what freedom means and what it costs, will keep that Pole in order, — for his own benefit!

Without respect to immigration, however, the strong tendency of nineteenth-century people to move into the city, nowhere stronger than in the United States, has thrown the nation temporarily off its balance: it has brought about great changes, social and industrial, while the needful intellectual and moral modifications of the former agricultural régime have not yet been made. In country life, formerly dominant over the whole territory of the United States, and seen at its best estate in the New England town, there is much practical equality and a large neighborly interest which disappear almost entirely in the great city. "A modern city is probably the most impersonal combination of individuals that has ever been formed in the world's history. People come to these centres from the most diverse quarters and with the most diverse aims. They have no sense of common interests or mutual obligations, but are drawn together simply by the magnetic force of industrial conditions."[1] The human sympathy which prevails under the simpler conditions of country living, and softens the inevitable inequalities of fortune, disappears to a very great degree in the city. The loss of it in large manufactories, where thousands are at work, and personal acquaintance between employer and employed is out of the question, is one great root of labor difficulties. The employer tends to think of his workpeople as a variety of machines, — much more troublesome, indeed, than those made of iron and steel; unable to conceive of themselves in this way, workpeople become more and more alienated from their natural leaders.

We may well consider for a moment how little the newspapers have to tell us of labor troubles among the many million persons in the United States who are directly concerned with man's original and perennial industry of tilling the earth, as owners of the soil, or hired workers, with their families. The American farmer who works with his hired men, or directly superintends them with a practical knowledge

---

[1] *Introduction to Social Philosophy*, by J. S. Mackenzie, p. 101.

of the business, commands, as a rule, their respect
and confidence. In these working associations the
feeling of partnership in a common lot reminds men
of fundamental equalities and insures peace and good-
will — the condition of lasting prosperity. The difficulties of the American farmer to-day — they are not
slight — are not due to artificially inhumane relations
with the workers he employs: they are mainly owing
to the fact that he sells his product, at home or
abroad, under one economic system and buys under
another. Conservative as the agriculturist naturally
and properly is, he is beginning to make himself felt
in such a reform of the tariff as will no longer allow
him to be ground between the upper millstone of protection and the nether millstone of free trade.

Difficult, then, as the problems raised by the mass-
ing of workers in factories and the crowding of people
into cities may be, we have to recollect, when fundamental solutions like socialism are proposed, that one
quarter part of the whole population of these States
lives in the country, under conditions which excite no
considerable longings for State control of industry,
and that three quarters are outside of the large cities
and towns where socialism finds its natural habitat.
The city will have to solve its peculiar difficulties,
and nothing is gained by misrepresenting these problems as if they directly affected the great majority of
the people, who live outside of cities. The manufacturing world will be obliged to meet and master its
own hindrances; here, again, it is irrational to propose a sweeping remedy altogether uncalled for by
the industry which employs more persons than any
other; agriculture, the basal career of mankind, is
conservative to the last degree, because directly sub-

ject to the most jealous taskmaster — Nature! Least of all men is the farmer a sentimentalist; least of all men is he likely to give up private ownership and the right of self-direction in his work without exceedingly solid reasons. The problem to be solved must be put in very tangible shape before he will meddle with it; when it is put in this form it will lose much of its difficulty, becoming in large degree a matter of character, in which each man must help himself.

The abolition of poverty and the introduction of general comfort is the aim of the socialist; it is just as much the aim of every one else who wishes well to his race. The benevolent desire to see every man obtain the substantial comforts which the majority now enjoy in this land — a house and home, work giving a return sufficient for a comfortable support, and leisure enough to keep the worker from becoming a mere drudge. These benefits have been attained by the great mass of the American people through the practice of certain simple but difficult virtues, — industry, thrift, skill and patience in the contest with natural obstacles to human effort. Doubtless these fundamental advantages may be rendered easier of acquisition in the progress of civilization; the rate of speed in the attainment of a moderate competence will certainly be quickened by invention and scientific discovery. But can the *method* be so far changed — from individual initiative, control and ownership, to governmental initiative, control and ownership — that *all* shall soon have what *many* now enjoy, without practicing the same difficult virtues or manifesting the same degree of ability? The State Socialist confidently answers this inquiry in the affirmative. Others must be pardoned if they fail to see that man's progress has thus far mollified the stern conditions of human existence sufficiently for the new method to work with such wide benefit.

The Socialist shines, as a severe critic, in pointing out the plain evils of the existing order; but as the constructor of a new frame of things which will certainly stand, and under which men will prosper, he has had no success worth mentioning. No scheme has been plotted out which even strikes as feasible sympathizing minds who remember the demands of physical and human nature. Easy is it to dream of a society in which all shall be intelligent and virtuous and prosperous; no one to-day can claim credit for repeating what many noble souls have imagined or prophesied in the past; he only makes the fair imagination a commonplace of thought. Much more credit belongs to those who help mankind a step or two nearer, in reality, to a better country. We may grant, as we must, we may even declare with fervor, as we ought, that a social gospel, in the broad sense, needs continually to be preached; but, as continually, the more difficult question arises, "What shall we do to-day?" The man who in any direction answers this question with wisdom will deserve our prime respect. He, and such as he, will, in all probability, teach us as wisely what to do to-morrow, when to-morrow comes, with its fresh strength and its larger opportunity. "Surely," as Mr. Besant says, "there has never been, since the world began, any dream more generous and noble than this of the Socialist, insomuch that there are some who think that it was first revealed to the world by the Son of God himself. It is so beautiful that it will never be suffered to be forgotten; so beautiful that mankind will henceforth be continually occupied in trying to make it a practical reality; and, with every successive failure, will always be drawing nearer and nearer to the goal, until at last, if the kind gods consent, even after many years and many generations, it shall be won, and with it the kingdom long talked of and little understood. But those who expect it in their lifetime might as well expect the kingdom of Heaven." [1]

The beautiful dream has its justification in its end, the welfare of all. The dreamer is usually mistaken when he descends to such less inspiring but unavoidable questions as how to begin, and how to continue on the heavenly road. Rarely are the dreamers helpful members of the committee on ways and means! The true-hearted prophet and the benevolent beholder of visions are an indispensable element in every society not wholly abandoned to the dull routine of Philistinism. For them, and for their high and generous office in warming the heart and stirring the conscience, we can never cease to entertain a sincere and deep respect. At the same time we assert the right of the statesman and the practical reformer to actual leadership in the difficult labor of progress toward the fair ideal. Many of the so-called reformers are plainly a part of things needing to be reformed. The social dream to-day attracts, as always before, a motley army. With a few Sons of God, the numerous followers of the devils of laziness and intemperance; sentimentalists of every degree, from the best to the cheapest; enthusiasts for change as change, since no change can be for the worse for their proved inefficiency; "cranks" of every variety of eccentric movement; men who have failed in the sim-

[1] *Children of Gibeon*, p. 205, American edition.

ple task of winning their own bread-and-butter, and
therefore feel themselves quite competent to lay down
the law to the world of the capable and successful; loud-voiced women who have yet to learn that
ignorant scolding is not an effective weapon of social
reform; a long array of lunatics and semi-lunatics,
rejoicing in the opportunity of moving about in
worlds unrealized and unrealizable, — it is, indeed, a
variegated host which follows the standard of social
reform! But this is the weak side of every gospel of
the ideal; with such allies the religion of humanity
has always been afflicted. When the simple precept,
"He that will not work, shall not eat," is declared by
practical Christianity, dismay falls heavily upon these
adherents with mingled motives. People who prefer
to beg fall away: the genial company of professional
idlers seek a milder climate, where the moral temperature is less exigent: the incapable fall to the rear,
and the drudgery of reform is left to the capable
minority who can both dream and plan and work.
In working, these show their true metal, easily counterfeited so long as words only are in demand, "a
futile currency of breath;" and they will turn for
direction, in a world of fact, to those who have had a
measure of success and know why they have succeeded. If there is some little truth in Disraeli's
saying that "the critic is a man who has failed in literature," so there may be as much in the definition
of the systematic socialist as a man who has failed in
social life. In his strenuous declamation against the
wealthy of his day, he is, too often, deeply desirous
of riches for himself: ideally arranging the republic
wherein all must work equally, he does not labor as
much as most of the "aristocrats" he denounces, and

he thus affords a living lesson of the probable effects
of a socialistic régime upon the failures of the present
order. Herein, perchance, is the chief reason of his
existence! The sincere and able apostles of socialism
and their earnest disciples must not be confounded
with these camp-followers.

Some plain words of caution will not be out of
order, however, addressed to the great body of thinking people in this country who more or less incline to
adopt State Socialism, as a creed to be put into practice as soon as may be. The clergymen, the teachers,
the philanthropists, the men of leisure, the men of
business (though these are few), and the very large
number of educated women, who hail the message of
socialism as heaven-sent, should pause awhile and
consider the duty incumbent upon them. In a country where public opinion is very powerful, these
classes have much influence in its formation. So far
as this influence has gone to break down the blind,
ignorant and unreasoning prejudice against Socialism as a theory to be soberly discussed that once prevailed, no rational mind can complain that the literary or educated classes (as we may call them, for
the sake of brevity, and without making invidious
distinctions) have done unwisely. A people that
refuses to talk of socialism declares its own Philistinism; a church that dreads to inquire how far Jesus
Christ was a communist has lost too much of his
spirit; and no class of men and women ought to give
their minds freer play over all social matters than the
literary class. But all must account before the bar
of reason for the use they make of their freedom of
mind, tongue or pen. They must be held to a wise
choice of leaders whom they will steadfastly follow.

To take a late example of unreason: "There has been no more curious psychological phenomenon in recent times," says an American economist of the most liberal temper, "than the wholesale hypnotizing of clever literary people by Mr. Bellamy's dazzling vision. When they come out of the daze and begin to resume their intellectual self-direction, they may be trusted to discover," for instance, "that equality of income and equality of satisfaction of legitimate desires are two different things." [1]

Literary and professional people, in accepting the author of "Looking Backward" as an authority on the feasibility of the socialistic scheme, make such a mistake as the business man would make in preferring Mrs. Southworth to Thackeray as a novelist. It is a striking commentary on the deficiencies of a "liberal education" in this country that it should leave most of the graduates of high school and college so ignorant of the elements of political and economic science that the first clever romancer who comes along can captivate their minds, if only for a time. One may be fully persuaded that the romancer does more good than harm in the end, since he sets people to thinking, and yet perceive the immediate injury that he does by leading many to suppose that these hard matters, which try the shrewdest trained intelligence, can be settled at once by the vivid rhetoric and the *ipse dixit* of a story-teller. The harm will be remedied in no long time, as "literary people" apply themselves for light to the study of political science and the elements of economics. They should never put by the appeal to reason and humanity, as the final

[1] Prof. F. H. Giddings, in the *International Journal of Ethics*, January, 1891, p. 242.

court in these matters; but reason includes science, and humanity itself cries out against guidance by sentimentality. "It is not only idle, it is positively mischievous, to delude ourselves with ideals which cannot be realized; because they blind us to actual improvements that might be made with such means as are even now at our disposal. We must prefer a candle and a plain road to a meteor and a marsh."[1]

The saner literature of fiction teaches this lesson: thus it is worded by the novelist whose "impossible story" (so his friends called it, but he was never able himself to understand why it was impossible) stands verified in the People's Palace of East London: "A mathematician tries his theory on elementary cases; socialism, and the ladies and gentlemen who construct with infinite labor constitutions, schemes and plans for the universal good, do not. The simple case is beyond them. They are full of rage against the old system, but their indignation is expended in deepening their political convictions. There was once another man who went down the Jericho road and fell among thieves. First, there passed by the priest, just as in the former case, his scornful chin in the air; and then the Levite followed. Now this Levite did not immediately pass by, but he stopped and inquired carefully into the particulars of the case, and made full notes of them, and then he went his way, and out of the notes he compiled a most tremendous oration, eloquent, fiery and convincing, which he delivered at a meeting of the Democratic Federal Union, on the wretched system under which robbers are suffered to exist, and propounded another system, by means of which there would be no more robbers in the land at

[1] *Introduction to Social Philosophy*, by J. S. Mackenzie, p. 282.

all. And yet the old system goes on still, and still we see coming along the hot and thirsty road the Samaritan with his nimble twopence."

Between such a realistic novelist, closely true to the sad facts of his surrounding world and able to suggest a feasible remedy for some of them, and the pure romancer of a distant future, there is a wide difference. One excites a proper human sympathy with present distress and points out a channel of use in which that sympathy may flow: the other caricatures the real world and lightly constructs one that he can approve, indeed, but which has the slight defect that it is out of connection with human nature and social law. The literature of enduring power in fiction speaks to-day through writers like Mr. Walter Besant: the author of "Looking Backward" has no such hold upon reality. The most noted writer to-day of "novels with a purpose" is true to the actual world when she makes David Grieve declare: "Socialism as a system seems to me to strike down and weaken the most precious thing in the world, that on which the whole of civilized life and progress rests — the spring of will and conscience in the individual. Socialism as a spirit, as an influence, is as old as organized thought, and from the beginning it has forced us to think of the many, when otherwise we should be sunk in thinking of the one. But as a modern dogmatism, it is like other dogmatisms. The new truth of the future will emerge from it as a bud from its sheath, taking here and leaving there."

In our day the novel is a favorite vehicle for the reformer; the story is often written simply to give a wider circulation to ideas of a new social order uppermost in the mind of the author. The political econ-

omists of the first half of this century would have
done well had they paid more attention than they did
to the influence of the essayist and the poet in forming public opinion. Economists and sociologists
make a mistake to-day if they slight the function of
the novelist, especially, in the progress of thought, or
are prejudiced against a new scheme of society because propounded by a man devoted to pure literature. That such is not my own temper the preceding
paragraphs will show. Literature, as distinguished
from economic science, has a most important office to
discharge in the origination, the treatment and the
conclusion of social discussion. The weight of the
novel must nevertheless depend on the closeness to
fact and the vigor of reasoning it exhibits. The many
who are fortunately awakened to a deep interest in
the lot of their fellow-mortals by the vivid pages of
the novelist will need to sustain it by recourse to
deeper fountains.

For such and for all, the prophet and guide of
American literature, Ralph Waldo Emerson, speaks a
counsel of perfection when, with many repetitions, he
declares the worth of the individual in contrast with
that worship of the majority which culminates in
socialism. His disciples stray far when they practically embrace the Owenite doctrine that circumstances
are all that we need to change, — the characteristic
article of the socialistic creed. What Emerson said
in 1844, reviewing the active reform period which
had then apparently culminated, we may well repeat
to-day: "I do not wonder at the interest these projects inspire. The world is awaking to the idea of
union, and these experiments show what it is thinking of. It is and will be magic. Men will live

and communicate, and plough and reap and govern, as by added ethereal power, when once they are united. . . . But this union must be inward, and not one of the covenants. . . . Government will be adamantine without any governor. The union must be ideal in actual individualism." Lecturing in London, in 1848, on Politics and Socialism, he "spoke well of Owen and Fourier, and said their conceptions should be gratefully appreciated; for they who think and hope well for mankind put the human race under obligation. They are the unconscious prophets of the true order of society, — men who believe that in the world God's justice will be done. Yet he protested against phalansteries in favor of the separate house, and declared it was individualism men needed, rather than having all things in common." [1]

When a lofty idealist like Emerson thus speaks of individualism, we know — whatever the qualifications of his doctrine in the direction of coöperation which we may need to make — that it is not a doctrine of greed or a spirit of low selfishness that he inculcates. The temper and the method, on the contrary, are precisely those which a materialistic Socialism should most carefully ponder. "Whilst I desire," says our great American teacher of the gospel of the soul, "to express the respect and joy I feel before this sublime connection of reforms, now in their infancy around us, I urge the more earnestly the paramount duties of self-reliance. I cannot find language of sufficient energy to convey my sense of the sacredness of private integrity."

The uncritical tendency to Socialism, visible among American men of letters, in the members of various

[1] *R. W. Emerson*, by George Willis Cooke, p. 94.

professions, and in many of their readers, needs more careful treatment than that which the novelist and the essayist, however capable, have supplied. The inquiry is very pertinent, how far the system is compatible with the genius of the American people, under the conditions which their natural environment and their political history have determined. To such an inquiry — obviously lying neither in the realm of fiction nor in the province of the moralist — we will now turn. The answer may not be derived from imaginations of a possible future, or from theorizing upon what we suppose ought to be; it is to be drawn from the history of the American people, issuing in its actual character as shown in the life of to-day.

CHAPTER III.

THE AMERICAN SPIRIT.

FEW tasks are more difficult than the accurate delineation of the character of a people as shown in the whole range of its activities. When the people belongs to modern times, and shares the complexities of a developed civilization, the national psychologist has a labor before him far greater than when he would depict, for instance, the typical Greek and Roman of antiquity. After he has thoroughly studied for years the literature and the history of Greece and Rome, making himself familiar with their laws, customs, art and religion, he may undertake with some confidence to sketch the main lines of the character of the men who have left such a record of themselves in word and deed. The literary record, however imperfect, is finished: the relics of the art are in our hands; the social frame is antiquated; the customs have vanished; the religion is no more. Roman Law and Greek Literature are our great inheritance from classic antiquity, and many historians, entering into these rich bequests, have set forth the chief lineaments of the Greek victorious in the fields of beauty and knowledge, and of the Roman triumphant in every art of conquest and government. Each successive painter has the benefit of the attempts of his predecessors; he learns from them to heighten or tone down his colors, to adopt a more just perspective in portraying the

individual against the background of circumstance,
and to realize the just image of a man once living,
however different he may have been from the Greek
or the Italian of to-day. There have thus been
formed generally accepted characterizations of these
two great peoples of antiquity, which have gradually
been cleared of conventionality, rhetoric and extreme
generalization, as the students of the whole record
have corrected mistakes of interpretation.

The typical Greek, then, we know and the representative Roman; and neither can rise from his grave
to correct our mistakes! We are not so free from
controversy when we endeavor to describe a people of
modern times. The gain in the nearness and fullness
of testimony is more than offset by the complexity of
the character of modern man and the national equa-
tion which the psychologist has to make, whether he
is portraying his own people or another. The bias
of patriotism and historic rancor forbid much expectation of an impartial picture of the Frenchman from
the Englishman, or of the German from the Frenchman. Neither of these, again, will describe his own
countrymen to the satisfaction of the judicial-minded
foreigner. Such attempts, indeed, are rarely made.
Far more common is incidental laudation of the virtues of his countrymen by the historian or essayist,
in contrast with the vices or weaknesses of people
across the Channel or over the Rhine. International
studies in psychology like Mr. P. G. Hamerton's
"French and English," or Mr. W. C. Brownell's
"French Traits," based on sympathy and familiar
knowledge, are few and far between; when the observer belongs, as Mr. Brownell does, to a nation
which has generally been on friendly terms with the

people he would represent, the antecedent probability is greater that he will do no gross injustice.

A writer who can justly describe the character of his own countrymen, free from both the partiality of the patriot and the bitterness of the censor, is more exceptional, perhaps, than a fair-minded exponent from another country. The task is not one which the discreet student will lightly undertake, so near are the dangers of eulogy and of fault-finding, — two occupations equally unprofitable. A justification for the attempt by an American to draw here some lines of the American character may, however, be found in the presence of a great problem that now confronts all civilized peoples. The inquiry is natural whether there may not be in the character and condition of the German, the Italian, the Frenchman, the Englishman and the American some special reasons of weight for expecting a specific solution in each country. The opinion on this matter of an enlightened foreigner who has carefully studied the United States, for instance, is of high value, for such a student will take points of view which the native's very familiarity with his own institutions leads him to neglect. But, in most cases, such an observer will commit mistakes impossible to one born and bred in the country; when the country is steadily progressive, he may fail to emphasize favorable tendencies much more important than existing phenomena of an evil appearance.

If an "inside view" can be corrected from the observations of an able and impartial outsider, the conditions are favorable for the study of a particular problem as determined, or likely to be determined, by the national character. These United States are here especially fortunate in the fact that such Europeans as Alexis de Tocqueville, Hermann von Holst, and, most of all, James Bryce, have devoted themselves to studying the American people and the institutions under which it lives, and which are the expression of its spirit. The problem of Democracy interests the whole world to-day, and America for this reason properly invites the attention of mankind. For Americans themselves, the question of the desirability and practicability of republican institutions is no longer open; it has long since been decided in the affirmative by "the grave mistress, Experience," as William Bradford called that best instructor of men, who has taught us Americans "many things." A much more recent problem, the desirability and practicability of Socialism, does present itself to America, as to other nations, for answer. If the response be anywhere favorable, a working programme would soon follow. Yet Socialism needs many factors for a full trial of its claims. The first of these is certainly a disposition in the national temperament to attempt radical solutions of existing evils, a willingness to revolutionize the prevailing order, however gradually, in a sure faith that the new principles will work out a better society than we now see. An inquiry, then, in this direction, into the actual American Spirit, made by an American, and checked by the reports of foreign students generally ranked as the most able and impartial, should have some little value in the discussion of Socialism.

I do not undertake, in the narrow limits of these three chapters, to trace the historical development of the American Spirit as it is in operation to-day, nor can I pretend to give an exhaustive exposition of all its elements. The temper and character of the American people at present, in such of its aspects as bear upon the question of the adaptability of Socialism, — this is the specific topic in hand, and the limitation may give one confidence in undertaking it. How the typical American thought, felt and acted between the War of the Revolution and that of 1812, Mr. Henry Adams and Prof. J. B. McMaster have lately informed us in some detail.[1] The conventional notion of the average "Yankee," of the later period from 1815 to 1860, formed by the Englishman, Frenchman and German of the same time, is not to be examined here. Socialism, especially in the United States, is a question of to-day, not of yesterday. The American who is to meet it is the American of a Union freed from the reproach of slavery through a tremendous civil war that deepened and purified the national consciousness, purged away many of the follies of youth and brought America into the front rank among nations in gravity of spirit. Before, she had excelled in aspiration rather than in the actual performance of high deeds the results of which endure in the memory of grateful mankind.[2] Considering, then, the institutions, the tendencies and the temper — intellectual, moral and spiritual — of the Ameri-

---

[1] "The traits of intelligence, rapidity and mildness seemed fixed in the national character as early as 1817, and were likely to become more marked as time should pass. A vast amount of conservatism still lingered among the people ; but the future spirit of society could hardly fail to be intelligent, rapid in movement and mild in method." H. Adams, *History of the United States*, vol. ix. 240, 241.

[2] " Earth's biggest country 's got her soul
And risen up earth's greatest nation."

Lowell.

cans of this generation, — how will they be likely to
solve the economic problem, now that the political
problem is virtually answered.[1]

The query will at once be raised, Is it possible for
any one to speak with authority for so complex a
body as the whole population of America, including,
as it does, millions of natives of other countries, and
scattered, as it is, over a territory so immense as to
give rise to many and notable local differences of
habit and temper? The attempt to speak with exact
comprehension of our North and South, East and
West, and of the Irish, German and Negro stocks,
— to name no others, — must be regarded, in truth,
as entirely unpractical; but the resource is obvious.
The omission of other elements in the American constitution than the English strain would render the
analysis imperfect in some degree; but if this English
element be left out, then we should be trying to produce our play without Hamlet! The master-force in
American civilization is the Anglo-Saxon spirit derived from our English forefathers who colonized the
New World. The new world presented new conditions under which a new form of government and a
novel social order were necessarily developed. The
Englishmen of the seventeenth century who settled
the new England, the new York, and the new Jersey
brought with them the habits, the ambitions, the
aspirations, of the many who remained in the parent
island. Here these habits were to change greatly;
here these ambitions and aspirations had an open field

---

[1] " The political problem the people of the United States do
appear to me to have solved, or Fortune has solved it for them,
with undeniable success." Matthew Arnold, *A Word More
About America.*

in which to run and be fulfilled. After a quarter-millennium, the American of purest English descent is another and very different person from his nearest kinsman the descendant of those who remained at home. The climate and other natural factors of the new physical environment have wrought out another physiological type; the novel influences of freedom, in a continent remote from contact with Europe and its secular civilization, have produced a type intellectually and morally new as well.

This nervous, quick and capable race, impatient of restraint and eager to explore every avenue of opportunity, has welcomed to its domain the sons of all the countries of Europe. Beside later accessions from the mother-country proper, the Scotchman, the Irishman, the Scotch-Irishman so-called, the German, the Frenchman, the Scandinavian, have come, in various degrees of force, to aid in building up the new nation. No recent difficulties, caused by the swarming into the United States of the less capable natives of Eastern and Southern Europe, can obscure the great part which the immigrants from Northern and Western Europe have played in building up the industrial and political power of the United States. But they have come hither not to transform, but to be transformed. The extreme preponderance of the English stock in America, before the Revolution which separated us politically from England, made a centre of influence irresistible in changing into its likeness all subsequent settlers. Since time began there has been no other such absorbing power as the English race domiciled in America, speaking the Anglo-Saxon tongue and developing the precedents of English freedom. It has suffered no other race to retain its mother-

tongue here for any length of time, however obstinate
the endeavor. By its free schools, its omnipresent
newspapers, its vigorous literature, its constant circulation of population from one part of the country to
another, and its equal extension of political rights
and responsibilities, it has broken down many division walls between the Irishman, the German, the
Frenchman and the Scandinavian on one side, and
the population already domiciled and Americanized
on the other. The mass of this transforming power,
increased every year by its conquests of new-comers,
is plainly inexpugnable. The few communities
where the language of Germany, Denmark or Sweden
is still currently spoken can cherish no reasonable
hope of long maintaining their isolation. All pre-
cedent is against them; the struggle, however mis-
takenly patriotic, must soon be abandoned before a
wiser view of manifest destiny.

The race that has victoriously practiced the Ameri-
canizing process, from the beginning of the United
States until now, is surely the one factor to be dis-
criminated from the whole multitude of present
Americans as the best representative of the American
spirit. It will, of course, be well to inquire later if
our conclusions respecting socialism in this country,
founded on a consideration of the Anglo-Saxon spirit
working under American conditions, need modification from the presence of large Celtic and Teutonic
elements, for instance, in our population.

It may reasonably be anticipated that such modifications will not need to be profound. The American
ambassador to Germany who assured the Emperor
that a large part of this country had been Germanized
was just then more intent on extending the market

for the American hog than on spreading exact knowledge! The "new Germany" or the "new Ireland," to be found in any part of the United States to-day, is a very unstable power. The habits of German and Irish communities in respect to the observance of Sunday, or the use of liquor, for example, are not, indeed, those of the communities where people of English descent predominate; but the difference, as experience shows, is not fundamental or incapable of disappearance through changes on both sides.

Puritan New England no longer exists in its primitive asceticism. It has been modified in many of its ways and customs by contact with less severe nationalities, but it has not surrendered its intellectual and moral leadership of the country. By means of its children who have remained in the six Eastern States, and fully as much by means of the larger number whom it has sent out to people the Middle and Western States, making there a Greater New England, the stock of the Pilgrims and the Puritans has exercised a controlling power in American history. Thus far it has been able to direct the forces of the national development wisely and morally, not indeed in the name of Massachusetts or Connecticut, but in the name of Anglo-Saxon pluck and respect for right. A desire to avoid provincialism of temper and rhetorical flourishes about Plymouth Rock must not lead us to undervalue the actual consequence in American history of the spirit of New England. If we eliminate some unessential traits, we shall find it a fit and proper representative not only of all the older portions of the country, but of the Great West as well. With every year the territory in which the New England way of looking at things is practiced steadily extends westward. Its power in the regions of thought and practice does not decrease but increase.[1] There is now no perceptible difference between the prevailing temper of the Northern States on the Atlantic coast and that of the rest of the country, in respect to attachment to free institutions and the most characteristic American usages. The refinement and thoughtfulness due to a longer history and a greater nearness to the Old World are only amused by exhibitions of the opposite qualities in "the wild and woolly West," — wherever this may now be located. They do not give way, but they rely upon perennial influences, working upon the same material, substantially, to produce a similar result in time, in the West as in the East. The University of Michigan, for instance, represents these influences, as Harvard and Yale do; the elements with which it has to deal are a little more crude, but fully as sound and vigorous.

Justification is not wanting, therefore, for the limitation, favored by considerations of practical convenience, of our usual view to the older part of our country, and especially to New England.[2] The Puri-

[1] It is a Kentucky orator by whom these words were spoken : "Standing here . . . in Massachusetts, the parent of all the North, when I consider her influence in the country as a principal planter of the Western States, and now, by her teachers, preachers, journalists and books, as well as by traffic and production, the diffuser of religious, literary and political opinion ; and when I see how irresistible the convictions of Massachusetts are in these swarming populations, — I think the little State bigger than I knew."

[2] The personality of an author who would expound the American Spirit is of less importance than the truth to life of his delineation ; but it may not be altogether out of place to say that the present writer, of unmixed English blood, so far as he knows,

tan colonists are not only easily separable, locally and logically, from the more commingled streams of the rest of the country; they have also shown, in New England and the other States largely peopled by them, the forcible qualities of leadership. Furnishing but two Presidents, Massachusetts, for instance, has produced the largest part of the enduring literature of America thus far, and has nearly always had a great rôle in shaping the social and political development of the nation. Since the extinction of the Federalist party, — in reality a "survival" from pre-Revolutionary times, — Massachusetts has had a conceded place as a chief advocate of reform. With New York, she has been the consistent upholder of established law in finance against the vagaries of other States temporarily given over to the so-called "Ohio idea," or some kindred folly. The lead in many reforms and philanthropies is confessedly in the East. These are not less, but more characteristically American because they originate in the older part of the country where the American temper has had a longer time to shake itself free of the crudities and conceits of its youth, and is now better able to appreciate its powers and responsibilities.[1]

was born on the Illinois bank of the Mississippi, spent four years of his boyhood in California, and three years, after thirty, in Ohio, and has passed the rest of his life between city and country in the three New England States bordering on the Atlantic Ocean.

[1] Mr. Andrew Carnegie, indeed, tells us in his fervid panegyric on "Triumphant Democracy," — speaking of "really able Britons" like Messrs. Froude, Farrar, Freeman, Bryce, Spencer and Arnold, — that "this class knows that until the Alleghany mountains are crossed, the real native is rarely to be met with." It would be difficult to substantiate this assertion from the writings of the English authors named : it is certainly "news" to New England and New York !

The beginnings of American literature were made in Massachusetts and New York, for one reason, because the material pressure involved in life in a new country was first considerably relieved in these two States. If any one would illustrate the most characteristic American thought and feeling from the literature of the United States, he turns, perforce, to Franklin, to Emerson, and to Lowell, apart from the statesmen of the early Republic and their successors. The blight of negro slavery too early caused the public men of the South to fall from their equal standing with the orators and legislators of the North. When Washington, Jefferson and Madison had passed from the earthly scene where they had fathered the Republic with John Adams, Alexander Hamilton and John Jay, Southern statesmen devoted themselves to the defense of an institution in no other respect so "peculiar" as in its entire opposition to all ideas distinctively American. The protagonists of these ideas were then exclusively Northern and Eastern, — such as Webster, Seward and Sumner, until they were joined by Western statesmen like Lincoln, Chase and Giddings, bred in the same school of respect for freedom.

I. *Love of personal liberty is the first distinctive feature of the American Spirit.* Tired of kings and weary of a blood nobility, the men of the Revolution and the Constitution fought and legislated for a very tangible freedom. They were roused to assert themselves by an injustice very palpable to men of English descent — taxation without representation. If in the Declaration of Independence the influence of Rousseau and other advocates of "natural rights" was evident, the Constitution, drawn up in the absence of

Jefferson from the country, — by no means altogether unfortunate, — bore, throughout, the impress of the practical English mind. It is ever to be remembered, with all respect to the men of 1776, that these United States live under the Constitution of 1787, not under the Declaration of Independence. If there is aught in American institutions to-day that conflicts or seems to conflict with the spirit-stirring words of the Declaration, we need not feel any necessity for apologizing. The Declaration must be interpreted in the light of the Constitution, when the actual American spirit is sought. The Constitution is the supreme law of the land, and no custom or institution may stand against it, so far as its clearly defined powers extend. The framers of the Constitution were, indeed, convicted, out of their own mouths, for they had waged war under the Declaration; when they recognized negro slavery and gave it privileges, they were well aware of the contradiction between their theory and their practice. But since this glaring inconsistency was rectified by the stern logic of civil war, we may properly say that the American people believe that the Constitution no longer needs radical amendment from the Declaration. American life is best understood by reference to the former, not by repeating "self-evident truths" of the latter, the applications of which are *not* self-evident, but most vigorously disputed.

The American people of 1787–89, anxious to "secure the blessings of liberty" to themselves and their posterity, knew that "a more perfect union" than that of the Confederation was necessary. They had in view, as the proximate end desired, the establishment of justice, domestic tranquillity, provision for the common defense and promotion of the general welfare. To this end, they defined, in plain and sober words, the strictly balanced powers of a threefold Federal government. The delegates to the Convention had seen enough in practice of the theory that liberty is freedom "to do as one pleases," whether the "one" be an individual or a Commonwealth. Consciously or unconsciously, they accepted the valid distinction which Governor John Winthrop made in his address to the Massachusetts Assembly of 1645: —

"There is a twofold liberty, natural (I mean as our nature is now corrupt), and civil or federal. The first is common to man with beasts and other creatures. By this, man, as he stands in relation to man simply, hath liberty to do what he lists; it is a liberty to evil as well as to good. This liberty is incompatible and inconsistent with authority, and cannot endure the least restraint of the most just authority. The exercise and maintaining of this liberty makes men grow more evil, and in time to be worse than brute beasts: *omnes sumus licentia deteriores.* This is that great enemy of truth and peace, that wild beast, which all the ordinances of God are bent against, to restrain and subdue it. The other kind of liberty I call civil or federal, it may also be termed moral, in reference to the covenant between God and man, in the moral law, and the politic covenants and constitutions amongst men themselves. This liberty is the proper end and object of authority, and cannot subsist without it; and it is a liberty to that only which is good, just and honest. This liberty you are to stand for, with the hazard (not only of your goods but) of your lives, if need be. Whatsoever crosseth this, is not authority but a distemper thereof."

Divested of its theological dress, this earliest definition of the civil liberty desired and attained by the American citizen is still one of the best. It was plainly acceptable to Washington and to John Marshall, his biographer, who wrote of him: "In speculation he was a real republican devoted to the constitution of his country, and to that system of equal political rights on which it is founded. But between a balanced republic and a democracy, the difference is like that between order and chaos. Real liberty, he thought, was to be preserved only by preserving the authority of the laws, and maintaining the energy of government."

"Liberty, Equality and Fraternity," — these three great words have had magical power over the French mind. In the United States the formula has had no vogue. The American, according to Mr. Bryce, "is capable of an ideality surpassing that of Englishmen or Frenchmen;" but in the political sphere, as elsewhere, he loves the concrete. Doubtless our earlier generations delighted in resounding declamation about Freedom. This rhetoric was a token of the lusty youth of a strong nation. The war which made the United States in reality a free country put an end to much of the previous rant and cant. In truth, the average man of Anglo-Saxon blood finds it difficult to-day to grow enthusiastic here over privileges to which he was born, as were his father and his grandfather before him. He is altogether willing to take liberty for granted; he is rather bored than otherwise if summoned to ecstasy over a blessing as familiar as air and sunshine. In full enjoyment of the thing, he is not anxious to be very often shouting the name. Civil liberty has been greatly extended during this century in the Old World, and the ground for much of our former national swaggering has disappeared. Beside this fact, of which educated Americans are well aware, the more mature spirit of the people is conscious that it has outgrown the raw conceit of its youth, and that it is time to put by such childish things as once formed the staple of Fourth of July orations.

The American of to-day takes a practical view of liberty. Of equality he is still less disposed to talk vaguely and rapturously. He is not at all inclined to dispute the truth, held to be self-evident by the signers of the Declaration of Independence, "That all men are created equal." [1] But he has too much respect for the obvious facts of human life to suppose for a moment that this equality is an equality in natural ability or in moral character, or that it is an equality in respect to property or social position, to be enforced by law. The actual extent of it is implied in the remainder of the second sentence of the Declaration: "That they are endowed by their Creator with certain unalienable rights; that among these are life, liberty and the pursuit of happiness." [2]

---

[1] "Who would dare deny this equality of universal humanity? — the right of every man to *live* without hindrance or question from others; the right of *freedom* in the use of his powers of body and mind, — freedom to make as much as lies within him of life and its opportunities, to make the most of himself as a man ; and the right to the fair procurement and enjoyment of all the happiness within his reach." *The United States as a Nation*, by Joseph P. Thompson, p. 68. This is, of course, substantially Napoleon's *la carrière ouverte aux talents.*

[2] Eighteen, if not more, of the State Constitutions declare that all men have "a natural right to acquire, possess and protect property."

The signers of the immortal document meant to affirm that no man's liberty or life should be taken from him except under conditions to which all men are uniformly subject, and that all men should have the same opportunity, so far as the government is concerned, to pursue happiness. They did not assert that no man's liberty should be interfered with under any circumstances, for they were as far as possible from being philosophical Anarchists. On the contrary, in order to secure the rights in question "governments are instituted among men." The signers did not declare that human life is so sacred that no government has a right to take it away, even in punishment for treason or murder. They did not believe it to be the business of Government or the State to guarantee happiness to each and every citizen. They would have accepted Emerson's saying that "America is another name for opportunity," but they could only have been amused by the notion that it is the function of government to go beyond securing an equal opportunity before the law for every man, and to provide work, food, clothing and other desirable things for the citizen, in order to complete his happiness.

It was not happiness but justice which the fathers of the American republic had in mind, in their opening affirmation. Of this justice they had no fanciful notions. It is enjoyed in substance when the life of the individual is secure, when his liberty of action is limited only by the need of preserving peace and order, and when his natural desire to seek his own welfare is allowed the freest scope consistent with the equal right of every other person. Jefferson and John Adams had a common faith in a natural, as distinguished from an artificial, aristocracy: "I agree with you that there is a natural aristocracy among men. The grounds of this are virtue and talents. . . . This natural aristocracy I consider as the most precious gift of nature for the instruction, the trusts and the government of society. . . . An artificial aristocracy founded on wealth and birth, without either virtue or talents, is a mischievous ingredient in government, and provision should be made to prevent its ascendency. . . . May we not even say that that form of government is the best which provides the most effectually for a pure selection of these natural *aristoi* into the offices of government? "[1]

In his famous Illinois Campaign of 1858, Abraham Lincoln defined his conception of the Declaration: "I do not understand the Declaration of Independence to mean that all men were created equal in all respects. They are not equal in color. But I believe that it does mean to declare that all men are equal in their rights to life, liberty and the pursuit of happiness." In Theodore Parker's often quoted definition of the American idea, in which he had been anticipated by Daniel Webster, and was followed by President Lincoln in his Gettysburg speech, equality of political rights is implied in the assertion that the people originate and maintain the government for their own welfare. "The people's government, made for the people, made by the people, and answerable to the people," said Daniel Webster, in his second speech on Foote's Resolution, January 26, 1830. "There is what I call the American idea. . . . This idea demands, as the proximate organization thereof, a democracy, — that is, a government of all the people, by all the people, for all the people; of course, a

[1] Jefferson to Adams, Oct. 28, 1813, *Works*, vol. vi. p. 223.

government of the principles of eternal justice, the unchanging law of God. For shortness' sake, I will call it the idea of Freedom: " so spoke Theodore Parker at the New England Anti-Slavery Convention in Boston, May 29, 1850. "That this nation, under God, shall have a new birth of freedom, and that government of the people, by the people, for the people, shall not perish from the earth," were Lincoln's undying words at Gettysburg, November 19, 1863.

The inequalities of a despotism or an aristocracy cannot exist in a democracy. But no American democracy has ever assumed the task of doing away with the inequalities for which differences in natural ability, in education, in family or in fortune are responsible. Very much to the contrary, it would secure opportunity by education and suffrage and then take its hands off:

> " Thet 's the old Amerikin idee,
> To make a man a Man, an' let him be." [1]

Equality before the law — a most desirable and fully attainable equality — is the kind at which we aim in these United States. A man becomes fully a man in the sight of his fellow-citizens when by his vote he gains a share in shaping the government. His ballot counts for one in deciding an election. Constitution and laws and public schools have brought him so far. As for any other kind of equality, they henceforth "let him be." The words of the Declaration may be styled "glittering and sounding generalities " or "blazing ubiquities," as one chooses his standpoint with reference to "natural rights." There can be no doubt as to the interpretation actually given them in American life.

[1] "Mr. Hosea Biglow's Speech in March Meeting." Lowell's *Poetical Works*, Riverside edition, vol. ii. p. 384.

Fraternity, the third member of the French political trinity, is the one least often mentioned by Americans under this name. But nowhere else is so much said in the churches of "the Brotherhood of Man" — the religious equivalent of the word, — and a true "enthusiasm for humanity," resting upon a sense of membership in one common family of man, characterizes the American spirit. We are a humane people, as the comparative mildness of the penal laws, the size and multitude of our philanthropic associations, and the popularity of such movements as that in behalf of kindness to animals testify.[1] We are a social people, and while little is expressly said or written about "fraternity," there is a great deal of practical and ready recognition of the manhood in every man and the womanhood in every woman as worthy of respect and kindness. In a nation of workers, living in a country possessed by the democratic spirit, the feeling of brotherhood is largely taken for granted. The unsentimental American is suspicious of the frequent preacher of the "fraternity of mankind;" but his hand is ready and his purse is open on every worthy appeal for aid to the suffering.

II. There has been a steady and very observable decline in the fondness for eulogy of liberty in the abstract which formerly characterized Fourth of July oratory in this country. *Practical conservatism is now a second prominent mark of the American Spirit.* The American has never cared much for ideal liberty. Like his English ancestors, he has usually been stirred to a public declaration of his "natural rights" by some gross invasion of his actual privileges. In the Declaration of Independence the very small pro-

---

[1] "None can breathe her air nor grow humane."

portion of general assertion of rights to specification of concrete wrongs is notable. When further invasion has been rendered impossible, the American abstains in State papers and elsewhere from declamation on the beauty of liberty and the vileness of despotism. He sufficiently resembles the Englishman for these words of M. Émile Boutmy to be altogether applicable both to the unwritten constitution of England and the written constitution of the United States. "Narrow but lucid realism, calm satisfaction or acquiescence in the arrangements of daily life, dislike to great schemes, to heroic remedies and actions which are naturally destructive of a somewhat complex equilibrium: these are the characteristics common to both the Anglo-Saxon Constitutions." [1]

The frame of government under which the American citizen lives, he knows, was deliberately adopted by his ancestors, under no constraint but that of the general human lot. It was their deliberate choice: it has been amended in successive generations, as time has shown the need of alteration. Theoretically, the same process can be applied to it in the most thorough manner by any generation when need arises; practically, such amendment is more and more rare and difficult in ordinary times. As Mr. Bryce has forcibly pointed out, there is no such natural tendency in a democratic country as theorists have assumed, to change institutions which the people have freely established and can revise at their pleasure, simply for the sake of change. The natural conservatism of human nature everywhere forbids such a useless expenditure of force.

The strong political instincts of Anglo-Saxon men,

[1] *Studies in Constitutional Law,* p. 166.

strengthened by centuries of freedom, lead them to cherish peace and order as the conditions of the happiness they seek in an active career. The American recognizes cheerfully that the liberty he desires to follow his own bent must be kept consistent with the equal liberty of every other person to do the same. The minimum of interference with his useful activity by the government which he has himself helped to establish has been, more or less consciously, his desire as a maker of laws and constitutions.[1] But he rarely thinks of rebelling whenever the government, in forming and maintaining which all have a part, simply comes in to provide equal opportunities for all to follow an unchecked career. Least of all men is the American able to find meaning in the maxim that "Government is a necessary evil." It has always seemed to him, as an acceptor of facts, a necessary arrangement for man; therefore it must be a good in itself. The question of the degree in which any specific government shall make itself felt in the private life of the citizen is another matter, to be determined as actual cases arise. Government is a necessary good. There must always be some kind of governing power to act as the instrument of that natural organization, the State. There is not, there never has been, any properly American theory as to the proper extent of State action. The dominant

[1] This aim was well stated in a political platform adopted in a Western State a few months ago : " We believe that in a free country the curtailment of absolute rights of the individual should only be such as is essential to the peace and good order of the community, and we regard all legislation looking to the infringement of liberty of person or conscience, not absolutely necessary to the maintenance of public order, as vicious in principle and demoralizing in practice."

feeling in the United States, however, has been and is that the American citizen owns the government, not that the government owns him. The people have made the governmental frame: the people can remake it. But they have deliberately restricted themselves to certain ways allowable in this remaking. In the exercise of that sagacity which has given them distinction as the best example of political liberty, they have chosen to make the process of important change slow and difficult. With every year of life under a constitution wisely framed, the disposition of the American people to political revolution, or even to any considerable measure of change, diminishes. Conservatism in the sphere of politics is as marked a characteristic of the American spirit as love of liberty. Conservative as respects its own environment, it is radical in its attitude toward Old World conditions with which it has nothing to do in practical life.

The reason for this conservatism fails to appear to many, but it is obviously this: "The sovereignty of the people," from which some, who have never lived under it, expect unlimited blessings, we have known as an actual fact for more than a hundred years. We have discovered many of its inevitable limitations as well as enjoyed its innumerable benefits. We have learned, roughly speaking, how much and how little to expect from a republican form of government, as such. We have come to realize, after a multitude of varied experiments, that republican government has practical limits to its efficiency, beyond which it is irrational to go, through any desire to be theoretically consistent. Many experiments are yet to be made, indeed, as material and social conditions alter and

new problems arise. But in making them we have
learned to be far more cautious than formerly. The
interests involved become each year more numerous
and more difficult to reckon with. Each specific
reform is more complicated with an immense network
of closely related interests. As the nation grows
older, there is less of that insurance against danger
which the unbounded resources of a new country have
hitherto provided. The conservative temper properly deepens as America waxes in power, wealth and
wisdom. There is, in fact, no characteristic of the
American political temper which more impresses keen
observers from Europe than the deep-lying respect
for law — the laws of nature, of human nature, and
of the statute-book — which the people as a whole
manifest. This respect is the very opposite of that
wild and irrational desire for change as such which
too many theorists have imputed to democracy as an
essential quality.[1]

The spirit of a race is always a much more important matter than the form of government under which
it lives. The American spirit is a lineal descendant
of the practical, law-abiding, freedom-loving English
temper. Whatever changes it has passed through, it
has not lost these qualities. By virtue of them, it
has succeeded. When freedom has been established
in the organic law of the new land, and a people, so
descended, inheriting age-long precedents of liberty,
has discovered and practiced for a century the art of

[1] Recent writers on Switzerland make prominent the conservatism of the Swiss people. Even the referendum has a steady-
ing effect on legislation. See Adams and Cunningham, *The
Swiss Confederation*, and Boyd Winchester, *The Swiss Republic*,
chapter I.

governing itself under the new conditions, a conservative tone toward proposals of fundamental change is simply a sign of rationality. The opposite spirit would imply the weakening of reason. "The American Republic," wrote Alexis de Tocqueville in 1850, in the preface to the twelfth edition of his remarkable work on "Democracy in America," "has not been the assailant, but the guardian of all vested rights. The property of individuals has had better guaranties there than in any other country of the world. Anarchy has there been as unknown as despotism. . . . The principles on which the American Constitutions rest — those principles of order, of the balance of powers, of true liberty, of deep and sincere respect for right — are indispensable to all republics. They ought to be common to all; and it may be said, beforehand, that, wherever they shall not be found, the republic will soon have ceased to exist."

M. de Tocqueville has properly been criticised for attributing to democracy, as their cause and origin, certain phenomena here in America which are due to quite other reasons. The extreme love of generalization which characterizes the French mind is responsible for this defect in his great book. But no equally competent observer since his time has called in question the correctness of the words just quoted. On the contrary, the latest eminent Frenchman to discuss our country, the Duc de Noailles, is even more explicit in praising the Constitution and the people on account of this conservative disposition. "This complex instrument," he says of the Constitution, "lends itself to different airs with very diverse variations and fugues: these are not free from false notes and discords, but, in the midst of them all, perpetually recurs the fundamental theme, what the Wagnerians would call the *Leitmoitif*, of conservatism." "Even in their errors, the Americans," he declares, "retain the conservative sense. . . . Nothing, with them, proclaims the spirit of the system-builder or the passion of the sectarian. Their failures and their falls are to be habitually referred to the enthusiasm of a democracy, young, exuberant, rash, and frequently led to deceive itself, but never anxious for anything more than for enlightenment, and always ready to return upon its errors." In the midst of the agitation, corruption and partisanship of American political life, "it needs attentive observation to distinguish the general conservative spirit which more or less inspires the nation, and keeps it in the right way or brings it back. This beneficent force, the result of acquired experience and a certain rectitude of judgment, has lost or gained ground according to time or circumstance. It has remained thus far the true moral force in American democracy and the essential cause of its success." The Duc de Noailles is impressed with the fact that this conservative disposition is shown by both political parties. Each includes representatives of all classes of the people, and thus "the United States have offered during three or four generations, the very interesting and very peculiar spectacle of a great country belonging to 'the right,' but interpreting and practising institutions of 'the left' in the French sense of these two terms. . . . Conservatism is diffused through the whole atmosphere in America. . . . It has no special history: the Americans are conservatives without knowing it."[1]

[1] *Cent Ans de République aux États-Unis.* Par le Duc de Noailles. Paris, 1889. Vol. ii. pp. 387, 388, 389, 405, 415.

To the same effect, M. Émile Boutmy speaks with admiration of "the gifts of prudence, moderation and political wisdom which a long parliamentary habit, acquired on the soil of Great Britain, has implanted in the instincts, and, so to speak, in the very blood of the emigrants whose descendants now people the United States." [1] He marks the very gradual nature of political changes in America: "Slow changes, careful transitions, which follow and reflect the natural progress of events, half-concealed and almost unconscious transformations which do not run counter to consecrated formulas until innovation has secretly gained over the instincts of the people and has allied itself with long custom, — all these different forms of growth take place more easily in England and even in the United States than in France."

To quote only one recent German student of America, Professor A. Sartorius Freiherrn von Waltershausen thus accents the conservatism of the American: "The American national character, which took shape under the earlier social conditions, has reached a certain fixity, that has thus far continued despite the changes in these conditions. It is active as an independent factor in the present social state. The reform movements of to-day and the reactions against perversions of existing law are affected by it. The. people are practical, and always ask for the attainable; when they have reached it, they go on to demand more. To claim everything at once they esteem folly; they will in no case give up what seems to them good at the time for anything which is not entirely comprehensible. Hence American workmen are very accessible to socialistic criticism of the pres-

[1] *Studies in Constitutional Law*, p. 102.

ent order, but they look upon the communism of the future with a skeptical eye."[1]

Our English kin are better fitted, naturally, than the French or even the Germans to recognize the essential spirit of the American mind in politics. No one has ever disputed the conservatism of the typical John Bull, and he knows his like when he sees it. He sees it all the more plainly when liberal in his temper and well acquainted with this country. Thus Mr. Bryce is more emphatic on this point than Walter Bagehot or Sir Henry Sumner Maine. But Mr. Bagehot could say: "The Americans now extol their institutions, and so defraud themselves of their just praise. But if they had not a genius for politics, if they had not a moderation in action singularly curious where superficial speech is so violent, if they had not a regard for law such as no great people have yet evinced, and infinitely surpassing ours, the multiplicity of authorities in the American Constitution would long ago have brought it to a bad end. Sensible shareholders, I have heard a shrewd attorney say, can work any deed of settlement; and so the men of Massachusetts could, I believe, work any constitution."[2]

[1] *Der Moderne Socialismus in den Vereinigten Staaten von Amerika*, p. 18.

[2] *The English Constitution*, p. xi. So, too, the Duc de Noailles observes, in words which I prefer to leave in the original : —

"La supériorité américaine paraît tenir à un don ou à un sens spécial, que l'on pourrait en quelque sorte qualifier de dextrine cérébrale et intellectuelle, fait mi-partie de droiture et de dextérité, valant moins que la première et plus que la seconde, espèce de notion spontanée de la direction droite, comparable à l'aimant dans la boussole, ou a l'instinct de l'hirondelle, qui sait toujours reconnaître le chemin du nord ou du midi, selon la nécessité de chaque saison. Aux États-Unis, en effet, ignorants et lettrés, corrupteurs et corrompus, ont naturellement l'esprit

Sir Henry Maine, to the same tenor, observed of our Constitution, "Its success, and the success of such American institutions as have succeeded, appears to me to have arisen rather from skillfully applying the curb to popular impulses than from giving them the rein." [1]

The difficulty is not small in choosing the most forcible passages from "The American Commonwealth" in regard to the disposition of the American people to hold fast to that which is good, and their unwillingness to jump out of the frying-pan, unless very sure they will not land in the fire. Mr. Bryce often recurs to this fundamental quality, and I must content myself with three quotations from the ablest and fairest survey of America yet made. Speaking of the fault, already noticed, which is supposed to inhere in a democracy, that it loves novelty for itself and has a passion for destroying old institutions, he inquires: "When the new order has been established, is there any ground for believing that a democracy is an exception to the general tendency of mankind to adhere to the customs they have formed, admire the institutions they have created, and even bear the ills they know rather than incur the trouble of finding some way out of them? The Americans are not an exception. They value themselves only too complacently on their methods of government; they abide by their customs because they admire them. They love novelty in the sphere of amusement, literature, and social life; but in serious matters, such as the fundamental institutions of government and in religious

droit. Ni les uns ni les autres ont portés d'attaquer ou à renier les principes fondamentaux de l'ordre social."

[1] *Popular Government,* p. xi.

belief, no progressive and civilized people is more conservative.[1] . . . The people are profoundly attached to the form which their national life has taken. The Federal Constitution is, to their eyes, an almost sacred thing, an ark of the covenant whereon no man may lay rash hands. . . . In the United States the discussion of political problems busies itself with details, and assumes that the main lines must remain as they are forever. This conservative spirit, jealously watchful even in small matters, sometimes prevents reforms; but it assures to the people an easy mind, and a trust in their future which they feel to be not only a present satisfaction, but a reservoir of strength."[2] "The Americans are at bottom a conservative people, in virtue both of the deep instincts of their race and of that practical shrewdness which recognizes the value of permanence and solidity in institutions. They are conservative in their fundamental beliefs, in the structure of their governments, in their social and domestic usages. They are like a tree whose pendulous shoots quiver and rustle with the lightest breeze, while its roots enfold the rock with a grasp which storms cannot loosen."[3]

III. *The American is supposed by foreigners, and by himself as well, to be nothing if not "enterprising."* He is usually energetic, pushing and capable in the conduct of his private affairs.[4] "Le go-ahead"

[1] *The American Commonwealth,* first Am. edition, vol. ii. p. 447.

[2] *Ibid.* vol. ii. p. 461.

[3] *Ibid.* vol. ii. p. 254. Mr. Bancroft emphasized American conservatism in beginning his *History of the United States.*

[4] "The Americans are, to use their favorite expression, a highly executive people, with a greater ingenuity in inventing means, and a greater promptitude in adapting means to an end, than any European race." Bryce, vol. ii. p. 44.

of the people has always impressed Frenchmen who have traveled in the United States. The phrase is one of the commonest of every-day expressions, and the "go-ahead" person is everywhere held in honor.[1] The disposition to take up with spirit and execute with fire the work in hand may be given as a definition of "go-aheadativeness." Holding the law in respect and orderly to the last, the typical American business-man greatly resents interference by Congress or the Legislature, or, as he would prefer to put it, "the politicians," in trade and commerce. He will not waste much time in simple denunciation of a meddling tendency; but, as a man of commercial talent, he is firmly convinced that business will flourish most when "the politicians" leave it alone.[2] He is usually more willing to endure a law which works poorly than to risk the substitution for it of a worse one, which might well be the effect of starting up the legislature or Congress to reform. Of the restless enterprise of the American, stimulated to the utmost by the practically unbounded opportunities which have hitherto

[1] "Circumstances had made the desire of gain, skill in acquisition, and a spirit of bold and venturesome enterprise the domineering and most striking traits of the national character." H. von Holst, *Constitutional and Political History of the United States,* vol. vi. p. 101.

[2] "The United States are primarily a commercial society, and only secondarily a nation, . . . not so much a democracy as a huge commercial company for the discovery, cultivation and capitalization of its enormous territory." E. Boutmy, *Studies in Constitutional Law,* p. 128.

"Their greatest achievements have lain in the internal development of their country by administrative shrewdness, ingenuity, promptitude and an unequaled dexterity in applying the principle of association, whether by means of private corporations or of local public or quasi-public organisms." Bryce, ii. 197.

prevailed, Mr. Ruskin, the least judicial of observers, has given a very unflattering estimate: "My American friends . . . tell me I know nothing about America. It may be so, and they must do me the justice to observe that I, therefore, usually *say* nothing about America. But this much I have said, because the Americans, as a nation, set their trust in liberty and in equality, of which I detest the one, and deny the possibility of the other; and because, also, as a nation, they are wholly undesirous of Rest, and incapable of it; irreverent of themselves, both in the present and in the future; discontented with what they are, yet having no ideal of anything which they desire to become." [1]

Change, indeed, has hitherto been the law in the United States, — change of business, change of home from East to West or from North to South, a readiness to "pull up stakes" and go out to build up a new country on the borders of existing civilization. But as the country has grown older and the West has filled up, this changeableness has visibly diminished, and it is likely to diminish still more. The intellectual restlessness of the American mind is a much more important matter. The American intellect is exceedingly active and versatile, and as accessible as the Frenchman's to novel ideas. [2] Doctor Holmes' good-natured satire could speak forty-six years ago of

[1] *Time and Tide*, Brantwood edition, p. 181.

[2] President J. G. Schurman of Cornell University has well stated some reasons for regarding the American as the Greek of the modern world. "Zeller finds the originating ground of Greek Philosophy in the numerous and happily combined endowments of the people ; in their practical address and active power ; in their æsthetic feeling and thirst for knowledge ; in the equipoise of their realism and idealism ; in their acute per-

> " A nervous race,
> Fretful to change and rabid to discuss,
> Full of excitements, always in a fuss."

But this superficial restlessness is accompanied, as we have seen, by a fundamental conservatism in respect to practice. There is a national dislike of extremes and revolutions. We have too practical a temper to commit ourselves with enthusiasm for any length of time to the guidance of one principle. The long distrust of "free trade" is an example of this characteristic.

The American is generally supposed by other peoples to have a genius for business and an extreme capacity for "turning off" work, as the phrase goes. American business methods always look to directness

ception of individuality and their harmonious conception of a totality, and in their openness to foreign influences along with the self-poised independence that enabled them to assimilate what they received. If this picture of natural endowment, to which might be added a unique vein of humor, be not the counterfeit presentment of the American temperament, there is certainly no other people of whom so many of the features are accurately descriptive. . . . On the one hand, Greek culture was characterized by freedom, — freedom of government for the city-states, freedom of action for the individual, and freedom of thought in religion ; . . . on the other, by respect for custom and law and by subordination of the individual to the whole. . . . If these favoring aspects of Greek civilization are not to-day reproduced in the American love of independence and the American respect for law . . . then one can scarcely imagine where they are to be found even in approximation among the peoples of the earth." (*Philosophical Review*, January, 1892, pp. 2–4.) That the American occupies a position between the Englishman and the Frenchman, intellectually at least, will be conceded by many who may not be prepared to go along to the end with President Schurman in his delineation of Americans as the Modern Greeks.

in reaching the object sought. Saving of time is the prime consideration. The one-price system is almost universal, little time being wasted in bargaining. To do the largest amount of business in the shortest possible period and with the least formality is the usual desire. New ways and methods are welcomed, and immediately and widely adopted, if they result in saving time or diminishing expense or increasing returns. The natural conservatism of business is probably less in the United States than in any other civilized country.

IV. The *love of competition* which characterizes the Anglo-Saxon race has probably reached its utmost pitch in America. The French proverb, "Nothing succeeds like success," Mr. Bryce declares, is more true here than in any other country. The shrewd and dexterous American is quick to adopt any new means which will put him in advance of his rivals in trade: the professions are crowded with men who are keen antagonists. It has not been shown that this zeal in competition has lowered the level of honesty in legitimate business, as compared with other commercial nations of the present day. The competitive spirit is inseparable from manly strength and self-reliance. "Self-help" has always been the motto of the American from the first settlement of the country down to the present hour, and he is distinguished by his capacity for adjusting himself to circumstances, and so mastering the situation.[1] Personal indepen-

---

[1] A striking instance of this readiness is related by Theodore Winthrop in his account of "Our March to Washington." "The Massachusetts Eighth Regiment found the railway track beyond Annapolis torn up in April, 1861. 'Wanted, experienced track layers' was the word along the files. All at once the

dence of others' aid has been his practical ideal. He
has been taught from the first that it is the business
of every man to make his own living; that the community is not bound to give him employment so long
as he is able to seek for it himself, or food and shelter
so long as he is able to work at all. Yet there is no
hesitation in America in helping those who are really
destitute and unable to help themselves. The humanity of the community and the independence of the
individual are not over-emphasized by President Eliot
of Harvard in writing of a Maine town: "Everybody
who has a domicile in the town is assured of a bare
livelihood at all times, and of aid under special misfortunes. The idea that it is the duty of the town to
take care of its poor is firmly planted in the mind of
every inhabitant. . . . Beside this idea of the town's
duty toward the unfortunate and incapable is planted
in the breast of the rural New Englander another
invaluable sentiment, namely, that 'to come on the
town ' is the greatest of misfortunes and humiliations.
Few aged people 'come on the town.' " [1]

Americans outside of the large cities are in the
habit of taking care of themselves without any help

line of the road became closely populated with experienced track-
layers fresh from Massachusetts — Presto Change ! The rails
were relaid, spiked, and the roadway leveled and better ballasted
than any road I ever saw south of Mason and Dixon's line. . . .
The engines had been purposely disabled. Here appeared the
deus ex machina. . . . He took a quiet squint at the engine, and
he found ' Charles Homans, his mark' written all over it. . . .
The old rattletrap was an old friend. Charles Homans had had
a share in building it. The machine and the man said ' how d' y'
do ' at once. Homans called for a gang of engine builders.
Of course they swarmed out of the ranks."

[2] " The Forgotten Millions," *Century Magazine,* August, 1890.

from policemen, the preservation of law and order being largely and successfully left in the hands of the individual citizen. There is no reliance upon a numerous constabulary for defense against private aggression. In the great majority of his daily doings, the American feels himself at liberty to follow his own bent, and nothing could be more offensive to him than the constant presence and intrusion of such a bureauracy as the patient, well-drilled German submits to. He desires neither the supervision nor the assistance of a governmental officer when he can help himself.[1]

Americans have a great respect for the strong man, probably all the more respect in political life because of the many limitations with which "one-man power" has been surrounded by the framers of our constitutions. American political life, unfortunately, gives too few opportunities for the manifestation of independence, but the representative who through sincere conviction opposes the opinions at any time uppermost in the minds of his constituency is apt, in the end, to gain more than he loses: the Governor or President who vetoes a bill is almost invariably popular because of his action. There is such a rooted distrust of

[1] "The two nations [England and America] alike prefer the practical to the abstract. . . . They set a high value on liberty for its own sake. They desire to give full scope to the principle of self-reliance in the people, and they deem self-help to be immeasurably superior to help in any other form, — to be the only help, in short, which ought not to be continually or periodically put upon its trial, and required to make good its title. They mistrust and mislike the centralization of power, and they cherish municipal, local, even parochial liberties as nursery grounds, not only for the production here and there of able men, but for the general training of public virtue and independent spirit." W. E. Gladstone.

"politics" and "professional politicians" in the common mind that the executive who resolutely opposes the legislature or Congress has the support of the people in nearly every instance. They know that compliance on his part with the majority in his party, the legislature or Congress would be easy, while resistance is more or less difficult. Under these circumstances "genuine, solid, old Teutonic pluck" wins the public admiration. The tendency is visibly strengthening in the United States to concentrate administrative powers in the hands of one man, and to hold him responsible for its wise and honest use. Diffusion of responsibility through a crowd of legislators has proved to be a deceptive method of securing the public welfare.

V. *Public spirit is one of the foremost of national characteristics in America.* In some parts of the country it is weak in consequence of the extremely cosmopolitan character of the population, but nowhere in the world, probably, is there a more general conviction that the public has a rightful claim on a large share, comparatively, of the time and labor of the individual citizen.[1] There is but a small class of professional philanthropists and reformers who are ready to join in every enterprise of public spirit; but the number of persons is great who are influenced by the special appeals of reform movements directed at particular abuses. Philanthropic undertakings and charities of a thousand kinds have no difficulty in

---

[1] "An American attends to his private concerns as if he were alone in the world, and the next minute he gives himself up to the common weal as if he had forgotten them. At one time, he seems animated by the most selfish cupidity ; at another, by the most lively patriotism." Tocqueville, vol. ii. p. 171.

rallying support and gaining the means necessary for presenting their programme to the public, for influencing legislation, and for reaching their object more directly. Associations for the general improvement of mankind have little attraction for the practical American spirit, but it is ever ready to take up a specific problem in reform or philanthropy, and to work heartily at its solution until this is attained.[1] The executive talent generally attributed to the American shows itself nowhere more strikingly than in the facile and effective creation and extension of voluntary associations of all kinds.[2] In politics, in philanthropy and in religion, coöperation and association are the first and most natural resort of the whole people.

VI. *The American is constitutionally an optimist.* He naturally inclines to take a cheerful view of the

---

[1] "Nor do their moral and religious impulses remain in the soft haze of self-complacent sentiment. The desire to expunge or cure the visible evils of the world is strong. Nowhere are so many philanthropic and reformatory agencies at work." Bryce, vol. ii. p. 248.

[2] "Americans, of all ages, all conditions, and all dispositions, constantly form associations. . . . I have often admired the extreme skill with which the inhabitants of the United States succeed in proposing a common object to the exertions of a great many men, and in inducing them voluntarily to pursue it." Tocqueville, vol. ii. pp. 129, 130.

"Associations are created, extended and worked in the United States more quickly and effectively than in any other country. In nothing does the executive talent of the people better shine than in the promptitude wherewith the idea of an organization for a common object is taken up, in the instinctive discipline that makes every one who joins in starting it fall into his place, in the practical, businesslike turn which the discussions forthwith take." Bryce, vol. ii. p. 239.

most desperate situation, morally or politically. Beyond a doubt, his optimism has thus far been justified by the result. He has unbounded faith in the country and the people (with a very large P), and this hopefulness is the reason for that good-natured acceptance of the will of the majority for the time being which is so marked a feature of our political life. The day after election is the one day of the year in which there is the largest exhibition of good-humor. The defeated party cheerfully accepts the situation, and resigns itself to its position in the minority until the next election, when it is hopeful that the popular verdict will be different. This faith in the people does not imply, especially with the reformers, a belief that the people are always right, but a belief that the people are always open to conviction, and that the side which has the strongest arguments will finally win. This belief is nowhere stronger than in the minds of the most thoughtful and independent American citizens.[1] Optimism is reinforced by the omnipresent sense of humor which, for instance, cheerfully accepts derisive political epithets in the course of the political campaign, such as "locofoco" or "mugwump," and is ready to laugh at its own expense when the popular vote has placed it in the minority. Party spirit in the United States goes to regrettable extremes, especially in the absurd decision of town and city elections according to national politics, but the prevalent good-humor and the

[1] "A distinguished American writer, to whose energy the cause of international copyright owes much, wrote to me in describing the final struggle by which the bill was carried, 'I have always said, never despair of America.'" Mr. Bryce in *The Speaker*.

thorough hopefulness of the national temper are alleviations of much practical consequence.

Nowhere in the modern world is the characteristically modern faith in Progress more profoundly rooted in the mind of the people than in America. "Some things can be done as well as others," is the homely way of expressing this conviction which Dr. Holmes quotes from Sam Patch, whom he calls "the Western Empedocles." The astonishing growth and development of Western States and cities, the marvelous progress of the whole country in every material respect, need only a passing mention in a work like the present, not devoted to sheer eulogy of "triumphant democracy," or to exposition of the dangers lurking or patent in our civilization. The forward look is characteristic of the American; he believes in Progress, if in no other god! A people saved by the locomotive and the telegraph from the otherwise probable disruption of its vast domain; a people inventive in the highest degree and carrying a practical temper into every field of science which its insatiable curiosity tempts it to explore — Americans have an almost boundless credulity concerning the power of science and invention to overcome all present evils and satisfy every carnal desire. For no class of persons have they a more sincere and abiding respect than for the men whose names are associated with the sewing-machine, the reaper, the telegraph and the electric light — to mention but four of the more notable inventions of the age. American history is an Iliad of invention, and its heroes have largely been its Howes, McCormicks, Morses, and Edisons. The actual confidence of the people of the United States in the power of plainly approaching applications of electri-

city to give a new lease of prosperity and to do away
with existing social troubles is extreme — and who
shall say that it is ill-founded, so far as it concerns
the material causes of moral difficulties? Electricity
may almost be called to-day the American Messiah!

The American's faith in political progress is in the
more thorough appreciation of principles already long
and widely accepted and in their consistent evolution.
He has ceased to expect that democracy will adopt
the same type of institutions everywhere else as in
America; but of the ultimate, universal prevalence of
the democratic principle he has no doubt. A faith
like the Frenchman's in "La Patrie" and a confidence in divine protection like the Hebrew's blend to
make his creed at once political and religious.[1] American patriotism has always taken the form, more or
less, of a belief in the "manifest destiny" of the
United States. Mr. Bryce, of all observers from
abroad, has treated this belief with the most respect:
"Foreign critics have said that they think themselves
the special objects of the protecting care of Providence. If this be so, it is a matter neither for surprise
nor for sarcasm. They are a religious people. They
are trying, and that on the largest scale, the most re-

---

[1] The influence of optimism on theology has been remarked
by M. Boutmy. "In a country where everything succeeds,
where at the feast of life there is room for all, it must be difficult to conceive a heaven with a narrow gateway and a salvation
limited to the few. The American is therefore naturally an optimist. He is accustomed here below to a comfortable income
and the prospect of a final surplus, and, being imbued with the
idea that this happy experience will be repeated in the world to
come, he is constantly wandering farther and farther away from
the state of mind that characterizes Calvinism." *Revue Bleue*,
Dec. 20, 1890.

markable experiment in government the world has yet
witnessed. They have more than once been surrounded by perils which affrighted the stoutest hearts,
and they have escaped from these perils into peace
and prosperity. There is among pious persons a
deep conviction — I have often heard it expressed in
sermons and prayers with evident sincerity — that the
nation has been, and is being, more than other nations, guided by the hand of God. And, even when
the feeling does not take a theological expression, the
belief in what is called the 'Mission of the Republic'
for all humanity is scarcely less ardent."

Although this feeling does not receive at present
such frequent or over-emphatic assertion as before or
during the Civil War, it is probably stronger; it par-
takes less of chauvinism and more of religious trust.
The fact that America has passed through the Puritan
discipline is the reason, to a large extent, of our confidence that we are a chosen people. The Puritans
were an Old Testament folk, and it was especially
noticeable how largely the Old Testament was read
in Northern pulpits during the Rebellion. The deep
experiences of the war, which tried men's souls as
they had never been tried before in the history of the
nation, issuing at last in a result of first importance
to entire humanity, have supplied an immovable foundation for this trust. It may be heard speaking with
the strongest conviction in the verse of our poets who
have written since the war; it is heard not only in
the poetry of Bryant, Emerson and Lowell, but also
in the mature strain of Oliver Wendell Holmes: —

> " This is the new world's gospel : Be ye men !
> Try well the legends of the children's time ;
> Ye are the chosen people, God has led

Your steps across the desert of the deep
As now across the desert of the shore ;
Mountains are cleft before you as the sea
Before the wandering tribe of Israel's sons ;
Still onward rolls the thunderous caravan,
Its coming printed on the western sky,
A cloud by day, by night a pillared flame ;
Your prophets are a hundred unto one
Of them of old who cried, ' Thus saith the Lord ; '
They told of cities that should fall in heaps,
But yours of mightier cities that shall rise
Where yet the lonely fishers spread their nets,
Where hides the fox and hoots the midnight owl ;
The tree of knowledge in your garden grows
Not single, but at every humble door."

The imperfect examination of the American Spirit
which this chapter has attempted has been purposely
confined to those deeper-lying qualities that have a
direct bearing upon the question of Socialism and
Individualism. If the exposition has not been altogether misleading, a person entirely unacquainted
with the history of the United States might at once
infer that no rigid theory of the relations of the individual to the State would find favor with such a people. Its moral and intellectual qualities are such as
to render extreme individualism and extreme socialism impossible for it. The most superficial view of
the American character discloses the union in living
practice of the traits which make the individualist
with those which make the socialist. Self-assertive,
but kindly and sociable; indisposed to "orate" about
equality and fraternity, but ever jealous of any
affront to his manhood as an equal citizen and voter,
and ready to give the most concrete exemplification
of the brotherhood of man on occasion; politically
conservative, but intellectually radical; "pleased with

his world, and hating only cant," but always ready to
see the self of to-day surpassed by the self of to-morrow, and more prone to bow in worship of Progress
than to practice adulation of a less spiritual deity;
ready to discuss every proposal of change, but in
practice shrewdly intent on the actual consequences
of any proposal; his motto apparently "every one for
himself," but very able and very willing to combine
with other men for a common advantage; distinguished alike by "go-aheadativeness" and by sagacious circumspection; disinclined to bow before dig-
nitaries not of his own making whom he can also
unmake at pleasure, but most ready to follow natural
leaders; a realist of the realists in politics and business; an idealist of the idealists in his visions of the
future of democracy, science and art; alert for his
private advantage, yet public-spirited in a large
degree; superficially irreverent, but fundamentally
convinced that he belongs to a chosen nation and a
peculiar people — the American is no mixture of incompatible characteristics, but a new type of manhood. He is neither individualist nor socialist, but
a very human combination of the qualities of both.
Let us first see what respect he has shown under
the conditions of his environment for the tendency to
individualism. Great as this has undoubtedly been,
it is a respect limited by his practical talent and his
political genius.

CHAPTER IV.

THE AMERICAN SPIRIT AND INDIVIDUALISM.

In more than one sense America may be called the paradise of the individual. No other country has held out such great prizes to private talent for the last century, or offered it a freer field to work in. A manly, capable and self-reliant people, Americans have had an opportunity the like of which is unknown to history.[1] Least of all peoples have they had reason to put their faith in governmental machinery, even that of their own devising, in preference to individual initiative and voluntary coöperation. Especially in the building up of great manufacturing industries and the development of immense transportation systems has the practical genius of the people asserted itself, with the results in gigantic operations and colossal fortunes which we see to-day, in all directions.[2] The American is always ready to receive

[1] " Americans are fond of representing their country as a theatre for the trial and development of liberty in every form and in every direction of speculative and practical life ; scarcely an American can be found who has not in his mind, in a more or less nebulous form, this idea of illimitable individualism and indefinite expansion." *Education from a National Standpoint*, by Alfred Fouillée, American edition, p. 6.

[2] " An American explorer, an American settler in new lands, an American man of business pushing a great enterprise, is a being as bold and resourceful as the world has ever seen." Bryce, vol. ii. p. 303.

help from the State in starting a railway or a steam-
ship line ("the old flag *and* an appropriation"); but
he is not at all inclined to consider the government
a proper agent for the management or ownership of
either. The working theory on which American
industrial life has been conducted is that stated by
President E. B. Andrews of Brown University: "In
all economic activity the presumption is in favor of
individual liberty and free competition." In the
absence of any sharply defined delimitation of the
two, there has been no general feeling that the interest of the individuals who make up the public and
the interest of the public are different and contra-
dictory.

The American patent system may well be selected
as an apposite illustration of the union of regard for
the individual and concern for the public. It derives
from the English practice of granting to inventors
and discoverers in the arts the exclusive control of
their inventions and discoveries. This practice, dat-
ing back to the time of Edward III., has spread from
England into all modern countries which protect the
inventor and discoverer. The patent is virtually a
bargain between the ingenious inventor or the fortunate discoverer and the government as the representative of the people. The man who, after long
months or years, has succeeded in making a sewing-
machine that will work, might keep his model a secret; mankind would be no wiser, and those who ply
the needle would not be benefited. If the new invention is to be open to appropriation by any and
every comer, without regard to the interests of the
inventor, there will obviously be very little inducement for the average man to invent a new machine or

seek an improved method of production. They are so few as not to need reckoning who will toil severely with head and hand, and devote their time and their money to inventions for lightening the labor or increasing the comfort of the public, without desiring any return. The benevolence of the inventor who would take out no patent on his Franklin stove was as rare as his scientific skill and his comprehensive patriotism. Ordinary justice rewards the public benefactors who invent labor-saving devices and useful machines with protection for their brain-product. It thus opens a sure road to fortune to the ingenious person who can invent a device, machine or process of value to civilized man. Such exceptional individuals, stimulated by the hope of wealth and reputation, and moved by the union of three strong forces, — innate intellectual energy, self-interest, and desire to improve the lot of their fellows, — have led the wonderful progress of modern times in arts and manufactures.

On the other hand, while the people at large regard a liberal compensation to the inventor as only a fair return for the great service he renders them, they do not consider that his exclusive right should be perpetual. A term is fixed within which he shall receive from the public a fee for each machine made, or for the use of his new process. In this time he is to secure for himself the reward for which a progressive people are sure to give him an opportunity by their patronage. After this period has expired, his invention becomes a part of the common stock of civilization. The community has protected him in the exercise of his individual talent and given free field to his ambition, considering such protection of ultimate advantage to all; now it withdraws its favor, as the object is achieved, and assumes to itself the invention for which it offered a stimulus and paid a reasonable reward.

The patent system of the United States, of which the centennial anniversary was observed in 1890, has been pronounced by the Commissioner of Labor "the most elaborate and the most complete of any in the world." A careful examination is made into the actual novelty and utility of the invention offered for inspection, and the inventor is secured in his exclusive right, after the patent is granted. In these two important respects the American is more careful than the Englishman even to encourage and protect the inventor. Jefferson, indeed, who, as Secretary of State, was practically the first American Commissioner of Patents under the Act of April 10, 1790, construed it with extreme rigor, in what he supposed to be the interest of the people, and only sixty-seven patents were issued in the years 1790–93. He opposed the very lax law of 1793 on the ground that the promiscuous granting of patents is "against the theory of popular government and pernicious in its effects." The stricter act of 1836 placed the system substantially on its present basis. Up to that year 11,384 patents had been granted: between 1836 and 1891 the "new series" increased to the astonishing number of 443,987 patents, — exclusive of designs, trademarks and labels.

This multiplication of ingenuities is the result of a consistent regard for individual talent on the part of the community from the beginning of our history. The General Court of Massachusetts Bay in 1641 gave to Samuel Winslow a monopoly for ten years in making salt by his process. In 1646 it granted a patent to Joseph Jencks for an improvement which "changed the short, thick, straight English scythe into the longer, thinner, curved implement with stiffened back, substantially the same as that in use at the present day." In 1652 the Superior Court made a decree in favor of John Clark, by which every family using his invention for "saving wood and warming houses at little cost" should pay him ten shillings a year. Connecticut provided, by the law of 1672, that "there shall be no monopolies granted amongst us but of such new inventions as shall be judged profitable and for the benefit of the country." Under this law patents were granted for making steel and glass, for tide-mills, and for a clock "that winds itself up by the help of the air, and will continue to do so without aid or assistance until the component parts thereof are destroyed by friction!"

The United States Constitution declares that "the Congress shall have power . . . to promote the Progress of Science and useful Arts, by securing for limited Times to Authors and Inventors the exclusive Right to their respective Writings and Discoveries." The first patent granted under the act of 1790, dated July 1, 1790, was to Samuel Hopkins of Vermont for making pot and pearl ashes. In 1890 the number of patents issued was 26,292. The figures mark the extraordinary inventiveness of the American mind, quick to realize the needs of a new country in which laborers have been few, and anxious alike to secure fortune and reputation for the individual, and ease and comfort for the community. The earlier inventors were naturally concerned largely with processes for subduing the wilderness and cultivating the new

land; but the whole field of invention has since been
explored by the American, with results known to all
men. The cotton-gin; the steamboat and the locomotive; the breech-loading rifle and the revolver; the
plow, the reaper and the mowing - machine; the
elevator; the steam fire-engine; the sewing-machine;
the printing-press, the type-writer and the type-set-
ter; the telegraph, the telephone and the phono-
graph; the electric light and the electric car; the
engraved bank-note and the machine-made watch, —
these are some of the achievements with which the
names of Americans are honorably associated, from
Eli Whitney to Thomas A. Edison. The quickness,
acuteness and ingenuity of the Yankee have become a
proverb, and the world gives him the credit of being
the most inventive of men.[1] His necessities were
great in the new country, and his talent has become
hereditary, now that the land is practically subdued.
In the further progress of invention the American has
a boundless faith; he looks to this quarter for relief
from many existing evils, and his belief is justified
by experience.[2] The inventor, for instance, who

[1] "Beyond question, in respect of mechanical appliances the
Americans are ahead of all nations." Herbert Spencer, *Essays,*
iii. 473.

[2] A striking anecdote is related of Dr. Thornton, for twenty-
six years the Superintendent of the Patent Office. When the
English troops captured Washington in 1814 and destroyed the
Capitol, it is said that a cannon was turned upon the Patent Office. Dr. Thornton threw himself before it and passionately
cried out, " Are you Englishmen, or only Goths and Vandals ?
This is the Patent Office, a depository of the ingenuity and
invention of the American nation, in which the whole world is
interested. Would you destroy it ? If so, fire away, and let
the charge pass through my body." His devotion was effectual
in saving the building.

shall surmount the difficulties of applying stored-up electricity as a motive power in transportation will probably make the largest individual contribution to the improvement of the tenement-house system. In the future, as in the past, the American patent system will reconcile the interests of the inventor and the interests of the community by a method that is, theoretically, neither individualistic nor socialistic, but is simply the outgrowth of a wise interpretation of all the facts of the situation. Practically, it respects all the interests involved, according to the method of the statesman.

The briefest survey of the situation will show that American practice has never been in accordance with the theoretical individualism of closet philosophers. The notion that a certain entity styled "the State" should be an object of suspicion to every individual has had no standing with the American mind since the days of Jefferson, when it was discovered, once for all, that the only power the people need fear is the people themselves in an irrational mood. No American State has been willing to confine itself within the narrow limits which the theorists of individualism would prescribe, and beyond which they can see only slaves and despots. Every Commonwealth of the Union has felt itself free to establish and maintain public schools, and it has never dreamed of apologizing to the taxpayer. If a community desires to support a free public library, it does this with no feeling that it is invading the supposed "rights" of any person, to the effect that he shall be free from contributing in this way to the general enlightenment. The town or city will establish parks and pleasure grounds, if it choose, for the sufficient reason that they greatly promote the public health and the general welfare. The State will legislate concerning the proper construction and the sanitary condition of factories and tenement-houses and feel no scruple. Without remorse it regulates the hours of labor so that no employer shall enforce an excessively long day.

As nearly every class shows a marked tendency to infringe upon the rights of other classes unable to resist to advantage, the people at large do well to act, through their agent, the government, so as to restore the balance. The object is to keep competition really as free and fair as may be, where the conditions are such as, without legislation, preclude an approximation to theoretical freedom. If the philosopher maintain that there is great danger from so loose a conception of governmental interference, and that the rights of individuals will certainly be outraged under it, the American would reply that "interference by the government" is a phrase that loses much of its offensive meaning with a people that governs itself; that mistakes will and must be made by any people in learning the art of self-government; that an intelligent, capable and fair-minded people will rectify these mistakes sooner or later, and will not be apt to repeat them; and that, where the utmost liberty of speech and the press is allowed, no aggrieved individual is destitute of means of agitating for redress. The court is always sitting, and appeals are ever in order. If an individual should, in effect, ask that the general principles and the common method of American civilization be set aside for his supposed benefit, he will not, indeed, be likely to obtain much consolation. The will of the majority is the one power that demands respect in a republic. The resource of the individual who believes that the majority at any time is mistaken is his ample freedom to argue the matter and convince the majority of error, if he is right. A fundamental belief in the reasonableness of mankind and its consequent openness to conviction lies deep in our American temper. If this had not been repeatedly justified by the event, our institutions would long since have broken down. Experience, however, has only strengthened our confidence. Taking pains to secure a wide spread of ordinary knowledge, and guarding individual rights by constitutional guarantees, — not to be evaded while Supreme Courts exist, and not to be removed altogether except by a slow process always open to the assault of reason, — we have a just feeling that the rights of individuals are, on the whole, well secured in this country.

If any person in the United States believes that the government invades his "rights" by taxing him for any other purpose than to keep the public peace and repel invasion, whether it be to pay for carrying the mails or for supporting free schools, he will probably be simply laughed at; yet no one has power to prevent him from expressing his opinion, by speech in private or public, by petition, or by printing his opinions in such form as he may desire, with a view to converting the public to his way of thinking. If he refuses to pay taxes for purposes which he deems illegitimate, he can appeal to the courts, — with no prospect, however, that they will exempt him from burdens which have been considerately undertaken and are steadfastly borne by the whole people. The rampant individual must allow a nation the right to develop its own genius! If he is a consistent individualist after Mr. Herbert Spencer's pattern, he will have the alternative set before him of paying taxes which he deems iniquitous or emigrating to a land — if he can find one — where intelligence is less esteemed and "cranks" are held in greater honor.

In point of fact, the number of extreme individualists in this country is, and has been, exceedingly small. Unwillingness to pay taxes for other than the most limited purposes of government is common enough, as in all countries, but it rarely seeks to disguise itself with a cloak of theory. The American people are public-spirited, and institutions like the common schools have become incorporated into their life, so that persistent unwillingness to support them may well seem treason against the public weal. Whatever element of socialism, so-called, has been deeply ingrained into our laws and constitutions, must be regarded as permanent by the few conscientious and rational individualists of the extreme type among us. Temporary tendencies that appear to go too far toward socialism to be in accordance with the national spirit, they may and should resist with vigor. If they are correct, they will check these tendencies in time; if they are mistaken, the processes will continue until their excess becomes patent to the majority. The individualist, careless of measure and degree, who refuses to pay taxes for schools or roads, will meet at last the prevailing argument of force, and be compelled to submit to full payment, with costs. Such cases have been extremely rare, so great is the respect felt for the will of the people, deliberately settled and long unchanged, and so common is submission under protest, loud or weak, to the actual law of the commonwealth. The protest invariably dies out in a short time; it is most often made by the new-comer not yet familiar with the logic of the country he has sought as the home of freedom — which he is apt to confound with license. Such a protest is quite absent from the lips or the thought of the American-born. The practical policy for those who lean to individualism in this country is not effort to abolish methods to which we are already committed as a people, but resistance to further measures supposed to be extreme in the direction of socialism.

The American intellect had formerly, if it may not be said to still retain, a natural propensity to such a general theory of the relations of the individual and the State as Mr. Herbert Spencer expounded, in his early work on "Social Statics," with a freshness and charm in strong contrast with the laborious pedantry of much of his later writing, and as that to which John Stuart Mill gave classic expression in his essay "On Liberty." The average American liked to do as he pleased, if any one did. He delighted to repeat that "one man is as good as another;" and his politics resounded with this slogan. Naturally dear to the American mind, therefore, has been the theory that every person has a perfect right to do as he pleases, so long as he does not infringe the equal right of every other person, and that governments exist to guarantee this right. Of a sweet savor in our nostrils was every doctrine asserting the beauty and the value of such individualism. For government in the abstract we had no partiality.

Most of the younger liberals of America would have professed themselves, twenty-five years ago, un-hesitating disciples of Mr. Spencer's political creed.

Such is no longer our theoretical position, even in appearance. American individualism is not that taught by Mr. Spencer. Our practice is far from being consistent with the rigor and vigor of the English philosopher of evolution. A brief examination of Mr. Spencer's essays on "The Man *versus* The State" should at once reveal to American Spencerians the gulf which yawns between his doctrine and the customs which they admire and support in their own land: they can no more belong to the sect of "Suspenceru maru-nomi" as the Japanese style it, "the man who swallows Spencer whole!" Published in 1884, these essays contain Mr. Spencer's most elaborate attack on modern tendencies in legislation, and the reissue of them last year, in connection with a revised edition of "Social Statics," shows that his attitude has not changed. Mr. Spencer himself is tolerably consistent; but his followers here too often assert his theoretical premises, while they heartily sustain institutions based upon entirely different principles, and favor movements inspired by a social temper quite alien to his. This being the case, a short review of "The Man *versus* The State" from the American standpoint will be in order.

"The New Toryism" is Mr. Spencer's epithet for the liberalism and radicalism in Great Britain which seek to promote the welfare of the people by positive legislation. "The Coming Slavery" is to result from the indefinite extension of such legislation. "The Sins of Legislators" are the ignorance and rashness which the writer considers inherent in law-making assemblies, while "The Great Political Superstition" is the supposed "divine right" of Parliament. These four essays are pervaded by a combative spirit

toward recent British legislation, which can be justified only by a thoroughgoing belief in the perfect
truth of the individualistic theory propounded in
"Social Statics," in complete allegiance to which the
author, indeed, seems never to have faltered. The
thesis which he maintained in 1860, in an article on
"Parliamentary Reform," he now holds, if possible,
with increased conviction: "Unless due precautions
were taken, increase of freedom in form would be followed by decrease of freedom in fact. Nothing has
occurred to alter the belief I then expressed. . . .
Dictatorial measures, rapidly multiplied, have tended
continually to narrow the liberties of individuals, and
have done this in a double way. Regulations have
been made, in yearly-growing numbers, restraining
the citizen in directions where his actions were previously unchecked, and compelling actions which previously he might perform or not as he liked; and, at
the same time, heavier burdens, chiefly local, have
further restricted his freedom by lessening that portion of his earnings which he can spend as he pleases,
and augmenting the portion taken from him to be
spent as public agents please."

The chief emphasis in the leading essay falls upon
that interference with individual liberty which consti-
tutes the first count in the indictment. An ingenious
attempt is made to fasten upon the Liberal party in
England the name of "Tory." The argument is that
the Whig party always endeavored to release individuals or classes from some positive restraint upon their
freedom, handed down from mediæval days. The
Habeas Corpus Act, the Emancipation Act and the
Reform Bills are among the instances quoted. Each
of these measures removed some previously existing

obstacle to the unhindered exercise of his powers by the person. It gave him nothing positive, but simply secured him, or enabled him to secure himself, from interference by other persons. To this negative conception of freedom Mr. Spencer would confine the mission of the Whig or Liberal party. When modern Liberals go on to provide free public schools or to protect workmen against the cupidity of manufacturers, he raises the cry of "Toryism." To him the fundamental quality of Toryism is that it always tends to restrict individual freedom in the interest of a class. If a restriction of children to a certain number of working hours is laid upon an employer by law, or if his factory is required by Act of Parliament to be kept in a clean and wholesome condition, we have Toryism, since the legislation is in the interests of a class, — the laboring class! It matters not, in Mr. Spencer's logic, that, in the absence of such positive legislation, a great number of people would become physically stunted or contract various diseases, to the manifest detriment of the public welfare.

To an American, it must be said plainly, this argument is sheer pedantry. "Liberalism," to be sure, means, etymologically, "releasing," and the Liberal under various names has largely labored up to this time to give a free field to individuals or classes virtually debarred from full liberty of exercising their powers. But this by no means demands that he shall never attempt any other task. If a fellow-man has been confined in a dungeon for years, — this is the reasoning, — you may bring him forth into the open air, and strike off his chains; but you must not feed him, you must not clothe him, you must not bind up his wounds, you must not give him instruction. This would be contrary to the theory of pure individualism, and to Mr. Spencer this theory is infallible and complete. Let those who have been set free politically take care altogether of themselves! Freedom is all the world owes them. If they cannot feed and clothe themselves, finding work and bread, the theorist should say, "Let them perish," in accordance with the tender spirit of the struggle for existence. He is too humane in fact to say this; but he does say that if they succeed in keeping themselves physically alive, they should have no schools and no books, except what they will themselves pay for. In the United States the impulse of humanity led the American people to emancipate the negro and give him a vote. They went on to help him obtain the elements of knowledge and to make the way easy for him to acquire a little property. This would seem incomprehensible to Mr. Spencer, who could only cry, "Tory," and predict a "coming slavery" for all such advocates of general education and a wider division of the land.

However much this matter may be confused in Great Britain, Americans can see plainly, in the light of their own experience, where the real slavery exists; it lies in narrowing the mind to a theory of the advisable functions of the State which is essentially false, if offered as a complete rule of practice. Our national life began on a field free from the survivals of feudalism. The work of simple liberation, which occupied the Whigs of Great Britain for two hundred years, was already achieved for us, or needed not to be done. Negative freedom abounded. "Compulsory coöperation" was conspicuous by its absence. Has there, then, been no reason here for a Liberal party as opposed to a Conservative party? Mr. Spencer's attempt to limit "liberalism" to the one task which has chiefly occupied it in England down to the middle of this century is irrational. The distinction between the Tory, or Conservative, who wishes, above all else, to preserve the *status quo*, and the Whig, or Liberal, or Radical who wishes, above all, to improve the *status quo*, is fundamental and permanent in modern society. The task of Liberalism varies according to its generation, but its spirit is ever the spirit of regard for the welfare of the whole people; the one task of Conservatism is to defend vested interests against what it considers dangerous innovation, and it is very apt to consider all innovation dangerous. The Liberal party in this country, varying its name, has always steadily improved upon negative freedom by successive additions to positive welfare. It has provided free schools, reaching a comparatively high standard; it has favored public libraries, as the nation has grown richer; it has guarded the public health, providing for sanitary inspection and control; it has established pleasure grounds in the cities; and it has opened the public domain freely to actual settlers. We do not repent of these measures. Such of them as were first carried by a scant majority have proved their wisdom to all, and there is now no cry for their abolition. This test of experience is the one test we have wished to apply to all schemes for promoting the public welfare by legislation. Countless projects, originating in too philanthropic brains, our Anglo-Saxon respect for self-help and individual initiative has rejected.

It is, however, precisely what Americans have done and proved to be good, permanently good, for the whole body public that has inspired much of the English legislation which seems to fill Mr. Spencer with horror. His theory so completely possesses his mind that he takes no pains to inquire how far the facts of American experience square with it. The simple fact that the prevailing tendency in England is against this theory is, apparently, enough for him. The American, familiar with the American wisdom of educating the people, smiles when he reads Mr. Spencer's melancholy account of what has been done so late in Great Britain to this end: "Legislators who in 1833 voted £20,000 a year to aid in building school-houses never supposed that the step they then took would lead to forced contributions, local and general, now amounting to £6,000,000; they did not intend to establish the principle that A should be made responsible for educating B's offspring; they did not dream of a compulsion which would deprive poor widows of the help of their elder children." But worse than this, it appears, is to come upon a modern civilized nation which has actually spent thirty millions of dollars in sixty years in providing school-houses. "There is a rising demand, too, that education shall be made *gratis* for all. The payment of school fees is beginning to be denounced as wrong; the State must take the whole burden." Nowhere does Mr. Spencer ask what has been the result of just such a policy in the United States as he bewails in Great Britain. Nowhere does he inquire if it may not be that the period of pure liberation from restraint was but one moment in the evolution of civilized society. Nowhere does the suspicion seem to cross his mind that this limited theory of the relation of Man and the State, a theory essentially insular, has been corrected and reduced to its just proportions by wider experience and more inclusive reasoning.[1]

By the verdict of experience, everything called "individualism" must stand or fall. So must all that is styled "socialism." But the measure of socialism which is incorporated in our American institutions has stood its trial. In vain will pure theorists denounce its gradual spread in the mother-country, where conditions are similar, in the shape of free schools, public libraries, factory inspection, regulation of the hours of labor, sanitary legislation, and the like. To the American eye the chief actual evil of those Mr. Spencer laments as resulting from this humane progress seems to be that his antiquated theory of individualism is rudely disregarded, and is likely to be disregarded a great deal more in the future. Hence these tears, shed over a sadly mangled system! That the masses in England have been raised somewhat above the brute-like condition; that they enjoy a larger access to health and knowledge because of favoring statutes, and that they prove their wisdom by asking the gradual extension of such legislation, — to the philosopher, intent not upon the welfare of the people, but upon the maintenance of his cherished theory, however partial it may be, and more ready to indulge in easy scolding than to investigate the condition of the largest Anglo-Saxon nation in the world, all this is beside the mark. We here

[1] Mr. D. G. Ritchie in his essays on the *Principles of State Interference*, well says that Mr. Spencer's "political individualism is inconsistent with the scientific conception of society which he himself has done so much to develop and to teach. It is a survival from the so-called philosophical radicalism which flourished in Mr. Spencer's early days, and it is a survival which vitiates his whole political thinking."

see a practical application of an ethics severely true to the natural struggle for existence in the inferior world, and applied to human affairs, as if the humanity of man brought in no higher element of compassion and no more penetrating spirit of helpfulness.

Mr. Spencer has a habit of evacuating the human problem with which he deals of its peculiar interest and character, in order to make it square with the most general of theories imposed upon the whole universe of things. The weakness of this method is obvious in his caricature of the State. The perpetual antithesis of the two types of society, the militant and the industrial, is made to drag along with it, in closest alliance, an almost absolute opposition of the Individual and the State. "It is unquestionably true," he says, "that government is begotten of aggression and by aggression." This very partial statement of the origin of government in primitive times, when man was but little above the brute, ignores the natural foundations of admiration, respect, affection and other sentiments which promote the proper leadership of the strong, the brave and the good. But, even were it a tolerable statement of the origin of rudimentary government, it is by no means a satisfactory account of existing conditions. Neither by aggression nor for aggression, chiefly, do men come together in historic times, but because of their social nature. "A conscious and reflecting society is a State," in the words of Mr. F. C. Montague, in his admirable essay, "The Limits of Individual Liberty." "Such a society has an intelligence and a will. It has a national character. It has an organ to express this: the organ known as government." Such a government is not the monstrosity always present to Mr. Spencer's imagination, as the perpetual enemy of the individual, constantly striving to do foolishly and wastefully what should be left to prudent personal initiative, and continually endeavoring to restrain and encumber the free play of personality.

The State is as natural as the individual: civilized man has come to be an inseparable part of it. To cleave the two sharply apart, and set government, the organ of the State, off on one side, over against the individual, making it a perpetual object of distrust and hostility, — an evil, and nothing but an evil, necessary in some slight degree, but to be kept within the most limited range of activity, — this certainly seems to the American mind a strange perversion of the truth. Accustomed as we are to the conception of government as the servant of the public, the natural agent of public opinion and the public will, it would be a monstrous error in us to condemn its essential nature and cast it out from the circle of human sympathies, dwelling monotonously upon all its blunders and all its weaknesses in the long past, as if these were the deeds of an enemy to be extirpated, and not simply the reflection of the common intelligence of the time in which they occurred. It is not strange that some sympathetic readers of Mr. Spencer's unsparing diatribes should, like Mr. Auberon Herbert, assert that the revenue of all government, central or local, should be left to purely voluntary payment. It is difficult to draw a logical line between such social anarchy as Mr. Herbert would thus produce and the "administrative nihilism" of a government which could only repel invasion and preserve order.[1]

[1] " These necessary limitations are not determinable by *a priori*

That the business methods of government may be made to approximate more and more to the standard of honesty and carefulness set in private business; and that, consequently, numerous tasks may gradually be intrusted to it which formerly were better done by private hands, if done at all, the extreme individualist will not allow. He grudgingly admits that government may carry the mails, but it should not control communication by telegraph as well as by letter, as this would be, in itself, an abomination. He would give the ballot to the most ignorant farm-laborer; but he would do nothing to preserve society at large from the evils of illiterate voting, by establishing free schools and enforcing attendance. He would permit carelessness and superstition to scourge a continent with small-pox, rather than abridge by compulsory vaccination the supposed delights of private liberty. The simplest instincts of self-preservation in civilized States have brushed away such nonsense, as it must be plainly called. A society is as real and as natural as the individual; it needs no justification when it compels every man to regard the public health as well as the public order, obliges him to know his spelling-book, if he would vote, or opens to him free libraries and reading-rooms.

The practice of the United States in regard to free schools and public libraries (fully considered in the

speculation, but only by the results of experience; they cannot be deduced from principles of absolute ethics, once and for all, but they vary with the state of development of the polity to which they are applied. The settlement of this question lies neither with the celestial courts of Poesy nor with the tribunals of speculative cloudland, but with men who are accustomed to live and work amongst facts instead of dreaming amidst impracticable formulas." Professor T. H. Huxley.

next chapter) is enough in itself to show that such thoroughgoing individualism as is advocated in " A Plea for Liberty " is entirely un-American. We have no sympathy, in fact, with the maxim that "government is a necessary evil." Belief in this dismal creed gives to the writings of Mr. Herbert Spencer a strange and peculiar tone of bitter hostility to the discharge by government of many natural functions of a civilized society. Here in the United States what we call "the government," at any time, is simply a set of agents elected to carry out the will of the people, under certain general regulations and restrictions imposed by the laws and the Constitutions, which were the work of the people in former years. Still, we are not ready to say that government is always a good; we see plainly that we may have too much of it, as well as too little, whatsoever the form of it may be.

There is an immense reserve of practical individualism in the American mind, in the feeling that the individual should be as free as possible to speak his own mind, attend to his own business in his own fashion, and enjoy his earnings in ways which he desires. But the American's respect for "the will of the people " is such that he rarely assumes the position of a perpetual opponent of governmental extension. The citizen is decided, in his attitude toward any proposed measure for enlarging the activity of the government, not by a rigid theory of individualism in politics and economics, but by the all-prevailing spirit of private enterprise and political sagacity. The first of these everywhere nourishes a deep feeling that the less the State, as a rule, meddles with the citizen, the better, on broad general grounds. One reason for this feeling, to name no others, is that the citizen wishes to take as little time as may be from his own affairs in looking after the agents appointed by the people to discharge those functions not left to individuals.

His political sense leads the American constantly to prefer local to centralized administration; he is willing that a town-meeting should place restrictions on the individual which he would not approve in the case of a State, and much less in the case of the nation. Mr. Toulmin Smith's two propositions commend themselves to our political temper: —

"Local self-government is that system of government under which the greatest number of minds, knowing the most, and having the fullest opportunities of knowing it, about the special matter in hand, and having the greatest interest in its well-working, have the management of it, or control over it."

"Centralization is that system of government under which the smallest number of minds, and those knowing the least, and having the fewest opportunities of knowing it, about the special matter in hand, and having the smallest interest in its well-working, have the management of it, or control over it." One of the most conspicuous failures in American politics has resulted from the occasional disregard of these maxims by State legislatures when they deprive cities of the choice of their police commissions.

Mr. Bryce would distinguish between the sentimental and the rational ground of the *laissez-faire* principle, — the former being an intense feeling of personal freedom, and the second a conviction of the comparative inability of government as such to do any kind of business as well as individual enterprise would effect it. Owing to the American respect for the majority, there is less and less expression of such a sentimental ground of individualism in these later years; there is evidently an increasing dislike of rhetorical generalities about personal independence, as the country grows older. The spirit of private enterprise is as strong as ever; but the arguments in opposition to any proposed measure of so-called "governmental interference" are more and more based upon "the rational ground," — a consideration of the comparative inefficiency of government by the side of private individuals in securing a certain benefit that is confessed by all to be desirable and feasible. However the case may have been in times past, the theoretical doctrine of *laissez-faire* is no longer predominant here. So many forces work in opposition to it that it is rarely potent in deciding a particular issue. The moral sentiment, for instance, pays little regard to *laissez-faire* when considering the evils that arise from the unrestricted sale of intoxicating liquors, in that part of the country where individualism is generally supposed to be most rampant. In the extreme Western States there is a readiness that is even amusing to try experiments in legislation which would vastly extend the sphere of the State and limit private enterprise correspondingly.[1]

The prominent matter in the minds of the American legislator is, usually, the obvious public welfare for the time being. As he is not, commonly, well-equipped historically or a careful student of political evolution, he is only too ready, when he sees an undeniable evil, to enact a law against it. Often he

[1] Compare the article by Albert Shaw, Ph. D., on "The American State and the American Man," in the *Contemporary Review* for May, 1887.

does not previously consider whether legislation may not even increase the evil; the proposed law may well seem, to deliberate students of sociology, politics or finance, an unwarrantable interference with the natural laws of these phenomena, which can only fail of its aim. The result of the different conditions of our many States is a great variety in legislation. It has lately seemed to the majority in Kansas that a strict prohibitory law will promote temperate habits; but the older State of Massachusetts has twice passed and twice rescinded such a law, and now leaves the matter of licensing the sale of intoxicating liquors to annual decision by each town or city. Usury laws fixing a maximum rate of interest appear to the people of Nebraska a step in the direction of the public welfare; but the experience of Eastern States shows that such legislation is usually a dead-letter. The humaneness of the American temper is largely responsible for the laws which exempt the homestead and a certain amount of personal property from attachment, thus apparently interfering to preserve the citizen from the consequences of his own recklessness or business incapacity. In another direction it is largely the reason of laws which provide that seats shall be furnished for women employed in shops or at certain trades, and that employers shall be liable for accidents to employees on the premises.

There is no sentiment of individualism in this country strong enough to discourage the activity of the State in quarters where it would obviously be helpful to a large number of citizens, and where these could not reach the desired result otherwise except at a much greater outlay of time and trouble. We consider that State inspection of stores, factories and steamers is a simple dictate of common prudence; that State analysis of drugs, liquors and various kinds of food preparations is plainly in the interest of the people at large; and that the collection of statistics of labor, transportation and manufactures may be easily, thoroughly and inexpensively done for the community by a State Board. *Prima facie*, it is most desirable that the farmer should be protected by a State analyst against the dishonesty of makers of artificial fertilizers; and that the butter which he puts on the market should not be counterfeited by even the most wholesome oleomargarine sold as butter. The Board of Agriculture does not displease the majority in any State by holding Farmers' Institutes, by making various experiments, or by publishing the results of these for the benefit of farmers. If the plains of a Western State are treeless, the legislature encourages tree-planting; if, as in New Hampshire, woodchucks are superabundant, it offers a bounty on their destruction, — in both cases, with the entire acquiescence of the people.

Practically, then, we may say that no American legislature feels itself trammeled by a theory of the functions of government tending toward individualism. The forces which generally keep it from going to extreme lengths are the universal opposition to class legislation, and the practical temper and political sense of the people at large, who rarely forget that measure and proportion are to be observed everywhere. If the rights of some individuals prove to be grossly infringed, they will be quick to complain, and the next legislature will repeal or modify a law which its predecessor may have passed with comparative unanimity. A statute originating in an excess of

philanthropic zeal may be found to be entirely un-
workable; if so, it will soon be quietly abrogated,
with little opposition. We shall see that such facts
as these are not to be explained by any bias of the
American legislature toward theoretical socialism.
In fact, socialism has been little known, and less
understood, in the United States, down to a comparatively recent period. Within this period, there has
been no change in the general scope of American
legislation. No party of considerable strength has
yet proposed in a State legislature or in the national
Congress a distinctively socialistic programme, and
there seems no prospect of such a party arising.
Whenever a measure has been adopted which the
socialist would call a step in the direction of complete
ownership by the State of the means of production, it
has not been passed as such, but purely on its merits
as an individual instance. Thus the Massachusetts
General Court of 1891 authorized towns and cities to
manufacture electric light under certain carefully
specified conditions; but the legislature was far from
giving this simple permission on the ground, expressed or implied, that, everywhere and always, the
State is to be preferred to the individual as a producer. On the contrary, in accordance with the
usual practice in such permissive legislation, it left
each local community free to decide for itself whether
to undertake the manufacture of electric light or not,
and to continue the business or not, according as the
results should be found to be favorable or unfavorable
by the community.

Briefly, one may say then, that neither a Herbert
Spencer nor a Karl Marx could legitimately extract
much comfort from the proceedings of our American

legislatures. Undoubtedly, on the surface, there would be many more indications of a "coming slavery" to disturb Mr. Spencer than of *laissez-faire* to arouse Karl Marx; but if either Mr. Spencer or Karl Marx should suppose that a consistent socialism or individualism underlies the doings of the legislatures, or is likely to result from them, he would profoundly mistake the situation. The issue has never been plainly raised between socialism and individualism as general principles; but wherever specific matters have come up for decision, in which the rights of the individual have been an important consideration, the result has usually been their final establishment, however grossly invaded they may have been at first. The absurd prohibition, for example, of the very manufacture of oleomargarine was an instance of extreme legislation in favor of the farmer; it had to give way to laws limited, for the most part, to preventing the sale or use of this product under the name of "butter." A practical conclusion has not so easily been reached in the much more important matter of the sale of intoxicating liquors. In a number of States prohibitory laws or amendments to the constitution have been enacted, and in most of these they have been repealed. The issue is still far from being taken decisively out of the hands of the State legislature; but, on the whole, local option, which leaves the question of the sale of liquor to the town or city, is the result which has best approved itself. Such a settlement would be in accord with the general feeling of the American mind, which endures with patience a larger amount of governmental activity as one comes closer home to the local administration.

If the reasonings in this chapter are not erroneous,

there is no propriety in supposing that the American Spirit is characterized throughout by Individualism, under any strict definition of this term. In the next chapter I shall show that the national temper is just as little in favor of a scientific Socialism.

CHAPTER V.

THE AMERICAN SPIRIT AND SOCIALISM.

THE phenomena of scientific socialism in this country were set forth in 1886 by Professor R. T. Ely in "The Labor Movement in America;" the new edition of 1890 was enlarged, but not revised to date. Professor A. Sartorius Freiherrn von Waltershausen in his elaborate work, "Der Moderne Socialismus in den Vereinigten Staaten von Amerika" (1890), is dependent upon Professor Ely for most of his facts. A foreigner easily commits the mistake of supposing that thoroughgoing socialism, such as Professor Ely investigated with much industry, is a threatening feature in the American situation. In point of fact, however, most of its phenomena are of a very obscure order, even now; and when they have been brought to the light of day, they have drawn from the American-born no expression of alarm, and still less of respect. Referring my readers to the two volumes, by the American and the German professors, for that exposition of the propaganda of strict socialism in this country which is no part of my purpose here, I shall best show my own estimate of its importance by another kind of presentation of the actual condition of affairs.

I. IMPORTED AND AMERICAN SOCIALISM.

Putting the situation in a concrete form, we may

say that the great majority of socialists in the United States is made up of two classes.

I. There is, first, the newly-arrived foreigner who has brought with him, more especially if he comes from Germany, a head stuffed with abstract theories of the right social order and a heart bursting with wrath against the existing government, because of its outrages on individual freedom. Two cousins, Johann and Wilhelm, land in a country where speculative thought is lightly esteemed, particularly in politics, but where the Anglo-Saxon instinct for liberty and order has established a government of the people, by the people, for the people, — where, in fact, the "government" is simply an agent of the people. The worthy Johann needs some time to adjust himself to the new atmosphere and the new earth. Free to talk to his heart's content and to print all the matter that he can pay for, in denunciation of every existing institution, he slowly learns the absurdity of much of his logic. His reasoning may pass muster in Berlin, where the Social-Democrats are largely a political party, asking for such reforms as have long been familiar to America in practice. The very premises of such reforms are lacking here, — the political repression, the crushing weight of an enormous military establishment, the remnants of feudalism, the career closed to the talent of the poor, and the spirit of profound social inequality. Johann soon votes on a political level with other American citizens. His ballot is as weighty as that of the richest man of the oldest family in the country. He is practically free from military service, and he is subject to no obligation of homage or obedience to an upper class. His children go to a free school in the Western town where he has settled on a farm, bought of the government at a nominal price, and they have an open field, as young men and women, to show what ability is in them.

Equality is the principle that pervades the political and much of the industrial and social life in which Johann takes a part. He is, perhaps, a good while in squaring his creed with his condition. As long as he draws his argument from his memories of the Fatherland (a step-fatherland, it was to him), he will enjoy his socialist newspaper and gladly unpack his heart of abuse for the tyrants that grind the faces of the poor and crush the people down. But when his little Karl has become a prominent brewer in the nearest city, and his Gretchen has married the lawyer of the town, — then, if not long before, the honest, thrifty, temperate Johann's reliance will be placed on observation, not on memory. Imagination will weaken, and common-sense rule the day. The American atmosphere is, finally, too much for theories of an order of things fundamentally novel. Johann forsakes the Socialistic-Labor party, and joins the party of sober reform, by whatever name it may be called.

The less industrious cousin remains in the city. Stimulating his imagination with copious draughts of lager beer, he declaims against the despots of the New World who keep his idleness dangerously near the starvation line. Johann has become that contemptible being, a capitalist, through his energy, thrift and industry; and he is so hard-hearted as to think that his now impecunious cousin should have done likewise, as the door of opportunity was equally open to both. For *such* equality, however, Wilhelm, the eloquent, has no relish. He continues in New

York, plotting a millennium in which the idle and the shiftless shall inherit the earth. His cousin has become "John," and John's children are "Charles" and "Margaret;" these names show that the second generation is Americanized in thought and feeling. Wilhelm's own children may have fallen away.[1] But he continues to be a prominent orator at the meetings, and a regular contributor to the journals of the socialists. He and his sympathetic countrymen refuse to become so far Americanized as to see things as they are, and adjust their futile theories to the successful practice of the more sagacious people into whose inheritance they have cordially been invited. They constantly lose strength, as the more capable of their number succumb to reason and prosperity; but their number is steadily renewed by more or less desirable new-comers. Thoroughgoing, scientific socialism finds its most convinced disciples in such a medium, in New York or Chicago. With the exception of the few individuals among them susceptible to argument, they are very poor material for American citizens. The policeman is the final argument that must be kept in readiness to prevent the practical application of their principles by violence.

II. A second and very different class of socialists proper in this country is made up of the American-born who have been converted, for a longer or shorter time, through their feelings. Intelligent persons

---

[1] As in the anecdote told in a newspaper not long since : " There is in New York a German Anarchist whose wife is of the same faith. The couple have three children, the eldest of whom is a masculine six-year-old ; he was asked by a visitor, ' What country do you belong to ? Are you from Germany or from Anarchy ? ' ' No, I 'm not,' shouted the boy, as he sprang from his chair and stood erect, ' *I 'm* an American ! ' "

who read much, they have had their sympathies
aroused by the sad details of the sufferings of East
London, set forth by the novelist and the philanthropist; they have learned to pity the hardships of
women-workers in the tenement-houses of New York;
they have waxed indignant over the "sweating" system; they have concentrated their attention on the
miseries and distresses of the poor throughout the
civilized world, and they have generously resolved
that something must be done forthwith to relieve this
great multitude of their brethren, now in want and
woe. Something must, indeed, be done: many things
must be done, at once, *and for a long time.* But the
first thing that our friend, the sentimentalist, needs
to do, if he would effect more good than harm, is to
reach a sound understanding of the actual situation.
A sober mind is indispensable in considering what
may be done to relieve social troubles. The difficulty
is not one of yesterday's birth. It is not at all probable that any generation will put an end to it completely. "There is no 'social question,'" said Gam-
betta, "there are social questions." There are many
of them, and no generation of mankind will answer
the last.

Among the socialists of this second class we do not
find any considerable number of those who know much
about poverty and vice, and have been active and
efficient in diminishing both, through the organization of charity and the removal of causes of crime.
"It is the fine people from Commonwealth Avenue
and Beacon Street," said a visitor to the poor in Boston, "who come down to the North End or the South
Cove, and in their kindness of heart take up socialism
as a cure for all the ills they see." The contrast is

very great between the luxury of one quarter and the poverty of the other. The charitable at once jump to the conclusion that the strongest visible power must be called in, to abolish poverty and do away with suffering. This power is supposed to be the state, — the government of the city or the commonwealth. Whatever difficulties or dangers immediately suggest themselves to those long familiar with the poor and the vicious, or to those who have carefully studied economics and politics, have little weight with persons whose lack of training disposes them to consider Mr. Edward Bellamy an authority in economics, or Mr. Laurence Gronlund a past master in political science. Such sentimentalists confidently settle offhand fundamental questions of the most complicated kind, which experienced statesmen and life-long students of society approach with diffidence, seeing that the way to a solution is obstructed by many unconquerable facts. No great problem has ever been solved well and finally, in this country or any other, by the sentimental method.

We have always with us, in every civilized state, the two factions, the Bourbons and the dreamers, — the Philistines, to whom whatever is, is right, and the Ishmaelites, to whom whatever is, is wrong. Until our nature radically changes its disposition to take up extreme positions, stolid conservatism and hasty radicalism will not vanish from the human world. The slow and often blundering progress of mankind is rendered secure by the intervention between these opposing forces of those who can both "feel deep and think clear." We of America are confronted to-day, like the rest of the civilized world, with social troubles which threaten, many think, to

" Rend and deracinate
The unity and married calm of states
Quite from their fixure."

Yet few sensible persons in this country view with
deep concern that future which, to men across the
Atlantic, seems big with trouble. We feel confident
that the true American spirit, the spirit of this intervening class, will prevail; that the right American
method will be applied, and that the last thing here
tolerated, for a moment, will be violence as a solvent
of social problems. We hear much, it is true, from
a certain class of minds, concerning a species of slavery said to be widely established at the present time.
The wages system is vigorously denounced by socialists of various kinds as a new serfdom, or slavery,
and possible slave-insurrections present themselves to
the imagination of the timid. But if we grant that
the wage-earner lives in a species of slavery, — a very
curious kind of "slave" he is, — how shall we deal
with such a widespread social evil? Here in America
— we say it in all cheerfulness and confidence — there
is every prospect that the solution will be peaceful
and rational, — rational *because* it is peaceful. The
few misguided spirits of foreign birth, ignorant of the
logic of free institutions, un-Americanized and un-
civilized, who would resort to dynamite to introduce
their kingdom of heaven *instanter*, will be immediately taught an effective object-lesson in democracy.
The policeman, the jail, and, in the last resort, the
gallows, are the inevitable and proper reply to violent
propaganda of anarchism, socialism or any other
"ism." Yet the wild German, the raw Hungarian
and the uncombed Pole may shriek themselves hoarse
in denouncing the tyranny of the freest government on

earth. The sentimental socialists who do not realize that personification is the thief of sense may paint the darkest pictures of the woes of a certain blameless being called "Labor" (he is largely mythological); of the utter wickedness of a personage of vice all compact, styled "Capital" (he is yet more of an imagination), and of the atrocious crimes of one "Competition" (the greatest myth of all.)

The typical American is not thus to be upset; he easily retains his mental and moral balance. He will express himself in reply, much in this manner: "Go on, ladies and gentlemen. Free your bosoms of all the perilous stuff that weighs upon them. Open speech is good for the soul. Print your diatribes, and advertise your panaceas in newspapers, pamphlets, and magazines to your hearts' content, not forgetting in your zeal for labor to pay the printer, and, possibly, the editor, although he is a being supposed to take more kindly than most men to air as a diet. Mentally rearrange the whole state of human things, from top to bottom. Reconstruct, in your imagination, the entire frame of society. See, in your mind's eye, every man and woman working two hours a day only, for two dollars or for ten, as you generously fix the figure. Take as many as you please of those masterly reviews of the world's past, in which you so delight, from the days of the megatherium down to the present hour. Invariably conclude that your pet schemes are the final and ripe result of time. Misrepresent the past, falsify the present, and prophesy a future that will never come to pass, — at your own sweet will. There are some things you cannot do, indeed; but you may try to do them as long as you like. You cannot permanently substitute rhetoric for reasoning, sentiment for fact, or personal inclination for disagreeable obedience to natural law. You cannot talk unreason in any degree, and rightly demand that it be accepted as the gospel of salvation for rational men. But there is one thing you shall *not* try to do in this American domain: you shall not make the least attempt to 'hale Utopia on by force.' My immediate answer will be superior force."

The American individualist who would be true to his convictions has little scope for practical expression of them here, except by refusal to pay what he deems unjust taxes. But the revolutionary socialist who considers it his duty to introduce the new régime of socialism by violence arrays against himself, at once, all the powers that be. If power is of the people and in the people, it is the people that immediately arise to extinguish his revolutionary ardor. The patience and coolness of the American in suffering the most incendiary appeals of the anarchist and socialist have been unexampled, — such faith has he in the curative effect of free speech and a free press upon unreason of every description; such confidence does he entertain in the irresistible power of America to convert to itself the rudest, rawest immigrant. Thus far, our confidence has been justified, though sometimes severely strained. But we have never bound ourselves not to use force, if necessary, in self-defense. The lesson of Chicago, we may trust, has been given with sufficient emphasis, once for all.

Revolutionary socialism has very little significance in the America of to-day, and it has small promise of a brighter time. Peaceful, evolutionary socialism is the only kind that can gain a hearing from the sober, order-loving American intelligence. I shall soon discuss in some detail the programmes of two organizations that represent most of the strength of socialism among the American-born population; I anticipate so far as to assert that these two movements will, in all probability, have no serious or immediate effect upon legislation. As a system, socialism has been developed chiefly by French and German thinkers, observing conditions which prevail in France and Germany, and suiting their remedies, such as they are, good or bad, to these conditions; English socialists have shown little originality, and American socialists less. Some of the proposals of the last-named will be carefully examined in the United States; a few will be tested here and there; further action will depend upon the practical results reached. Whatever progress "Nationalism" or "Christian Socialism" makes, however, will be in the direction of social reforms advocated by liberal economists for years before the appearance of these two movements. It will come moderately, step by step, and it will not come as a series of steps which must inevitably be continued in the same direction until Socialism, fully developed, rules the hour. As Professor William Graham has well said of the extension of government management in the sphere of industry: "This is pre-eminently one of the cases where an induction from the part to the whole would be fallacious, where what would be true for part of the field of industry occupied by the Government would not be true if it were universally occupied." [1]

[1] *Socialism New and Old,* American edition, p. 264.

II. The Free Public School System.

After the preceding rejection of developed socialism, which many will doubtless regard as all too summary, I would illustrate the characteristic regard for
experience that leads the American mind to prefer
its teachings to any rigid theory by contrasting our
practice with the ideas of Mr. Herbert Spencer in respect to State Education. Here is a great country,
largely settled in the first place, and dominated since,
by men of English blood. For more than a hundred
years the American people has been the foremost
teacher of the modern doctrine of democracy. During all this time, leaders and followers alike have
never wearied in praise of free public education as
the necessity and the ornament of an enduring republic. That freedom and knowledge must go hand in
hand is the most elementary principle of American
doctrine. It is a principle not grounded upon a
peculiarity of the New World or of the people who
inhabit it, but upon primary facts of human nature.

The American system of free public instruction
offers probably the most striking example of the spirit
in which the American mind has solved, in more than
one direction, the problem of the relations of the State
and the individual. This free school system did not
originate in a theory that the State is bound to fully
enlighten the individual citizen and give him a complete intellectual outfit. On the other hand, no
American commonwealth has been withheld from establishing public schools through fear of trespassing
on the liberties of any property-holder, in taxing
him for their support. Our public schools had their
origin in a clear perception, by the fathers of the Re-

public, of the simple necessity of widely diffused education to the very existence of a free state.[1] It is not needful for the perpetuity of republican institutions that there should be a small number of highly educated persons in the nation, however desirable this may be; but it is a first need that there should be a very general education in the elements of knowledge. Thus the United States Commissioner of Education, in his letter accompanying the "Statement of the Theory of Education in the United States" issued by the Bureau in 1874, declares that "the existence of a republic, unless all its citizens are educated, is an admitted impossibility." Ignorance and disorder are inevitable companions. In these United States the riots which have threatened the safety of New York, Chicago, Pittsburgh and Cincinnati in the last thirty years have been, in a very great degree, the work of the foreign population untrained in the public schools. Simply as a matter of police regulation, popular education is worth all it has ever cost any nation. In a civilized country, apart from the love of knowledge in itself, the founders of a republic can do no wiser thing to preserve order and secure life and property than the establishment of a system of free instruction for all the people. The American commonwealths which have most thoroughly carried on such a system were, indeed, founded by men who had almost a passion for knowledge. The members of the General Court of the struggling Massachusetts Bay Colony were determined that learning should not be buried in the graves of their fathers. Massachu-

[1] John Adams said that "this government stands on four corner-stones, — the church, the school-house, the militia, and the town-meeting."

setts Bay, like the later colony of Connecticut, cherished education with a zeal that has never been surpassed. The contrast between the North and the South in colonial times has often been illustrated by the different responses which the Governors of Virginia and Connecticut made to the English Commissioners for Foreign Plantations, when questioned in regard to education in their communities. Sir William Berkeley could say: "I thank God there are no free schools or printing presses, and I hope we shall not have any these hundred years," although he subscribed in 1660 toward the erection of a college. The Governor of Connecticut replied: "One fourth of the annual revenue of the colony is laid out in maintaining free schools for the education of our children."

It is important to remember, in this connection, — as most foreigners need to be told, — that there is no American school system established and controlled by the national government. All the original thirteen States had made provision for popular education, in various degrees, before the national Constitution was adopted; the matter was left to each State to regulate for itself. North and South, there was a thorough recognition of the necessity of free schools if the republic was to endure. The Virginia School Act of 1780, in granting land to Kentucky schools, used this language: "It being the interest of this Commonwealth always to promote and encourage every design which may tend to the improvement of the mind and the diffusion of knowledge, even among its remote citizens whose situation in a barbarous neighborhood and a savage intercourse might otherwise render unfriendly to science." In his "Notes on the State of

Virginia," published in 1787, Jefferson declared. "Every government degenerates when trusted to the rulers of the people alone. The people themselves, therefore, are its only safe depositories. And to render even them safe their minds must be improved to a certain degree." (This was an anticipation, in the eighteenth century, of Mr. Robert Lowe's famous epigram, "We must educate our masters;" here in America our masters are ourselves, the whole people.) To the same effect, the Constitution of Ohio, adopted in 1803, reiterated the Ordinance of 1787; "Religion, morality and knowledge being essentially necessary to good government and the happiness of mankind, schools and means of instruction shall forever be encouraged by legislative provisions not inconsistent with the rights of conscience." So Washington had previously declared to Congress: "Knowledge in every country is the surest basis of public happiness." There is no idea which can be called more distinctively and fundamentally an American idea than belief in public education. The conviction of its supreme importance has increased and deepened with every generation. The statistics of pupils, teachers, and the amounts expended for the support of schools throughout the whole country are a most striking proof. The latest report of the United States Commissioner of Education (November 17, 1892) says that there were enrolled in the elementary and secondary grades, in the year 1890–91, 13,203,170 pupils, forming over 21 per cent. of the population in 1890. The average daily attendance of pupils was 8,404,228; the average length of the annual session (1889–90) was 134.3 days; and the number of teachers was 363,922. The whole amount expended for

public school purposes was $148,173,487, a sum equal
to $2.36 per capita of the population.

In considering the system of free education which,
with many variations in detail, prevails throughout
the United States, it is especially needful to distinguish between the respective spheres of the National
government, the State government and the local government, — in county, city, town or township. The
national government, as we have said, has no control
over the educational system of any State, but it has
shown the universal American interest in education
in various ways, not authorized, perhaps, by a strict
construction of the United States Constitution. The
National Bureau of Education was established by an
Act of Congress approved March 2, 1867, in response
to a memorial from the National Association of
School Superintendents. The function of this bureau
is simply the collection and dissemination of information in regard to education in the United States and
elsewhere; the amount of its activity has depended
chiefly upon the generosity of Congress shown in the
annual appropriations. Congress has control of public education in the District of Columbia and the
territories; the Constitution authorizes it to dispose
of public lands and other property belonging to the
United States. The Congress of the Confederation,
by the Northwest Ordinance of 1787, set apart the sixteenth section in each township for the support of public schools, in order to carry out its declaration that
schools and the means of education should forever be
encouraged; beginning with Minnesota in 1858, the
thirty-sixth section was added. These two sections
are sold, and the proceeds go to form a State Fund
for the support of education. In 1862 Congress

established the system of endowing colleges of agriculture and mechanical arts in the various States with grants of public lands. The total amount of land thus bestowed down to 1871, upon common schools, universities and agricultural and mechanical colleges was 78,576,794 acres; the territories which have become States since 1871 have enjoyed the privileges of the same legislation. Notwithstanding this generous interest of Congress in public instruction, there is no feature of the educational system in the United States more diverse from the systems which prevail in Europe than its entire lack of centralization in the national government.

The same general principle holds good in the relations of a Commonwealth, like Massachusetts or California, to the towns and cities within its limits. The State, indeed, being much nearer to these communities than the national government, does correspondingly more in the way of support and regulation of schools; but its powers are limited by the constant feeling of the supreme desirableness of local responsibility. The income of the State Educational Fund, where there is one, is divided among the various communities, in proportion to their needs, as a supplement to the sums raised by local taxation, *never as a substitute*. The State law fixes the grades and the range of study, the minimum length of the term, and, where the principle of compulsory education is adopted, makes certain additional regulations as to attendance and truancy. Like the National Bureau, which was modeled upon them, the State Boards of Education are active in obtaining and publishing statistics and other information in regard to the schools of the State; but they have no legal power over any community to fix the amount of money to be raised, to arrange the details of the organization, or to determine the discipline or the special course of study in the local schools. This limitation does not prevent the State Board from exercising a great moral influence, especially in the country districts, through its agents, who offer their advice and assistance in the towns which they visit, and hold "institutes," which are largely attended.

Local option in education extends in each town or city to the farthest limit compatible with a regard to the demands which the State law makes. The principle of local self-government is predominant. The town or city chooses its own school board, or school committee, to which it intrusts the organization and oversight of the schools; it raises such a sum of money for their support as it deems proper; but, almost invariably, this sum reaches the minimum fixed by the State as the condition of obtaining a share of the School Fund. Through its school committee or board, the community chooses the teachers, determines the course of study, and arranges all the details of organization and discipline. In the annual bill of expenses of the town or city the appropriation for the support of schools takes a prominent place, throughout the United States, both as respects popular interest in it and its proportion to the other appropriations.[1]

The wisest authorities among American educators agree that nothing should be done to weaken the

[1] In the city of Newton, Mass., to take the nearest specific instance, the appropriation for schools for the year 1892 was $128,000 out of a total levy of $700,816, — no part of the amount being for the erection of new school-houses.

strong feeling of local responsibility for the generous support of schools which now exists in most parts of our country. Occasionally an observer from abroad, noticing the inadequate provision made in a few States, more especially in the South, regrets that there is not some central power to supplement the action of the local authorities. Even Mr. J. G. Fitch made this mistake; but Rev. Mr. McCarthy, the head-master of King Edward's Grammar School, Birmingham, in comparing the educational systems of the United States and England, does better to inquire, "May not Englishmen admit that our policy also has its elements of weakness as well as of strength; that too much centralization or too little trust in local interest in education is the characteristic note of our system, just as too little of the former and too much of the latter is of theirs." Mr. Fitch himself is aware that "the one great safeguard for the continued and rapid improvement of education in America is the universal interest shown in it by the community." He has well been reminded by the leading journal of this country that "this very interest is in great degree due to the autonomy of the local authorities in educational matters. . . . Probably such a general interest in the public schools and sense of individual responsibility for their welfare as prevailed in New England towns under the district school system has never existed elsewhere in this country or in England. Elaborate educational machinery will not atone for lack of popular interest in the schools." [1]

[1] "It is a curious and instructive fact that while the primitive ideal of self-government had become obscured both in English counties and in English boroughs, it not only survived but ac-

The common school system of America, prevailing from the Atlantic to the Pacific and from Mexico to British America, unsectarian and open to all without expense, has thus been kept by the people under their immediate control as nearly as possible. A system created by the democratic idea, it is the centre of an immeasurable interest on the part of the people at large. No reproach can be cast upon any political party in a campaign more likely to injure it, — if thought to be well founded, — than that of infidelity to the free public school system, and no party is willing to rest under such a suspicion. There is a true enthusiasm in America for education as a civilizing force, and the American tendency is to place too much, rather than too little, confidence in popular education as a preventive of crime. The results of the prevalence of this system for a hundred years have been stated by Mr. Bryce: "The Americans are an educated people, compared with the whole mass of the population in any European country, except Switzerland, parts of Germany, Norway, Iceland and Scotland; that is to say, the average of knowledge is higher, the habit of reading and thinking more generally diffused than in any other country." Necessarily, the education given by the public school system is elementary, and so far superficial; but, even if we exclude the High Schools and the State Universities from view, we may declare that the system attains the main object for which it was founded. The public schools preserve republican institutions by means of a general education of the people in the elements of knowledge. So Daniel

quired a fresh vitality in the Colonies of New England." George C. Brodrick in the *Cobden Club Essays*, 1875, p. 25.

Webster has said, "America has proved that it is practicable to elevate the mass of mankind, — the laboring class, — to raise them to self-respect, to make them competent to act a part in the great right and the great duty of self-government; and she has proved that this may be done by education and the diffusion of knowledge. She holds out an example a thousand times more encouraging than ever was presented before to nine tenths of the human race who are born without hereditary fortune or hereditary rank." Theodore Parker's saying is true, — although the latter part of it is less pertinent now than when he said it, — that in this country every one has a taste of knowledge while few persons get a full meal. In compliance, however, with the usual American unwillingness to lay down a rigid limit for the education given at the expense of the public, the curriculum of the public schools has scarcely anywhere been confined to the simplest elements of knowledge. The high school is to be found in all sections of the United States as well as primary and grammar schools, and, everywhere, it is free like them. The proportion of scholars who go through the high school is rendered small by the necessity that comes upon the graduates of the grammar schools, in a great majority of cases, of earning their own living at an early age; but in every considerable town and city in the United States the high school at least offers a good secondary education, free of expense, to young people who are not obliged to support themselves. The principle of free instruction has been carried farther by the establishment of normal schools for the training of teachers, and, in the western parts of the country, of State Universities where no tuition is charged to students resident in the State. The University of Michigan is a typical and admirable example of this highest grade of free education.

A recent modification of the free school system, continuing the logical application of its principle, has been the purchase of text-books and stationery for the use of pupils at the public expense. This system has prevailed, indeed, for seventy years in Philadelphia, and for fifty years in New York. In Massachusetts, the act of 1873 allowed cities and towns to provide text-books, or not, at their pleasure. This law was strongly opposed by many educators; but its working was so successful that in 1884 a second act made the supply of free books and stationery compulsory on all cities and towns. This decision was reached, not by balancing theories of socialism and individualism, but from simple observation of all the consequences of the system. It has been found, in fact, that there is a large saving of expense to the community as a whole, since the books are purchased in large quantities on advantageous terms by the school boards; that they are handled with at least as much care as before, and that most of them are available at the end of one school year for the scholars who enter the next year. The disagreeable necessity that formerly came upon some of the poorer parents of obtaining books free on the plea of poverty, disappears, and there is no peculiar feeling of dependence on the part of any, since text-books are supplied to all the pupils. The Boston School Committee declared in 1887 that "the free text-book act has undoubtedly been a large factor in filling our high schools and the upper classes of the grammar schools." In these grades of the school system the expense of text-books formerly operated to diminish considerably the number of pupils. While the total cost to the community is lessened by this measure, the opportunities of the public schools are now more largely enjoyed by the poorer children. The system thus becomes logically consistent, as no scholar is obliged to pay for any requisite of the course. For these reasons it is probable that the system of providing free text-books will make its way throughout the country.

The individualism which opposes free public education, disregarding the fact that it is a vital measure of self-preservation in a modern republic, has been outgrown in these United States so far as it ever existed. The opinion had, indeed, more or less strength in the early years of some of our Western States. From the "Life of Ephraim Cutler," one of the early settlers of Ohio, for instance, we learn (p. 174) that "the prevailing sentiment as regards the support of schools by taxation was that it was a violation of individual rights for the State to take one man's money to pay the school-bill of the neighbor's child. The common adage was, 'Let every man school his own children.'" The voluntary system, which men like Mr. Cutler set in operation in their respective localities, in order to secure the education of their children, was found to be wasteful and ineffective. One of the most generous supporters of this system while it was the only one practicable, Mr. Cutler pressed with vigor the adoption of the public school system finally established by the Acts of 1821 and 1825. When Peter Cooper, the founder of the Cooper Union, was born in New York, in 1791, that city of 27,000 inhabitants had not a single free

school. The first Free School Society was incorporated in 1805 at the instance of De Witt Clinton,
and its first school-house was built in 1809. The
Society, of which Peter Cooper was a trustee for fifteen years, continued its work until united with the
Board of Education, established thirty-seven years
later, in 1842. The first free school in California
was opened by J. C. Pelton in San Francisco, December 26, 1849, with three boys and one girl as
pupils; the number soon increased to three hundred.
For a time the school was conducted at private expense; but it was not long before the town council
adopted it.

As in California, Ohio and New York, so it has
been elsewhere in the United States; wherever public-spirited citizens have conducted or supported
schools on the voluntary system, the community has,
sooner or later, seen the necessity of the State as-
suming the obligation. The words of Washington's
Farewell Address have never failed of a response:
"Promote as an object of primary importance, institutions for the general diffusion of knowledge. In
proportion as the structure of a government gives
force to public opinion, it is essential that public
opinion should be enlightened." These are the words
of the statesman, not of the doctrinaire. No institution but the public school, it is probable, could have
preserved the United States a nation, substantially
such as the English settlers founded it, under the
enormous immigration from Europe. As Professor
Alexander Johnston, one of the ablest students of
American history, has observed: "Their absolute
democracy and their universal use of the English
language have made the common schools most success-

ful machines for converting the raw material of immigration into American citizens. This supreme benefit is the basis of the system and the reason for its existence and development, but its incidental benefit of educating the people has been beyond calculation." [1]

The American common school system is fundamental in the American State. An institution that more fully justified its own existence was probably never devised among men. It did not spring from a theory that it is the duty of the State to make the most of every citizen all through his life; and its steady advance has never been perceptibly checked by objections to the effect that it interferes with individual freedom. American experience has amply demonstrated that the modern republic rests safely upon popular education. In common schools the doctrine of that equality which is essential to the perpetuity of a free country is enforced upon the minds of its future citizens at the most susceptible age. The schools are the schools of the whole people, and they represent the State to boys and girls, not as a power to be distrusted or defied, but as the instrument of the will of the whole people, working for the enlightenment of all. In them the State helps, in Hosea Biglow's words, "to make a man a man;" and when the boy has gone through the public school course, it wisely "lets him be." [2] The makers, as well as the obeyers of the law, are trained in the common schools, and wisdom has dictated that the

---

[1] *Encyclopædia Britannica*, vol. xxiii. p. 765.

[2] "Though the people support the Government, the Government should not support the people." President Cleveland in his veto of the Texas Seed-Bill, 1887.

elements of the history and the government of the country be there taught to all. The system is so decentralized that many of the objections to national education made abroad do not apply here. Each community is free to carry the instruction given in its schools to the highest pitch that public sentiment therein will warrant. Such additions to the course of study as music, drawing and manual training depend upon converting, not the National or the State government, but the people of the community, to a conviction of their desirability. Thus the salutary principle of local self-control is deep-rooted in that American institution which might most plausibly be termed "socialistic." The public schools, moreover, have greatly aided in impressing a general note of intelligence on the population at large: "the whole American nation may be called intelligent, that is, quick," wrote Matthew Arnold. While the education imparted in the common schools has its obvious limits, the privately endowed colleges and the State Universities bring it about that "in no country are the higher kinds of teaching more cheap or more accessible;" our American universities are to-day "supplying exactly those things which European critics have hitherto found lacking to America." [1]

When, in any quarter of the world, the democratic spirit asserts itself with power, and ancient institutions — monarchic or aristocratic — begin to suffer modification in the interest of the people at large, the example of America naturally comes to the front. The sound doctrine that increase of the power of the people in government should be accompanied by an increase of general enlightenment impresses at once

[1] Bryce's *American Commonwealth*, vol. ii. pp. 534, 553.

the mind of the true conservative in such a situation. The statesman and the practical reformer join in advocating an extension of free schools in proportion as the right of suffrage is broadened. Especially when the suffrage is extended in England is the warning most pertinent which the American publicist gives of the necessity of popular education to freedom, so many and so great are the similarities between the two countries. The closeness of the similarity may be denied, indeed, by some; still one of the first demands to be met in the rational discussion of public education in England would seem to be a consideration of the results reached in a hundred years' trial of the system in the United States. If its effects have been bad here, then the opponents of free schools in Great Britain would have the strongest argument against the system. If its effects, on the other hand, have been good here, then an argument of much weight is plainly ready to the hand of the English advocate of free education. The one procedure which, to the American at least, must bear the mark of insular irrationality is an entire neglect to consider our experience. Recourse to such a prominent example, either for warning or for instruction, would appear to be unavoidable.

Yet, in the most important recent volume emanating from English thinkers who style themselves individualists, there is scarcely an allusion to the existence of public schools in this country, and not the slightest attempt is made to consider the general question as illuminated by American experience. Mr. Thomas Mackay, the editor of the essays collected under the title "A Plea for Liberty," brings this indictment, in the preface, against the English system of educa-

tion — the defects in which he probably exaggerates:
"If men will grant for a moment, and for the sake
of argument, that, as some insist, our compulsory,
rate-supported system of education is wrong; that it
is injurious to the domestic life of the poor; that it
reduces the teacher to the position of an automaton;
that it provides a quality of teaching utterly unsuited
to the wants of a laboring population which certainly
requires some form of technical training; that here
it is brought face to face with its own incompetence,
for some of the highest practical authorities declare
that the technical education given in the schools is a
farce; that therefore it bars the way to all free arrangements between parents and employers, and to
the only system of technical education which deserves
the name; if this, or even a part of it, is true, if at
best our educational system is a make-shift not altogether intolerable, how terrible are the difficulties to
be overcome before we can retrace our steps and fos-
ter into vigorous life a new system, whose early beginnings have been repressed and strangled by the
overgrowth of Governmental monopoly."

Mr. Mackay is reinforced by Mr. Charles Fairfield,
who declares, in considering "State Socialism at the
Antipodes:" "Of all State Socialistic measures
Free Education seems to be the most enticing. A
political party could hardly choose a more attractive
dole or bribe for the electorate. Its success, however,
is cumulative, and it is only after some years' experience that parents appreciate thoroughly what it does
for them. Cash outlay to pay for the feeding, clothing and education of children is to selfish and self-
indulgent parents a constant source of irritation.
The small sums which should go to buy bread and

butter, boots or bonnets for youngsters, or to pay for
their schooling, may be much needed by the male
parent for tobacco, drink, and perhaps 'backing
horses,' while the mother constantly needs new articles of dress and amusements. Free Education, at
the expense of that pillageable abstraction 'the general tax-payer,' thus appeals to some of the strongest
modern instincts." Such a caricature of rational
argument I quote here simply for the amusement of
American readers: it has the familiar ring of all opposition to the advance of democracy. But Mr. Herbert Spencer falls into a rhetoric as amusing, in the
introduction to the same volume: "On the day when
£30,000 a year in aid of education was voted as an
experiment, the name of idiot would have been given
to an opponent who prophesied that in fifty years the
sum spent through imperial taxes and local rates
would amount to £10,000,000, or who said that the
aid to education would be followed by aids to feeding
and clothing, or who said that parents and children,
alike deprived of all option, would, even if starving,
be compelled by fine or imprisonment to conform,
and receive that which, with papal assumption, the
State calls education. No one, I say, would have
dreamt that out of so innocent-looking a germ would
have so quickly evolved this tyrannical system,
tamely submitted to by people who fancy themselves
free." [1]

In his more recent volume on "Justice," Mr. Spencer speaks, in a similar strain, of "the cases in which
men let themselves be coerced into sending their children to receive lessons in grammar and gossip about
kings, often at the cost of underfeeding and weak

[1] *A Plea for Liberty,* p. 16.

bodies. . . . The so-called political rights . . . may even be used for the establishment of tyrannies." [1] The wondering American will search these writings of Mr. Spencer to find some explanation of the long duration in the United States of such a system of education as he denounces. A peculiar light, however, falls upon Mr. Spencer's claims to be an inductive philosopher when we note the entire absence of allusion even to the probable sufferings of the American people under "tyranny" of this kind. He has here been a singular instance, indeed, of arrested development. The fallacies which crowd each other in the chapter on National Education in "Social Statics," and which, assuredly, never originated in the study of existing systems in a judicial spirit, are still rampant in his latest pages. Mr. Spencer has had in America his warmest reception and his largest audience. As the foremost living teacher of the philosophy of evolution, a philosophy thoroughly in accord with the hopeful and progressive American spirit, he commands a deep respect which, as a believer in evolution from the first, I have no desire to diminish. But when we compare the political and social system which we have been erecting, in the true spirit of evolution, from the first settlement of America by Englishmen, with that State which Mr. Spencer would have revert to practical nonentity, we must consider his rank as a political philosopher to be far from the highest. American practice has never agreed with the "administrative nihilism" of Mr. Spencer's prejudices, to which he gravely gives the name of the philosophy of political evolution. The American generation now in middle age drew its

[1] *Justice*, pp. 178, 179, American edition.

formal doctrine of the functions of the State from John Stuart Mill and Mr. Spencer when its youthful ardor for consistency was strong. But between this doctrine and the customs and institutions which we advocate and applaud there is a chasm deep and wide, as I have before pointed out.

The public school system has further lessons for the socialist and the individualist. When the proposal is made by philanthropists more ardent than observant that free dinners should be provided for all the scholars in the public schools whose parents are, apparently, unable to provide them with a sufficient noonday meal, the American mind does not immediately acquiesce. Obviously, such a provision would forcibly emphasize the distinction between the well-to-do and the poor, and, just as evidently, it would be susceptible of the greatest abuse by the indolent and improvident. Wherever it is found that any children attending school are suffering from the real inability of their parents to provide them sufficient food, the resources of charity and philanthropy are entirely adequate, in every part of our country, to meet the evil. Another proposal, sometimes found on the programme of socialists in this country, is that the limit of the school-age be raised, up to which a child must attend a certain number of weeks in the year. This measure has, in itself, nothing objectionable. Thus far, however, the demand for the change has not come from educators familiar with the whole situation, but from kind - hearted persons who consider only the general desirability of fuller education for the children of the poor, and do not bear in mind the usual necessity, in a poor family, for the wages which the young people over fourteen might earn.

An important limitation of the free public school system, which the practical American mind has observed, respects the publication of text-books. The books used in the public schools have been published by private firms thus far; but within the last eight or nine years there has been an agitation in some parts of the country for State publication. Professor Jevons used to lament the absence of a country which might serve as a kind of "experiment station" in legislation for the benefit of other countries. Here in the United States we enjoy most of the advantages of such a plan through our federal system. Innumerable experiments in law-making are tried in one part of the country or another, by this or that State; consequently it is a common practice for the opponents and the advocates of a certain measure in one Commonwealth to agree to wait for the results of a similar measure passed by another State. The publication of text-books by the government is an instance very much to the point. In California, amendments to the present constitution obliged that commonwealth in 1884 to embark in the business of providing the text-books used in the public schools. In Ohio, a State school-book board was appointed in 1890, and this board made an investigation into the results of the California system. The investigation had a very discouraging effect upon further agitation of the plan, and Ohio is now trying a State contract system, like several other States.

Since the manufacture of school-books by the State is obviously a step in the direction of socialism, which no other feature of the American common school system renders necessary, it will be profitable to give in some detail the chief facts relating to the California method.[1] The first estimate made by the State printer was not ten per cent. of the actual cost. Publication began in 1886, but the series of State text-books is still incomplete in some important respects. Ten books have been issued, and the State Superintendent in 1888 admitted that "it costs the State more to manufacture the books than it will cost the private publishing house." California, rather curiously, is not one of the States that furnish school-books free to pupils; hence the Superintendent goes on to say, "but the consumer is interested, not in the actual first cost of the books, but in the cost to him," and he claims that the pupil or consumer pays the private publisher, or the retail dealer, from thirty to sixty cents more than he is required to pay the State for his text-books. Professor Jenks, however, reduces this saving considerably by his criticism, and thus concludes: "If we take into account the difference in the number of books and the quality of the work, to say nothing of the contents, it seems clear that at present, at any rate, a State, if California is typical, can contract with publishers to furnish it with text-books at a cost as low as that at which it can manufacture them, and can thus escape all the risk and trouble of the manufacture and save the interest on the investment." (The prices of school-books, it should be said, have been lowered by prominent firms within the last two or three years.)

If the experience of California can be trusted, the experiment of State publication of text-books is a fail-

---

[1] See, for full particulars, an excellent article in the *Political Science Quarterly* for March, 1891, on "School-Book Legislation," by Prof. J. W. Jenks. My quotations, when not otherwise credited, are from Professor Jenks' article.

ure, on the ground of economy. But a more important matter is the quality of the school-books thus
published. The following resolution, passed almost
unanimously on December 3, 1890, by the biennial
convention of California school superintendents, is
apparently decisive on this point: "Resolved, that
while certain of the State text-books — notably the
primary language lessons and the elementary geography — have met the approbation of the public school
teachers of the State, we desire to record our severe
criticism and disapproval of others of the State series,
and express our judgment that their thorough revision
by competent authorities, so as to adapt them to the
wants of the schools, is imperative and should be
entered upon at once." The Eastern States, like
those which make up New England, some of which
have had a leading position in educational reform,
have seen no serious agitation for a system of State
publication. It is probable that the experience of
California, showing that the State can buy school-
books of good quality and well manufactured more
cheaply than it can publish for itself, will discourage
further trial of the system. In Ohio, where the question has been agitated, the State supervisor of printing estimated that the cost of manufacturing and
distributing school-books, under the favorable labor
conditions which prevail in that State, as compared
with California, would still be greater than the expense of books of higher quality and better manufacture furnished by private publishers. Mr. Hirsch
substantiated this judgment with a number of those
practical considerations arising from the special nature
of the business of which the thoroughgoing advocate
of socialism is apt to make no account, but which the

matter-of-fact American mind is likely to consider quite decisive. Mr. Hirsch closed his report by calling attention to the political dangers inherent in such a system. It may not be inappropriate to call the attention of the reader to the fact that the objections are made by a German citizen of Ohio. "To my mind there are greater objections to this proposed undertaking by the State than mere material or mechanical difficulties. It would be an innovation or departure in the workings of our simple form of government which would be dangerous in many ways. It would open new and devious avenues to reach the public treasury. It would create a new State board, a bureau of officers, and a long line of contracting agents. It would subject our public schools and our school-books to partisan influences and control. It would engage the State in a form of business difficult, delicate and hazardous, and in competition with private citizens and private enterprise. And it would embark the State in an enterprise or undertaking which would be a never-ending source of perplexing difficulties, political spoils, partisan investigations, annual appropriations, and perennial deficiencies."

To the same effect "The Publisher's Weekly" of New York thus states its position as to the manufacture of text-books by the Commonwealth. "The State cannot, and never can be in the position to, make a text-book that can compete with one produced by private enterprise. Not that the State might not command the intellect necessary for the purpose, but for the reason that the office would, in a short time, become tainted with the bane that has made the present method of supply objectionable in many respects, — namely, politics. The safeguard, or at any rate one element of safety, in the present system of private enterprise, is the possibility of competition. Such a factor would never enter into a State institution — at any rate not for generations to come."

Thus the case stands with reference to this particular step in the direction of state socialism. The publication of text-books by the State of California was undertaken with a public opinion favorable to it; it was carried out with entire friendliness and faith in the system by the State board of education and the State superintendent. The result has been such that it is improbable that any other State will follow the example of California, whatever may be the future of the system there. We may here see how helpful an actual experience in any one State or group of States is, in determining the advisability of a measure of a socialistic complexion, and how inevitably the American will decide upon it, not according to theoretical preconceptions, but according to the plain results of experience. Such results under existing conditions of the political situation are likely to be even more unfavorable in respect to the quality than in respect to the cost of State text-books. Any one familiar with "practical politics" as carried on in a great majority of our States may be pardoned for the broad smile likely to overspread his face when he thinks of the character of the text-books likely to be produced under the supervision of the "machine," whether in New York or in Pennsylvania. In the educational direction state socialism has apparently no future in America.

III. The Free Public Library.

Let us turn to another institution which the high-strung individualist would rank at once with free text-books and State publication of school-books, — the free public library. This is, in fact, an extension of the public school system, and it has usually been advocated on the same general grounds, by persons prominent in educational reform. As in the case of the publication of school-books, we have here the advantage of considering a quite thorough adoption of a system by one State, in theory and practice. The result has been entirely different. The State of Massachusetts does not monopolize the public libraries of the country, but it is said to have more than one half of the entire number in the United States, and it is undoubtedly the leading commonwealth in the Union in this direction. It was the first State to establish a free public library commission, in 1890, being closely followed by New Hampshire, in 1891. The New York library laws of 1892 are now the best in the country. The first report of the Massachusetts Commission, dated February 1, 1891, thus describes the progress of the free library system in the Commonwealth in the last fifty years. "In 1839 the Hon. Horace Mann, then Secretary of the Board of Education, stated, as the result of a careful effort to obtain authentic information relative to the libraries in the State, that there were from ten to fifteen town libraries, containing in the aggregate from three to four thousand volumes, to which all the citizens of the town had the right of access; that the aggregate number of volumes in the public libraries, of all kinds, in the State was about 300,000; and that but

little more than 100,000 persons, or one seventh of
the population of the State, had any right of access
to them. A little over a half century has passed.
There are now 175 towns and cities having free public libraries under municipal control, and 248 of the
351 towns and cities contain libraries in which the
people have rights or free privileges. There are
about 2,500,000 volumes in these libraries, available
for the use of 2,104,224 of the 2,238,943 inhabitants
which the State contains, according to the census of
1890."

Massachusetts had a considerable body of legislation in reference to social and public libraries, beginning with the act of 1798 in favor of proprietors of
social libraries, before the act of 1890 established the
Library Commission and authorized it to expend a
sum not exceeding a hundred dollars for books to
establish a free library in any town destitute of the
same. The act obliges the town to provide, to the
satisfaction of the Commission, for the careful cus-
tody and distribution of the books thus furnished, and
to make an annual library appropriation not smaller
than fifteen to fifty dollars, according to the latest
assessed valuation. In February, 1891, one hundred and three towns in Massachusetts, having less
than one sixteenth part of the entire population, were
without public libraries. "These are almost without
exception small towns with a slender valuation, and
sixty-seven of them show a decline in population in
the last five years." Up to the 29th of October,
1892, fifty-two of these one hundred and three towns
had accepted the provisions of the State act and organized library boards. Massachusetts has thus
advanced from the public library act of 1851, which

authorized any city or town in the commonwealth to establish and maintain a public library at a certain expense, in proportion to the number of ratable polls, to a statute which formally adopts the system as a State institution, so far as to help establish libraries in small towns with a gift from the State treasury. The library system in Massachusetts is, however, predominantly due to the towns and cities themselves, reinforced in an extraordinary degree by the generosity and public spirit of individuals.[1] The endowment of a free library may be said to be one of the most popular forms of donations for public purposes with wealthy citizens of the State. According to the report of the Commission, "the gifts of individuals *in money*, not including gifts of books for libraries and library buildings, exceed $5,500,000." Without doubt, the public library system is one of the features of Massachusetts civilization upon which the citizens of the State most pride themselves. An objection to an annual appropriation by the town or city for the support of the free library already established is almost unknown; it is very rarely made on the ground that the local government has no right to tax the citizen in order to supply reading matter gratuitously to all. Such is the situation of free libraries in a characteristically American State.

The position of writers like Mr. Herbert Spencer

[1] "There is no way in which a man can build so secure and lasting a monument for himself as in a public library. Upon that he may confidently allow 'Resurgam' to be carved, for through his good deed he will rise again in the grateful remembrance and in the lifted and broadened minds and fortified characters of generation after generation. The pyramids may forget their builders, but memorials of this character have longer memories." James Russell Lowell.

and the other contributors to "A Plea for Liberty"
is sufficiently in opposition to this Massachusetts faith
in free libraries. Mr. M. D. O'Brien, who writes
the special chapter on this subject, is apparently
as free from the virus of knowledge of American experience as any one could desire. His whole argument shows a really delightful bigotry and insular-
ity. He defines the free library as "the socialist's
continuation school," which is supported by "the advocates of literary pauperism." "It is true the free
library party strongly repudiate the charge of dishonesty; but it is difficult to see any real difference
between the man who goes boldly into his neighbor's
house and carries off his neighbor's books and the
man who joins with the majority, and on the authority of the ballot-box sends the tax-gatherer around to
carry off the value of those books." Mr. O'Brien's
objections to free libraries are mainly to the effect
that the reading is chiefly novel-reading, which he
considers a luxury; that libraries are the resort of
loafers, and that forty-nine out of every fifty work-
ing-men have no interest whatever in them. He
pathetically inquires why, if the book-reader is to
have his hobby paid for by his neighbor, other persons should not be entitled to the same privilege.
"A love of books is a great source of pleasure to
many, but it is a crazy fancy to suppose that it should
be so to all." Every successful opposition to free
libraries is, to Mr. O'Brien's mind, "a stroke for
human advancement. This mendacious appeal to the
numerical majority to force a demoralizing and pauperizing institution upon the minority is an attempt
to revive in municipal legislation a form of coercion
we have outgrown in religious matters. . . . When

the socialistic legislation of to-day has been tried, it will be found in the bitter experience of the future that for a few temporary, often imaginary, advantages we have sacrificed that personal freedom and initiative without which even the longest life is but a stale and empty mockery." These quotations will inevitably have a comical sound to American readers who have been brought up under the common school system, which Mr. O'Brien regards as equally dishonest, and especially to those who have lived in towns where public libraries have been long established.

Mr. Thomas Mackay, the editor of "A Plea for Liberty," is, however, equally serious in his denunciation of "the attempt of free library agitators to make their own favorite form of recreation a charge on the rates . . . as unjust to those who love other forms of amusement and . . . contrary to public policy." According to Mr. Herbert Spencer, "The expediency politician, if it is a question of providing books and newspapers, in so-called free libraries, contemplates results which he thinks no doubt will be beneficial, and practically ignores the inquiry whether it is just to take by force the money of A, B, and C to pay for the gratifications of D, E, and F."

The free public library system, like every other human institution, is imperfect, but it is under the control in the United States of a body of librarians and friends of public education who are making it a valuable adjunct to the free school system. A very large proportion of the pupils in our public schools leave them early to engage in active life, and the American believes that the public library does well to furnish this class of persons, if no others, with the means of progress in knowledge. The public library is, in a sense, the people's university. Wherever this institution is found in a New England town, it is correctly considered by the traveler a sure sign of a higher level of general intelligence, public spirit and peace and order than prevails in most towns destitute of such a feature. It would be more easy to attack the public library with a show of reason from the standpoint of the publisher and the author, who may complain that their sales are diminished by the spread of this institution. The author and the publisher, however, are usually the last persons in America to raise such a complaint. They know full well that the taste for reading grows by what it feeds on; that it is better for people dependent on public libraries for their books to read a large proportion of fiction than not to read books at all; and that the public libraries of the country will gradually come to afford a sure and steady market for the best class of works. Reading is not regarded in this country — by the New Englander at least — as an amusement or a hobby. On the contrary, the American, in his zeal for knowledge, believes that the habit of reading has a highly civilizing effect. In coping with the illiteracy and ignorance of the foreign element, in enlightening the great mass of voters as to the history and logic of the institutions under which they live, and in forming a sound and vigorous public opinion on subjects of current or enduring interest, the free library has a great part to play in the United States.

Here in America the public library system has the unanimous indorsement of educators and the professional classes. Only a few years' experience in a town where a public library has been established

would be needed to convince the thoroughgoing individualist that its advantages far outweigh its disadvantages. It is surely an important factor in promoting the public welfare of a curious and civilized
people, eager for knowledge, and anxious to apply all
their knowledge to the improvement of their circumstances. Yet I do not argue that support of a free
library at the expense of the town or city or State
is preferable to endowment by a private individual.
On the contrary, the establishment of public libraries
by individuals of wealth is one of the most praiseworthy forms of private generosity. There is no
sufficient ground for the feeling that the rights of any
person in the town are outraged by taxing him for the
support of the public library; but considerations
relating chiefly to individual donors, and to men of
wealth as a body, favor private endowment. The free
public library system has passed beyond the stage of
argument, in the State of the Pilgrims and the Puritans; it is deeply rooted in the social system of Massachusetts, and its good effects in promoting public
intelligence, order and progress are indisputable.

The establishment and ample endowment of public
libraries by the rich is the most advisable method.
In many cases, however, individuals have simply presented library buildings to the town, and it may be a
question whether a lively interest on the part of the
citizens is not better preserved where an annual appropriation for the purchase of books and the care of
the library is thus rendered necessary. The maxim
is usually sound, that "what one pays for, he cares
for;" a town might profit more by a library toward
the support of which it makes a regular appropriation,
though not large, than by one purely and wholly a

gift. But, whether the free public library is entirely the gift of an individual citizen, or the joint result of private generosity and a municipal grant, or altogether the creation of the town or city, it is a perfectly valid institution; its logic is sound and its good results are amply and undeniably apparent. In the gradual extension of the free public library system from the larger cities into the smaller towns will, in fact, be found one of the surest guarantees of the perpetuity of the American Republic. The Republic has always depended for its very existence upon the intelligence of its citizens, and in the years to come the questions, economic and social, which must find their solution at the hands of the great mass of voters will make a severer demand for knowledge than has ever yet been made. The conditions in the United States are in this respect very different from those which have prevailed in England: but the theoretical individualism of Mr. Herbert Spencer and his school is opposed to the dictates of enlightened statesmanship in every free country.

IV. AMERICAN OPPORTUNISM.

Scientific Socialism has no more hold upon the America of to-day than thoroughgoing Individualism. On the other hand, the American would be untrue to himself were he not, continuously and persistently, a social reformer, welcoming, in this perpetual task, the aid of science and philanthropy alike. It would not be proper to call the characteristic American temper a compromise between Individualism and Socialism, though, logically, it may lie anywhere between these in specific cases. We do not consciously balance in our practice the claims of the individual and the claims of the government or the people. We do not philosophically choose the middle way, because it is such, between the two tendencies, any more than the good man, in his daily conduct, incessantly chooses between the dictates of pure selfishness and those of pure altruism. Behind the man and behind the nation there lies a past rich in practical direction. The instincts of a masterful race, sagacious in action, private and public, and docile to fact, commend to it the way of reason, in most cases as if by intuition. In the New World the field for experiments never made in the Old World, and much less safe, probably, to try there, is large and enticing, and a self-confident people will be sure to attempt many new ways. Not a few of these in all likelihood will be found to have been marked by Nature "No Thoroughfare;" some will lead to loss; others will issue prosperously; of all, we may be confident, not one will be attempted in a spirit of revolution.

If a name be needed to mark the temper of the American people in social reform, Opportunism may serve as well as any other word to denote its desire to consider soberly the present and its actual needs, and to adopt only well-considered and moderate measures. Franklin, perhaps on the whole the best representative so far of the practical American genius, was an opportunist from first to last. Washington and Lincoln were both content to serve their own time, and to make haste slowly; otherwise, a lasting progress seemed to them impossible.[1]

The American would undoubtedly give the individual the first chance in every new field. To such a

[1] Professor Henry Sidgwick's *Elements of Politics* shows throughout that opportunism is the English method as well.

race, marked by great business capacity and a genius
for self-help, the presumption is always in favor of
private enterprise. If experience shows that much
injury to the public arises from combination or competition between persons or corporations, however
closely checked here or there, a fuller control will be
reluctantly assumed by the people. This reluctance
is not theoretical; it is solidly grounded on the fact
that each enlargement of the sphere of a republican
government increases the burden of political duty laid
upon the citizen. The new functions must be discharged by agents whom he knows he will need to
watch with vigilance. As I have had occasion more
than once to repeat, there is no American theory of
the State, there is no philosophical system, generally
accepted by the people, limiting the functions of the
State or the freedom of the individual.[1] Under our
republican institutions, the government for the time
being is simply a set of agents of the people, put into
power to carry out certain principles which have been
approved at the elections. The government is not a
power looked-up-to as wiser than the average voter;
it is a body of delegates chosen to carry out a certain policy and manage the public business for a limited period.

Government is necessary; as it is necessary, it is
good, but it is not a good the type of which has been
fixed once for all. The American is one of the last
of men to suppose that the State has found its final

---

[1] " In the United States democracy . . . has never allowed
itself the luxury of a philosophical theory. It has remained
eminently realistic, strictly practical." E. Boutmy, *Studies in
Constitutional Law*, p. 127. " Doctrinairism is there so uncommon a fault as to be almost a virtue." Bryce, vol. i. p. 664.

form; that its powers and functions have been definitively determined. On the contrary, the new political, social and economic phenomena of our time will,
in all probability, considerably affect his view of the
amount of power which he thinks it advisable to in-
trust to his agent, the government. The people of a
State or of the whole Union have a plain right to protect themselves against new dangers arising from vast
increase in the city population, and from new evils,
latent or patent, due to the immense accumulation of
wealth in private hands. We have never tied ourselves down, in theory or practice, to refrain from
experiment in what may be called, loosely or accurately, the "socialistic" direction. We shall not be
in any degree terrified by the declaration that a certain measure has a socialistic bearing; the one question to be settled will be the preponderance of good
or evil likely to result from its enactment as a law.
American legislatures, as I have before said, are
only too likely to anticipate the slow development of
society, and, under a strong philanthropic feeling,
pass measures which do not find adequate support in
the common conscience and public opinion. But if
the American legislator were very much better acquainted with theoretical socialism than he is, and
very much more inclined to practical socialism than
he has yet shown himself, it is still probable that he
will stop short of statutes marked by the peculiar
note of collectivism.

State ownership of the means of production has
usually been limited in the United States to the manufacture of a few classes of goods in prisons, where
every dictate of wisdom teaches that the convict
should be employed in some useful occupation. The

American legislature is quick to respond to the demand for the inspection and the minor regulation of
industry, in behalf of those employed in it, or of the
general public; but it is reluctant to take business
out of the hands of private persons, in order to carry
it on as a state industry. There is a very broad line
of distinction between inspection or regulation of
production by a government, acting simply as the
agent of the people to promote the public welfare,
and the assumption of actual production, under the
supposition that the State can more profitably and
equitably accomplish the work than the private person or the corporation, operating under the present
competitive system. In Mr. Bryce's great work
may be found a very instructive table showing in a
large number of important points the extent to which
American State governments regulate production,
trade, commerce, the professions and general industry. In a vast majority of these instances the legislature is simply a convenient agent, doing for the
people certain things which, it is generally confessed,
should be done, but which common-sense realizes are
not likely to be done effectually if left to the conscience or the sense of honor of private persons.
Thus it is of manifest importance to the people that
unwholesome substances should not be sold for food;
that adulteration should be diminished as far as possible; that buildings, especially in cities, should be
constructed in ways likely to insure the safety of
their occupants, and that certain sanitary precautions
should be observed by every householder. It is
highly advisable that teachers, lawyers, physicians
and surgeons should produce visible evidence of education and capacity, in the form of a license from

some competent authority. Whatever view one may take of the feasibility of prohibiting the sale of intoxicating liquors, it is evident that, if the traffic is allowed, it must be stringently regulated in numerous ways, to secure the public peace and order. The interests of the people at large as depositors in savings-banks, stockholders in financial institutions, or members of benefit or coöperative building societies are evidently in need of protection by statute; and it is a necessity wisely laid upon the managers of these institutions to publish their accounts, or to keep them always open for inspection by State officials or their own members.

No argument would seem to be needed in support of the plain right of the State to regulate railroads, either by acts of the legislature or through boards of railroad commissioners. The steam railway is one of those developments of modern civilization to which the theory and the practice of modern legislation have not yet been completely and logically adjusted; but a commonwealth, as it gives a railway company special and exclusive rights, obviously retains the power to defend itself against abuse or extortion on the part of this same company. Paying due respect to the rights of the stockholders, the legislature may properly fix maximum rates and the reasonable facilities to be afforded the public. It is only discharging a simple duty to the public when it requires the railway company to use such brakes, couplings and heating apparatus as will best insure the safety of passengers and trainmen. The legislature is within the limits of practical wisdom when, as in Massachusetts, it demands that the railway employees shall be free from color-blindness. The inspection and regulation of transportation by water are equally duties of the legislative power. The government, as the agent of the people, should assure the safety of vessels, so far as oversight of their building and equipment can do this. Regulations as to the number of passengers to be carried by a steamer, life-saving appliances or officers' licenses stand in no need of justification. The inspection of mines and factories, to provide against explosions and fires and secure a good sanitary condition, is one of those functions of government, acting again as the agent of the whole people, which have been found eminently sensible. The general advisability of limiting the hours of labor in factories has been approved by American experience, as by English. The community has a right to regard the future welfare of the State, which will be injuriously affected by the employment of men, and especially of women and children, for a working day of extreme length and under conditions detrimental to health. Regulations with this end in view are not discriminations against the personal liberty of the manufacturer, and they are not made to secure "privileges" to the employee; their justification is the enlightened instinct of self-preservation on the part of the whole community, which cannot regard with complacency the exploitation of the great mass of working people to gratify the greed of a few persons. The establishment of State Boards of Arbitration, as in Massachusetts and New York, is another advisable step in behalf of that public welfare which is injuriously affected by every species of "labor difficulties." Acceptance of the proffered arbitration should usually depend upon the free will of both parties to the dispute, — the action of the State being limited to the proffer of capable and disinterested arbitrators, who seek only to further the welfare of both parties and of the State at large.

We shall consider more in detail hereafter how far it is advisable to extend the present functions of towns and cities; here it may be remarked that it is eminently conducive to clearness of thought to distinguish between the functions which commonwealths and nations may profitably undertake, and those much more numerous and more detailed offices which the strictly business administration of a town or city may well attempt to discharge. In America a large number of practices meet no special opposition from citizens of the community which it would be difficult to justify on any rigid theory of the duties of the State or city. In one town, for instance, a town history is published at the expense of the tax-payers; in the adjoining city, fire-works, athletic sports and balloon ascensions are provided at public expense for the celebration of the Fourth of July; in another city, free band concerts are given in the open air during the summer season. The institution of parks and pleasure grounds is sometimes defended in the United States on the ground that they increase the value of adjacent taxable property; but the argument that they tend to preserve the public health is usually considered sufficient.

One who has only a vague notion that "socialism" includes any and every exertion by the government of powers intrusted to it, by the people living under it, will see in the measures named in the last paragraph so many conscious steps toward the socialistic régime proper. But even if we should add to these the large number of attempts, generally futile, every year

made in different parts of our country to check this
or that social evil by legislation, we must still emphatically repeat that such a generalization is unjus-
tified. Far from this, the characteristic temper and
spirit of the American would need to be revolution-
ized before he could thoroughly adopt the programme
of scientific socialism, or favor these very measures
as "steps" toward it. On the other hand, it is
equally true that the American mind is not easily
frightened away from the consideration of a new
measure of State regulation by the declaration of its
opponents (or of its friends) that it will inevitably
lead to State Socialism. We are entirely able to go
a certain length in legislation and no farther; to retrace our steps, if found advisable, and to give up
experiments which have not resulted favorably.

A very recent instance will show how little public
opinion cares in this country about purely socialistic
or individualistic argument for, or against, a particular measure. In the Australian ballot system,
which has been established, with such good effect, in
thirty-five States of the Union in the last five years,
there are, to one who will stop to consider, some
plainly "socialistic" features, if we mean by socialism the substitution, in a particular instance, of the
agency of the State for the agency of the individual.
The State has taken the manufacture and distribution
of ballots entirely out of the hands of the political
parties, and it has prohibited certain customs at the
polls which until yesterday were of the commonest.
Superficially, this may be thought to be an instance
of state - production, as the ballots are supplied at
the expense of the whole State to each community;
the resemblance, however, is superficial only, for the

reason that the ballots are printed, on contract, by private firms. The practical considerations which commended this system at first, and which have already given it a secure place in our institutions, are such as these: The new method, while it restricts the liberty of a few persons to electioneer at the polls, very much enlarges the freedom of the great body of voters themselves from the officious interference of party agents; it secures the voter in the enjoyment of entire secrecy of the ballot which he has cast, so that, whatever his color or degree, he is virtually freed from intimidation previous to the election and from punishment by his political opponents after it. In respect to the mere expense of providing ballots, there is a great saving to the whole community from the small number of ballots now printed, in comparison with the large number wasted under the private system. The indirect benefits of the new ballot system in promoting the purity of elections, in discouraging corruption and bribery, and in encouraging independence of party, are inestimable. If serious argument had ever been made against the system on the ground of its socialistic tendency, these benefits would still have won for it general approval. The point important for us here is that among the crowd of objections, wise and foolish, made against the Australian system, not one, so far as I know, was based on the ground that the new method is "socialistic."

V. Socialism and Politics.

The American socialist will naturally welcome and support every new measure tending to enlarge the sphere of government in State or Nation which the untheoretical temper of the legislatures or of Congress

may allow to pass without criticism. Now that the
question of the socialistic trend of legislation is more
commonly raised, the believers in individual initiative
will be more watchful in observing and more vigilant
in opposing measures leaning unduly to state control.
The political bearings of socialism in general have
not yet received from friend or foe the consideration
which they deserve, and which they will inevitably
attract if socialism ever becomes a living issue in the
politics of the United States. In Germany it is evident to the American observer that the "social-demo-
cratic" programme is very largely political in its
demands; most of the institutions advocated we already possess in this country, having enjoyed them
for a long time. American socialism, largely for this
reason, has thus far been almost purely economic in
its bias. But as certain great political changes
would be inevitable even in preparing for the economic régime of socialism, it is in order to inquire
how such changes would strike the American mind.
A few words on the history and the position of the
two great political parties in the United States may
serve to indicate what promise there is for socialism
in the political field.

No party in the United States has ever had occasion to style itself socialistic or individualistic (except
in the latest times, and in the case of a very small
faction); individualism and socialism, as strict theories, have been entirely absent from American politics. There have been, however, almost continuously from the adoption of the national Constitution,
two great parties especially distinguished by their
attitude toward the national government at Washington. Under one name or another, there has always

been a party which has either consciously endeavored to enlarge the powers of the central government, or has viewed without concern any tendency that way. There has never failed to be another party which, for a variety of reasons, has viewed with distrust the enlargement of the sphere of the national authority, and has asserted, over against it, with more or less vigor, the importance of the States. Obviously, of these two parties, that which favors centralization commends itself more to the socialist as likely to pave the way for the incoming of a developed and scientific socialism. Any party strongly favoring the localization of power would naturally obstruct the advance of socialistic theories. The Whig party of former days was identified with the policy of "internal improvements" by the general government; it rested heavily on the "general welfare" clause in the preamble to the Constitution. The Democratic party, on the other hand, which has endured from the days of Jefferson, and is now apparently renewing its youth, maintains the policy of "strict construction;" it points to the definite specification of powers allotted to the general government by the Constitution and emphasizes the reservation to the States of all the powers not thus conceded.[1]

[1] Jefferson's statement of what he considered "the essential principles of our government, and, consequently, those which ought to shape its administration," was reasserted by one of the ablest leaders of the Democratic party in the last Presidential campaign. This is it : —

"Equal and exact justice to all men, of whatever state or persuasion, religious or political ; peace, commerce, and honest friendship with all nations, — entangling alliances with none ; the support of the State governments in all their rights, as the most competent administrators of our domestic concerns and

Two parties thus contrasted, by whatever name they may at any specific time be called, are the natural results of the federal system. But that alien element in our national life, the institution of African slavery in the Southern States, greatly interrupted the development of politics to be expected. It even went so far as to array the two great parties against each other almost as if each had come to occupy for a time the position of the other. The tremendous slavery struggle was a kind of Hamlet-Laertes combat in which each party took up the sword which the other had dropped. The party that stood, historically, for local liberties became the thorough advocate of slavery as a national institution which the central government should protect. The

the surest bulwarks against anti-republican tendencies ; the preservation of the general government in its whole constitutional vigor, as the sheet anchor of our peace at home and safety abroad ; a jealous care of the right of election by the people, — a mild and safe corrective of abuses which are lopped by the sword of revolution where peaceable remedies are unprovided ; absolute acquiescence in the decisions of the majority, — the vital principle of republics, from which there is no appeal but to force, the vital principle and immediate parent of despotism ; a well-disciplined militia, — our best reliance in peace and for the first moments of war, till regulars may relieve them ; the supremacy of the civil over the military authority ; economy in the public expense, that labor may be lightly burdened ; the honest payments of our debts and sacred preservation of the public faith ; encouragement of agriculture and of commerce as its handmaid ; the diffusion of information and the arraignment of all abuses at the bar of public reason ; freedom of religion ; freedom of the press ; freedom of person under the protection of the habeas corpus, and trial by juries impartially selected, — these principles form the bright constellation which has gone before us, and guided our steps through an age of revolution and reformation."

Whigs and their successors, the Republicans, were far from advocating the abolition of slavery by the national power; their declared intention was to limit it to the territory already its own. The force of circumstances obliged the party of the North in the Civil War to abolish slavery as a "war measure;" only through the imperative need of self-preservation did the utmost power of the Nation over the State come to be exercised. When slavery was abolished and the element which had swerved both parties from their natural development was thus removed, the Democratic and Republican parties resumed their characteristic courses. Inevitably, the prevailing tendency for a long time after the war was to the exaggeration of the functions of the national government; these had been so strained in the conflict of North and South that a pronounced exercise of them seemed in no need of excuse. This tendency culminated in the conditions demanded for the readmission of the "reconstructed" Southern States.

The special reason for the existence of the Republican party passed away in the death of slavery. The Democratic party, the party of strict construction, survived, as its alliance with the slave power had never been logical. Shifting its ground, through the natural unwillingness of a political organization to acknowledge that its mission has been discharged, the Republican party has emphasized the tendency to centralization to a degree which was certainly not in the minds of its founders. It has become, especially in the last ten years, a party advocating an extreme policy of high protection to native industries. The policy of "protection" is plainly, so far as it goes, a feature of "paternal government," while the opposite policy, "revenue reform," or "free trade," is more in harmony with regard for individual freedom. Speaking very broadly, then, one may say that the centralizing tendencies of a party of "protection to home industries" are favorable to socialism, while a party which supports a "tariff for revenue," or "free trade," is likely to be hostile to socialism. Viewing the situation more closely, one sees that a pronounced revival of State feeling is already evident in the discussion of the tariff; and this complicates the political situation. The interests and the natural policies of Massachusetts and Pennsylvania, for example, as industrial Commonwealths are far from being identical, at least on a superficial view. The manufacturing East and the agricultural West take different attitudes toward protection in accordance with their special interests. The high protective policy has been repudiated in the recent election, and a tariff for revenue, tending gradually toward free trade, is the probable outcome of the existing situation. If this be so, any tendency to socialism that may have been indicated by the long prosperity of the party of centralization will encounter a very considerable check.

There is little, however, in the fundamental temper of either party to encourage the hopes of the scientific socialist. The party of centralization has drawn to its membership, since it became the party of protection, the vast majority of the manufacturers of the country; at the same time, it has been strong, from its earliest days, in its hold upon the great agricultural element of the country. The latter joined the Republican organization in order to check slavery, and it has but lately discovered that its interests do not lie with a party of protection. The party of centralization is thus, comparatively speaking, the party of the large property-holders of the country, a great preponderance of wealth being, at present, on its side. Whatever inclination, then, to measures of a supposed "socialistic" complexion the Republican party may have, the favor it shows to centralization of power and protection to home industries is, after all, much more than counterbalanced, when a developed socialism is under discussion, by the profound conservatism of the property-holders, — the farmers and the manufacturers alike, — who make up so large a part of its membership. There is, of course, no horizontal line of party cleavage in the United States between rich and poor. So far, indeed, as there has been an approximation to such a division, the situation in one part of the country has been precisely the reverse of that in the other part. The Democratic party in the South has been a party of property, as well as the Republican party in the North; but the Democratic party, for various reasons, has enrolled the great multitude of Irish immigrants; it includes much the larger number of persons who might be ranked in the "proletariat" of America, if we had any considerable body of persons deserving such a name, as we have not. Thus the party of "strict construction," favoring limitation of the central authority, is also the party which includes the elements that elsewhere tend to extreme assertion of the national power. The party of "loose construction" and protection would be found fundamentally opposed to any greater degree of socialism than goes to favor manufacturers. The notable absence of distinctive party policy in regard to such proposals as those for a national telegraph system or a national railroad system indicates how slightly State Socialism has yet affected American political thought. The party which has always favored localization of power and is now contending for great reductions in the duties on imports would surely be stultifying itself if it favored the wide extension of governmental authority implied in a national railroad system. As a matter of fact, while the demand of the socialists as such for a national system of railways makes small progress and attracts inconsiderable attention, the expressed opposition to it thus far comes more largely from the Democratic than from the Republican party.

The "independent" element in American politics, embracing a large part of the reformers of the country, is a growing power. As a whole, it is decidedly opposed to any considerable extension of the sphere of government, at least until there has been a thorough reform in the civil service. The Puritan conscience, which was awakened to life by slavery, has revolted at the corruption and favoritism of the spoils system, and it naturally tends at the present day to favor local rather than paternal national government. Until the civil service of the Nation and of the various States has been thoroughly rid of the spoils virus; until it is accessible to all citizens without regard to politics and conducted honestly and efficiently, the Independents in politics will vigorously oppose measures which would increase to any marked degree the number of employees of State or Nation. In proportion, however, as the reform of the civil service is actually accepted by both parties and consistently practiced, this particular opposition to measures having a socialistic tendency will decrease.

The existing political situation in the United States

has, then, little promise for the thoroughgoing socialist, if I am not much in error. To repeat in other words facts usually overlooked by those who take a purely economic view: The party of loose construction which has been in power most of the time for thirty years is distinctively the party of large property-holders, and naturally opposed to fundamental change. The party of strict construction, which embraces the greater number of small property-holders is, both historically and logically, the party of individual liberty and State rights. Finally, the Independent element, which is happily coming to hold more and more the balance of power, is thoroughly opposed to any increase of the civil service of the State or the Nation until a great reform has been accomplished, beyond dispute, in the distribution of the multitude of minor offices. There is a powerful and growing tendency in the United States to take "out of politics" the public charities, the free schools, the public libraries, the public parks, and numerous other features of municipal administration. To take anything "out of politics" in civilized countries means to take it out of corruption into honesty, out of failure into efficiency, out of a condition on which corruption fattens into a condition in which office is regarded as a public trust for the benefit of the whole people.[1]

[1] Only one who has lived for some time in the United States and has had considerable experience of the actual workings of American political institutions will sufficiently realize the force of the common contrast between "the people" and "the politicians." It is purely in imagination or theory that the politicians are faithful representatives of the people. The busy, "driving" American citizen is apt to feel that he has no time to watch the people who make a profession of running the political machine. His own private business, with which government, as a rule, has

The precisely contrary tendency of socialism would be to bring more and more activities into politics. Until, then, the civil service reform is much farther advanced than now, the great weight of enlightened public sentiment in America may be expected to oppose any large addition to the present duties of our various governments. Until the administration of our cities, especially, is freed from its unnatural union with national politics and put upon a more consistent business basis, will there be a deep-seated hostility on the part of all who are not strict partisans to any increase in the opportunities for corruption and inefficiency in office, already too plentiful. When I come to describe the so-called "Nationalist" movement in the United States, I shall properly discriminate between the full programme of "scientific socialism" which I have, thus far, chiefly had in mind, and certain specific measures looking to the extension of the functions of the Nation, the State or the city, which are not, inevitably and inseparably, parts of the scheme of such a socialism.

VI. THE BETTER WAY.

In the last three chapters we have been occupied with socialism conceived from the allopathic standpoint. Thus conceived, as a complete and elaborate system of ownership by the state of all the means of production, *Socialism has no hold upon the distinctively American spirit.* Socialism declares, indeed, that it

---

little to do, tends to absorb his thought; he even prefers too often to be heavily taxed in direct consequence of political corruption, rather than take the time from his private affairs which would be needed to overthrow the " machine " and keep it in permanent exile.

is Republicanism applied to industry, and that a democratic people must constantly incline thereto. This involves, however, a pure assumption on the part of the socialist — an assumption which the American will be one of the first of men to perceive and disallow — that the people never need to be guarded against themselves. The American political scheme, on the contrary, is full of devices by which, in Lowell's phrase, "the people's will is protected against the people's whim, and full opportunity given of appeal from the people drunk to the people sober." Crazes of various kinds, political, financial and social, have had much currency at times in the United States, but there is no country in which they more quickly subside. The older the nation is, the more will the shrewd and practical American mind realize the necessity of interposing obstacles and delays between such temporary discontent, however widespread, and the fundamental change in the political or industrial order which the like discontent in a pure democracy, living under no written constitution, would immediately bring about.

In subsequent chapters, I shall have frequent occasion to recur to the various traits of the American Spirit to which we have been attending, or to allude to others upon which it is not needful to dilate here. Closing this rapid and incomplete survey of it, let us conclude with considering some fundamental matters. For a socialistic system to produce even a moderately successful result, as compared with the present industrial scheme, a very strict regimentation of industry would be absolutely necessary. This much is certain, although the weakest side of socialism, — as every one knows who has endeavored to acquaint himself with its practical programme, — is its attempted construction in detail of a system at all adequate, even in theory, to realize the blessings it promises. As a critic of the existing order, the socialist shines with such brilliancy as to delude many; but as the expositor of a new order, he has had no success. Karl Marx contented himself almost entirely with destructive criticism. It was left for a German economist, not a socialist, to draw from the fundamental ideas of Marx and the numerous writings of his school the most consistent outline of the socialistic state yet made. But whether we take Dr. Schäffle's picture, or Mr. Edward Bellamy's, or Mr. Laurence Gronlund's, is here a matter of comparative indifference. A very profound change would need to come over the American before any such picture could seriously attract him. A transformation of the national genius hardly less than complete would be demanded before it could approve the socialistic ideal presented by either of these writers. A society in which a highly centralized government would be the one employer of labor, the one producer, the one manufacturer, the one transporter, and the one distributer; in which there would be no trade and no competition; in which there would be no room for voluntary coöperation; in which the individual would inevitably wither and the government tend to be all in all, — such a society has in it nothing to inflame the American imagination, even in comparison with the present imperfect system. It is a depressing ideal of monotony and uniformity which "Looking Backward," "The Coöperative Commonwealth," and even "The Quintessence of Socialism" present to us. The active and laudable individualism of the energetic and capable American mind revolts at the necessary industrial and political despotism of such a state, and the conservative element in his political temper is as much repelled by the destruction of time-honored political institutions absolutely requisite for the mere erection of the socialistic state. Mr. Gronlund has been the most specific of Socialistic writers in acknowledging the chief changes in our political fabric which socialism would involve simply as preliminaries. These are so great that it requires a vivid imagination to suppose that the American mind will seriously consider them. A radical upheaval would be necessary for the sagacious American temper to rashly surrender the ample benefits which political freedom now secures, simply in order to discover whether or not the economic blessings promised by Mr. Bellamy and Mr. Gronlund have any existence outside their imaginations.

There is an attraction for a brief time, it is true, in the notion of equality of reward; but speedy second thought convinces the American that this is not a thing which he has ever desired under the existing system, and which it is not at all likely that he would desire under one to come. Equality of reward could be secured only by a regimentation which would raise in revolt every Anglo-Saxon instinct of personal freedom. The utter inability of the socialist to work out a scheme of compensation for the many kinds of labor needful in a civilized state, on any other basis than that of equality, becomes obvious to the quick-witted American as soon as his attention is called to it. Equality of reward for unequal talents and despotic regimentation in an "industrial army" are two features of constructive socialism which utterly fail to captivate his mind.

With great propriety one can retort upon the socialist that he repeats the error of the orthodox political economist in imagining an "economic màn" who never existed. The person who could be happy and contented in the imaginary Boston of the year 2000, or in Mr. Gronlund's coöperative commonwealth, would be devoid of life and spirit, as compared with the American of to-day. Weak in self-assertion, stunted in personal ambition, and deprived of the immeasurable incitements of individual interest and voluntary coöperation, the citizen of the socialistic state may well appear to the actual American a puny creature. Of all dwellers upon this round earth the American is least likely to be consumed with desire of shrinking to such pitiful dimensions. A cultivated socialist like Mr. Sidney Webb comes over here from England, to be sure, and finds everywhere many persons ready and desirous to hear all that he has to say about present evils and their remedies. In one city and another he has a friendly reception. Thoughtful American men and women are glad to meet him, hear his views, and discuss his proposals in the most open way. But, when it comes to approving his conclusions and accepting his remedies, or even confirming his statements of the situation and of the prevailing tendencies, — to say nothing of working out his plans, — he feels a dismal change in the temperature. Mr. Webb laments over "the general content and light-heartedness he observes in Americans: he wants to inspire them with a divine discontent. They think happiness is the end and aim of life, whereas it is the worst possible sign of the condition they are in." He continues pathetically: "One can tell Americans anywhere: they are always laughing and smiling and looking so pleased with themselves, because the public treasury is full and the country bursting with corn and wine and oil." Mr. William Morris, whose poetry we admire heartily, though opinions may differ as to his wall-papers, prefers to stay at home like Mr. Ruskin, and construct his ideas of America from the depths of his own consciousness. This country is to him "the apotheosis of commercialism, the awful example among nations; and he predicts for its present political and social system a violent overthrow. He thinks the United States, with its conservative Constitution, its huge monopolies, its millionaire senators, no more 'free' than Germany or Spain."

We entirely agree with the opinion that inspires these doleful utterances. Mr. Webb and Mr. Morris are convinced that America is a very poor field for socialism to cultivate. Mr. Morris plays Cassandra because he believes that the United States will stand out against socialism longer than any other nation, with correspondingly bad consequences. Mr. Webb cannot stomach our American optimism, for a certain degree of pessimism is essential to the mental make-up of a socialist. The socialist like Mr. Edward Bellamy is so far from cheerful in his views of things that he starts a new journal with the express design of showing that the existing order is "radically wrong in morals and preposterous economically." This modest indictment of civilization certainly goes some distance on the road toward the declaration that this is the worst of all possible worlds. Optimism and conservatism, however, are fundamental and related characteristics of the American social spirit. The man who believes that things, on the whole, are not in a very bad state, and are always likely to become better, is the man least of all disposed to denounce them by wholesale and propose fundamental change. If we see ourselves aright, as others see us, if M. de Tocqueville, the Duc de Noailles, M. Boutmy, Professor Waltershausen, Walter Bagehot, Sir H. S. Maine, and Mr. Bryce are not mistaken in their unanimous and weighty verdict on the main temper of our people, the bearing of this conservative and optimistic spirit on the socialistic proposals of the day is obvious. The State socialist would find it a primary necessity to his scheme of abolishing private capital in production to establish some new form of government. Republican institutions, as we have had them in this country for a century, are plainly incompetent to the enormous task which the State operation of all productive industries would lay upon the central authority. An administration numbering millions of officers, centralized in the highest degree and dispensing entirely with all our familiar checks and balances of power, would be the instrument imperatively needed to carry out the socialistic idea. Only the rigid discipline and despotism of an army could hold such a multitude of officials together and insure the obedience of every citizen. The socialists, therefore, who have worked out their conception on the line of an "industrial army" have been most consistent. But no conception could be more radically opposed to the political ideas under which we live. The complete demolition of the structure of Anglo-Saxon freedom, painfully reared through centuries, would be the initial task in the socialistic reconstruction. The machinery of the collectivist State needs broader and deeper foundations than have yet been laid by any free people: its weight and jar would soon bring down in ruin the walls of the present political fabric.[1]

Socialism demands an entirely new frame of things, political as well as social and industrial. The political change would need to precede the industrial. America as at present constituted "is made all of a piece: its institutions are the product of its economic and social conditions and the expression of its character."[2] If these economic and social conditions are to suffer a thorough transformation, a political revolution is requisite in some early stage of the process.

[1] " A government might perform the part of some of the largest American companies, . . . but what political power could ever carry on the vast multitude of lesser undertakings which the American citizens perform every day, with the assistance of the principle of association? . . . The task of the governing power will perpetually increase, and its very efforts will extend it every day. The more it stands in the place of associations, the more will individuals, losing the notion of combining together, require its assistance; these are causes and effects which unceasingly create each other. Will the administration of the country ultimately assume the management of all the manufactures, which no single citizen is able to carry on? . . . The morals and the intelligence of a democratic people would be as much endangered as its business and manufactures, if the government ever wholly usurped the place of private companies. . . . A government can no more be competent to keep alive and to renew the circulation of opinions and feelings amongst a great people than to manage all the speculations of productive industry. No sooner does a government attempt to go beyond its political sphere, and to enter upon this new track, than it exercises, even unintentionally, an insupportable tyranny; for a government can only dictate strict rules, the opinions which it favors are rigidly enforced, and it is never easy to discriminate between its advice and its commands." Tocqueville, vol. ii. pp. 132–134.

[2] Bryce, vol. ii. p. 473.

The probability of such a revolution here in America is of the very slightest. Some possibility of its consideration by a small party there might be, were a programme drawn up which should show how it might be effected by many successive steps of evolution from our present system, each being, in itself considered, not difficult to take. Such a programme, in order to inspire the respect of a shrewd and practical people, should proceed from persons who have repute as competent students of economics and political science, and whose credentials are clear as men knowing the past well, describing the present fairly, and outlining the future modestly. That socialism in this country has any number of persons thus qualified is far from obvious.

On account, then, of the character of the American Spirit, the United States is the country in the civilized world in which collectivism will make the least progress, — the country in which, as a consistent system, it will fail to receive even a trial. The national temper must fall much below its present pitch of cheerful confidence before socialism can get even a serious hearing as a practical remedy for existing evils, — such a curious compound is socialism of superficial optimism and fundamental pessimism. Its writers depict a condition of universal felicity, in one or two or three hundreds of years from now, as the sure result of the adoption of their schemes. A very sanguine disposition appears in this high rating of the value of a great increase in the governmental regulation of society. But how deep is the pessimism which asserts that the "existing industrial system" — an integral part of a civilization wrought out by thousands of years of effort — is "radically wrong in morals and preposterous economically "! How can such a bungling humanity be expected to set everything right in a few decades, if in tens of centuries it has succeeded no better!

The American mind will not be taken in by such sophistry. Its optimism does not blind it to the evils of the present time; but it relies for their cure on the forces of good which human nature has been displaying for many centuries, which have brought us thus far on the right way, and will bring us much farther, if we remain true to reason, to science, and to conscience. A scientific method will ascertain the facts and laws of the situation: a heart never destitute of sympathy for the weaker members of the one family of humanity will adopt every means for their permanent relief which careful study commends. What the American social spirit has done for two centuries, it will continue to do. It will give equal rights before the law to every man, an equal education in the public schools to every child, and a refuge to the infirm and incapable. It will clothe the naked and feed the hungry who cannot provide for themselves, and will enlarge the opportunities of work for those who can work.[1] It will hold back the State from no field which the State can cultivate better than private persons, singly or in companies, because of any theory of individualism. It will close no career to lawful enterprise and private talent because of any theory of socialism. It will be content to be opportunist and

---

[1] "The genius of the country has marked out our true policy, — opportunity. Opportunity of civil rights, of education, of personal power, and not less of wealth ; doors wide open. . . . Let all compete, and success to the strongest, the wisest and the best." Emerson, *The Fortune of the Republic.*

serve its own time, as it can live only in the present. It can be said with entire confidence that American legislatures make no laws out of an unquestioning adherence to a rigorous and vigorous theory; nothing has occurred, since socialism has been more warmly discussed here, that indicates any fundamental alteration in the temper or the tendency of the American people. They have legislated for their own actual condition, with no particular reference to individualism or socialism. They have been guided and governed by the political instincts of the Anglo-Saxon race, a race which has shown itself, thus far, in the history of the world, the most able to establish political freedom on solid and lasting foundations. The fathers of the American Republic, in Lowell's words,—

> " More devoutly prized
> Than all perfection theorized
> The more imperfect that had roots and grew."

Their genius for politics has always led the American people to respect the limits of the practical and the attainable. In the future, we have a full right to expect the same quality will be displayed in regard to any steps yet to be taken.

America will, indeed, show mankind a more excellent way than socialism. The world over, democracy has no more insidious enemy to fear, so surely would socialism issue in despotism, grossly discrediting political liberty as it does, while it would endeavor to lay upon a republic burdens impossible to be borne. The federal system is the only one open to America, a sober system of checks and balances, regardful of the individual, regardful, too, of social needs.

"America holds the future," said Matthew Arnold. If American conservatism and optimism have not here been overrated, then socialism will not prevail in the United States or elsewhere. No more will a narrow individualism be the heir of all the ages. Undivided and inseparable, society and the individual will respect each other's rights and functions, increase their attention to their diverse duties, and steadily lift mankind into more resolute life, "im Ganzen, Guten, Schönen."

CHAPTER VI.

NATIONALISM IN THE UNITED STATES.

THE so-called "Nationalist" movement in the
United States furnishes a pertinent occasion for applying, in a critical manner, the conclusions to which
we have arrived concerning the American spirit.
This specific movement originated in the ingenious
and widely known novel, "Looking Backward," picturing life as it may be in Boston in the year 2000
A. D. Mr. Edward Bellamy is, or was, a novelist
by profession; he has continued the line of literary
men who, for more than a century, have had great influence in calling public attention to social questions.
Prof. William Graham, in "The Social Problem,"
declares that this problem largely owes its existence,
under its present form in modern society, to men of
letters from Rousseau to Carlyle, and from Shelley
to Victor Hugo; they have exercised the function of
prophets of a higher, more moral civilization with
rare power and great effect. A previous chapter has
made sufficiently plain, I trust, my appreciation of
the important part played by literature in social progress. "Nationalism" in this country is, thus far,
largely a literary and personal matter, centring round
Mr. Bellamy, who has written its one book of consequence and now edits its most important newspaper:
he is the recognized father of the Nationalist Clubs
formed after the book was published in January,

1888, and has supplied much of the inspiration of the movement since.[1]

Edward Bellamy was born, in 1850, in Chicopee, Mass., of clerical stock, his father and his maternal grandfather having been Baptist ministers. Dr. Joseph Bellamy, the friend of Jonathan Edwards and the instructor of Aaron Burr, was his Revolutionary ancestor. Mr. Bellamy took a partial course at Union College, studied for a year in Germany, read law and was admitted to the bar. He soon found more congenial work on the staff of the "Evening Post," of New York, which he left in 1872 to become assistant - editor of the Springfield "Union." He abandoned journalism in 1876, and devoted himself for the ensuing twelve years to the writing of fiction. His first book, "Six to One: A Nantucket Idyl," had some strong touches indicating the writer's special talent as a story-teller; this lies more in depicting peculiar characters and describing strange situations than in the artistic reproduction of common life. In "Dr. Heidenhoff's Process," a second novel, for instance, the hero dreams of procuring the extirpation of certain memories by passing a current of electricity through a portion of the brain. In "Miss Ludington's Sister" the author develops with remarkable ingenuity his heroine's notion that each human being, in the course of his life, has a number of selves, corresponding to the various periods, and that these are all immortal. Mr. Bellamy has been prolific of short stories, which have been printed in the leading American magazines. In these, as in the

---

[1] In the *Quarterly Journal of Economics* for October, 1889, may be found an article which I have reproduced to some extent in this chapter.

novels, the felicity of expression is often great; the
situations described are usually peculiar, if not fantastic, and the portraiture of character is external.
Fond of pursuing an odd idea to its remotest consequences, the writer fails to set before us, as a rule,
the full personality of his men and women, with the
force of life. They are more or less wooden puppets
operated to develop a curious dream or an *outré* conception. Ingenuity, occasionally somewhat strained,
is the note of Mr. Bellamy's earlier literary product.
The writings just mentioned belong chiefly to the
school of fanciful idealism, rather than to that of careful realism. They rightly procured for their author
a high place as a writer of short stories in a country
noted for the excellence of its literary product in this
direction, but they did not indicate the advent of a
great novelist.

"Looking Backward," judged from a literary point
of view, does not lead to any reversal of this estimate.
The characters are few and rather mechanical; the
romantic interest of the story was deliberately sacrificed to the philanthropic purpose, and the book
would have been more effective, from any point of
view, had it been shorter. Published in January,
1888, the novel had but a limited circulation for some
months, although highly commended by the literary
critics. But the earnest feeling with which it was
written coincided remarkably with a new and pronounced public interest in social problems; after a
time it began to sell largely, and its author soon became a notoriety. The ingenuity with which the
story was developed within the narrow limits of its
meagre plot and its few characters, and, much more,
the forcible expression given to its conceptions of a

new society, painted in roseate colors, attracted a great multitude of readers. In the next two years the publishers sold over 350,000 copies of the book, most of them in paper covers. The story was "the book of the hour" in the United States; regarded simply as a literary sensation, it succeeded "Robert Elsmere" and was followed by "The Kreutzer Sonata." How much more than a literary sensation it should be considered is a question: the sensation subsided, and "Looking Backward" has had a moderate sale in the last two years. America has thus had the distinction of having produced the socialistic romance of modern times which has been read and talked about by millions of people, in the Old World as in the New. In the United States, indeed, the book made socialism run for some time the course of a "fad." Mr. Bellamy became an extreme convert to his own doctrine, as he was writing his romance, and there were not lacking persons who were convinced, by the sale of a third of a million copies of "Looking Backward," that there were at least a million, if not two million, thoroughgoing socialists in the United States, — all of whom might be considered ready to inaugurate "nationalism" at the earliest possible moment. Such methods of taking the intellectual census of a civilized people were sufficiently amusing at the time; only a few months have been needed to convince even the takers that they were over-hasty in substituting a simple process of multiplication for a house-to-house canvass. Very slight reflection shows any one acquainted with American life that the enormous sale of "Looking Backward" indicated the existence of a million or two of convinced socialists no more than the larger sale of "Robert Elsmere" indicated that countless Americans were ready to join a new sect in Christianity, holding the beliefs of the author. "Looking Backward" was issued at a time when public attention was eagerly directed toward social questions; and sixty millions of people, readers of the newspapers and patrons of the railway bookstands, soon absorbed many editions of a volume written with fervor and conviction. It has led to the production of a very considerable number of imitations and supplements by authors much less talented than Mr. Bellamy, who considered that the interest in "Looking Backward" was a plain invitation to the sentimentalists to come to the front and take charge of modern civilization.

The book soon led to the "Nationalist" movement, — a movement which has probably, through Mr. Bellamy's notoriety and the adhesion of a considerable number of young journalists in the East, made more noise with less reason for it than any other agitation of the day. Its name is appropriate to its ultimate aim, — the entire control of production by the Nation, — but very inappropriate to its present working programme of enlarging the functions of the towns, cities and commonwealths of the Union. Its present intellectual capital is chiefly borrowed from writers like Prof. R. T. Ely, who have no sympathy with its ideal of complete state socialism; the membership of the clubs devoted to its propaganda is small and of little weight, and the movement, so far as it has any specific life of its own, is steadily losing ground. As an intellectual ferment, it has had its part to play. The confusion of logical distinctions which leads its speakers and writers to label as a "Nationalist" any person who believes in social and industrial reform is evident to one at all willing to discriminate. Its chief interest for us here lies in its un-American spirit and the impracticability of the proposals it has added to those made by writers who had previously favored municipal or State control of "natural monopolies."

The description of the social and political condition of Boston in the year 2000 A. D., which "Looking Backward" gave, is not, of course, to be taken as the full and minute platform of the Nationalists. But Mr. Bellamy is a believer in the complete desirability and feasibility of such a State; he is the one authoritative exponent of "Nationalism," in his speeches, in his various articles in the newspapers and periodicals of the day, and in "The New Nation," the weekly paper established by him in Boston in February, 1891, of which he is the editor. He has retracted none of the characteristic ideas set forth in the novel; these are still the substance of the ideal state toward realizing which he would have the Nationalists direct their efforts. But in order to pave the way to the new régime, Mr. Bellamy and his followers have appropriated the proposals of much abler American thinkers like Professor Ely, and characteristically proceeded to ignore all questions of more and less: perhaps this was the only method whereby "Nationalism" could escape inanition in its cradle.

A number of Bostonians, enthusiastic believers in the programme set forth in "Looking Backward," established, in September, 1888, the "Boston Bellamy Club," which was reorganized in the following December as the "Nationalist Club." Its constitution declares that, "The object of this club shall be the nationalization of industry, and thereby the pro-

motion of the brotherhood of humanity. The economic tendency of the age being favorable to this end,
this club seeks to promote its practical adoption by
familiarizing the people with the beneficent idea underlying it, and by encouraging national and local
measures tending in this direction." The motto of
the club is "The promotion of the brotherhood of man
through the nationalization of industry." Following
the example of the Boston Nationalists, a considerable
number of other clubs were organized. They were
distributed unevenly through our American cities and
towns of all sizes, in various parts of the country.
Outside of four or five large cities in the East, a large
proportion of these clubs was soon to be found in
California, perhaps the most excitable State in the
Union; it was stated in June, 1890, that one third of
all the clubs in the country were in this State: the
same proportion held true of theosophical societies.
The contemplated "nationalist league" of clubs has
not been formed. The number of clubs has not much
increased of late; statistics are not published, and
probably at least as many clubs have disbanded as
there have been new ones formed: the tendency to
organization early reached its climax. The Boston
club has always been the leading body and the chief
force in the movement. This club, "The First Nationalist," includes very few "business men" actually
engaged in production or distribution; its membership is largely composed of women. A considerable
number of clergymen, with a few physicians, journalists and lawyers, have been on its list, — some of the
clergymen being active leaders in the Christian
Socialist movement, which I shall describe later.
The list of regular members includes hardly a man of

distinction, and but few women widely known as philanthropists. The club, however, hospitably welcomed as "associate members" every one who "believes in the nationalization of any special industry not already under the control of the nation." (As if one should be admitted to a church on accepting a single article of its creed, and that not the central dogma!) This elastic provision admitted Colonel T. W. Higginson, for instance, as a believer in the advisability of adding the telegraph to the post-office administration of the country, and Rev. Dr. E. E. Hale, who declares that the strengthening of the State governments is one of the chief needs of the time. Mrs. Mary A. Livermore and Miss Frances E. Willard have been connected with this club. Their labors in behalf of prohibition of the liquor traffic and woman's suffrage have given these ladies a great reputation, but they have not won repute in any economic sphere. With the exception of the persons above named or alluded to, the list of the Nationalists of Boston is one of comparatively unknown persons; among these there is, very naturally, at least the usual proportion of professional hobbyists and instantaneous world-regenerators, — that is, to use a common and very expressive word, "cranks." Every organization of this general description attracts such persons by its novelty, if for no other reason, to the very small help of the more capable promoters of the movement. Few programmes, indeed, could be imagined more likely to excite the ardor of philanthropists of this order than the comprehensive scheme of "nationalism."

The Nationalist magazine, started in May, 1889, was published monthly until February, 1891; its

early death could not be ascribed to the disease which
is said to have carried off one of the numerous queens
of King Henry VIII. We are told that Queen
Katherine Parr "died of thought;" the "Nationalist"
seems to have died of rhetoric. A certain species of
literary brightness and cleverness in its pages was
not accompanied by any serious or thorough discussion
of particular problems, economic or social. "Bal-
lades of an Outcast" alternated with fervid "Pleas
for the Brotherhood of Humanity;" and there was a
conspicuous lack of careful consideration of such
questions as a national telegraph or municipal gas-
works. For a number of months Nationalism was
characterized mainly by a literary spirit. Originated
by a clever novel, it excited the special interest of
numerous persons more or less literary, in disposition
or occupation, who had a philanthropic turn and a
general attraction to social problems, without any
particular knowledge of economics or politics. To
the lively young journalists and the warm-hearted
women who contributed most of the matter in "The
Nationalist," "the author whose pen of fire had drawn
pictures of inextinguishable flame on the mind-canvas
of his continually increasing audience," — to quote a
few words from the magazine, — appeared as the legislator of a new and better era, in which a complete
transformation will pass over the institutions of mankind, — political, industrial and social.

The literary class in the United States has, however, gradually reacted from its temporary fascina-
tion by Mr. Bellamy's scheme, through the rational
study which many have been led to make of social
problems. Little study, indeed, is needed to make
one discount the exorbitant pretensions made in "The

Nationalist" and "The New Nation." Goethe once said, "When Byron reflects he is a child." When Mr. Bellamy develops in the chapters of his romance of the future the ingenious imaginations of an ardent mind, peculiarly gifted in picturing eccentric characters and extraordinary situations, we read with interest his brilliant pages. We cannot fail to be conscious of the extreme injustice of his representation of existing society where all is wrong and outrage, compared with his cheerful delineation of a future where all is bright and right; nothing could well be more partial than his metaphor of the "coach" of civilization. But as a provocative to thought, as a brilliant dream which forces us to inquire more closely into the justification of existing institutions, the book entertains and edifies. We read it with an eagerness proportionate to our youthfulness of feeling and our respect for the ideal as compared with the actual. Few persons take up the book a second time except for critical study of the scheme embodied in it. As a stimulator of thought through the imagination, its author has performed a great service for his generation. This is, indeed, the one valuable contribution which Nationalism and Mr. Bellamy have made; they have drawn popular attention to social and economic problems, arousing discussion and agitation. But Mr. Bellamy is thoroughly a man of letters, not an orator of the millennium; he is a man of rare imagination, but political sense and economic sagacity are not prominent in his writings. When he prophesies "he is a child." The reputation in the field of letters which he had made, and to which "Looking Backward" contributed much, lends no justification to the extravagance of his subsequent course as an editor.[1] The man who practices medicine according to the method of intuition receives a common epithet. Any man who without careful study undertakes the cure of social disease — at least as difficult a task — deserves the same name.

The Nationalists gave their hearty adherence to the so-called "People's Party" which formulated a platform in a meeting at Cincinnati, May 19–20, 1891, and which figured in the recent Presidential election, carrying a few of the extreme Western States. Under whatever name, the "Nationalists" proper are plainly more noisy than numerous in the East, according to the returns of the votes cast November, 1892, which indicated 517 supporters of the "People's Party," in Boston for instance, while the 170 "scattering" included the votes of the Socialistic Labor party. A party which is able to keep its countenance while singing "My Country 't is of Thee, Land of Lost Liberty, Of Thee we sing," in Faneuil Hall, where Mr. Bellamy was introduced as the "hero of a million homes," is not likely to "pan out" well at the polls in a sensible American commonwealth like Massachusetts.[2]

[1] The *New Nation* has lately remarked that though the Homestead strike is dead, its soul goes marching on; that the shots fired by the strikers at the Pinkerton police, like those of the embattled farmers of Lexington, were heard round the world; that if the conflict between labor and capital, of which the Homestead strike was an incident, is not soon solved by ballots, it will be by bullets, etc., etc.

[2] The author of *Looking Backward* has little sympathy with American optimism. Last October he wrote : "In view of this situation, it seems to me that the condition in which the 400th anniversary of Columbus' discovery finds America should suggest, instead of jubilation and cannon firing, a season rather of fasting and prayer, that God may save the great experiment of human liberty from a disastrous ending."

The People's Party is the result of a temporary union of a great number of elements of more or less rational discontent which are not satisfied with the policy of the Republican, the Democratic or the Prohibition party, and which are very unlikely to continue in alliance for any length of time. Mr. Bellamy himself holds that it is the natural successor of the Granger movement, the Greenback party and the Butler party of Massachusetts. The relationship is, indeed, obvious and undeniable. The severe adverse verdict which time and reason have passed on the previous movements is likely to be repeated in the case of their successor. The People's Party is not much concerned about the reform of the existing tariff, but it is in favor of free coinage of silver, and of the issue by the national government of treasury notes as a substitute for national bank notes as legal tender in payment of all debts public and private. These notes "when demanded by the people, shall be loaned to them at not more than two per cent. per annum upon non-imperishable (*sic*) products as indicated in the sub-treasury plan and also upon real estate." The financial folly of this crazy movement needs no comment.[1]

The general character of Mr. Bellamy's social dream will be sufficiently indicated here by a simple reference to his "industrial army" which would enforce a service for twenty-four years of each person's life, — from twenty-one to forty-five, — with the exception of those who take to professional careers, but

---

[1] A speaker at a recent People's Party convention is reported to have appropriately concluded a vigorous harangue thus : " I don't know what it is we want, but we want it right away, and we want it bad."

are still under control of the State; to the disappearance of political life in a purely industrial organization of the nation; to the entire abolition of money, of trade, of private business enterprise, and of individual property, with the exception of a limited amount of personal belongings and household furniture. Absolute equality of recompense, without regard to the kind or quality of the product or service of different individuals, is the rule. Each person, man, woman or child, is guaranteed by the government nurture, education and maintenance through a yearly allotment which is the same for all. Mr. Bellamy has been no more successful than previous socialists in devising a scheme of credit-cards to take the place of money. In his new Boston, money is entirely absent. Of course there is no need of it on the part of the nation, as almost all property is its own, and it can command the services and possessions of its citizens for public purposes to any extent. The explanation of the absence of taxes and of a national treasury is apparently satisfactory to the author, but Mr. Bellamy is so little of a political economist that he finds himself obliged to use the word "dollars." His Dr. Leete says that the credit-cards are "issued for a certain number of dollars. We have kept the old word, but not the substance. The term, as we use it, answers to no real thing, but merely serves as an algebraical symbol for comparing the values of products with one another. For this purpose they are all priced in dollars and cents just as in your day." How a meaningless term, answering to no reality, can fix the value of commodities or services, and serve as an aid in distribution or exchange, one fails to see: the "algebraical symbol" remains an x always undeter-

mined. Mr. Bellamy informs us at least twice that
money — that is to say, gold and silver — is "a
merely conventional representative " of food and other
commodities; it seems plain, therefore, that he accepts "the greenback heresy" in finance, and holds
that only the government stamp gives value to what
we call money of any kind. When he thus dismisses
money entirely from his Utopia, and makes the service of one individual as good before the law as that
of another, we easily perceive that he will have a
difficult task in explaining the meaning of "cost,"
"price" and "value." The services of A, in this
year of grace 1893, are worth ten gold dollars a day,
and the services of B but two dollars, judged by the
usefulness of the product of each to the community.
The problem for Mr. Bellamy is how to define cost
and value when A is rewarded precisely the same as
B, all discrimination in recompense having been
abolished, and when there is no common standard of
exchange that is a measure for services and commodities. The "algebraical symbol" throws no light on
the solution of this question; the subject on which
it does throw much light, however, is the novelist's
qualifications for discussing economic subjects.

Mr. Bellamy's Utopia is a nation in the highest
degree centralized, — the government being the one
employer of labor, the one producer, distributer,
transporter and publisher. If the author of this
scheme of despotism in government[1] and a close approach to communism in property-holding had simply
presented it as an imagination, serious criticism of

[1] " Everything that crushes individualism is despotism, by
whatever name it is called and with whatever disguise it adorns
itself." J. S. Mill, *On Liberty.*

its economic or political shortcomings would be out of place. Taken by itself, "Looking Backward" does not commit the author to a belief that the scheme he describes will ever become a reality. It might have been written as a purely ideal construction on paper, with a view to stimulating mankind to think upon the possible improvement of its lot. It would then have been subject only to a demand that the representation hold together artistically and logically, the premises being granted. But Mr. Bellamy soon persuaded himself that the mantle of a genuine prophet had fallen upon him, and that "Looking Backward" is an inspired account of the order of things to be expected in the twentieth century. In March, 1888, he declared that "'Looking Backward,' although in form a fanciful romance, is intended in all seriousness as a forecast, in accordance with the principles of evolution, of the next stage in the industrial and social development of humanity, especially in this country; and no part of it is believed by the author to be better supported by the indications of probability than the implied prediction that the dawn of a new era is already at hand, and that the full day will swiftly follow." His confidence as a prophet seems not to have diminished as time has gone on. In May, 1889, he wrote: "My conviction as to the shortness of the time in which the hope of nationalization is to be realized by the birth of the new and the first true nation, I wish to say, is one which every day's reflection and observation since the publication of 'Looking Backward' has tended to confirm. [It then] appeared to me reasonable to suppose that by the year 2000 the order of things which we look forward to will already have become an exceedingly old story."

Mr. Bellamy would parallel from history the extreme speed of such a peaceful revolution within the next fifty years, resulting in a thorough change of the existing industrial order. He considers that the independence of the United States, the unity of Germany and of Italy, and the abolition of African slavery in this country are instances in point to show that the industrial revolution would demand comparatively a short period. That all these changes were primarily political, and consequent upon wars of long duration and enormous cost, he does not seem to remember. His tendency appears to be to shorten rather than to lengthen the limit allowed to the existing system, for he has repeatedly declared within the last four years that "Plutocracy or nationalism is the choice which within ten years the people of the United States will have virtually decided upon. There is no third choice." Four years of these ten have passed, and the slight progress which nationalism has made does not encourage a belief that the next six will see the choice fully made. Mr. Bellamy's amusing inexperience as a social reformer is sufficiently obvious in the emphasis with which he thus stakes his reputation upon the period within which "nationalism" will be the prevailing system in this country.[1] No man's prophecy of the future of human society is worth much unless it is confined to such generalities as the declaration that progress will probably follow the well-known lines of average human nature; this is the

---

[1] Mr. Hosea Biglow was less sanguine : —

> " Not thet I 'm one thet much expec'
> Millennium by express to-morrer ;
> They *will* miscarry, — I rec'lec'
> Tu many on 'em, to my sorrer."

conclusion to which they usually come who compare
the past with the actual situation of civilized mankind.

What has the American spirit to say to Mr. Bellamy and his scheme of Nationalism? He must be
ranked as a clever exponent of methods and ideas that
are extremely un-American. There is no point, indeed, on which he lays more emphasis than the supposed essential Americanism of his imaginary society.
The nationalists repeat that, as we have achieved political freedom in the United States, so we are now
to achieve industrial freedom; and that as the first is
realized in a government of the people, by the people,
and for the people, so the people will bring about
"industrial liberty" by taking the whole control of
business. That many of the undeniable corruptions
of our political life result from the equal suffrage
of all men, without regard to education or capacity,
and that we have escaped our greatest dangers as a
people through the counterbalance afforded by the
free play of natural aristocracy in the industrial world,
— these are considerations of the utmost importance
which the nationalist neglects.

America is fully committed to political equality;
with all its disadvantages, its benefits are far prepon-
derant. No person who understands the American
spirit or the American situation would dream of taking any backward steps in this respect. But it is the
plain duty of every rational American to perceive the
important practical difficulties and dangers of political freedom and to lend his aid in counterbalancing
them, as far as possible. One might well suppose,
from reading the writings of Nationalists, that, in order to have any kind of work done wisely, honestly

and efficiently, it is only necessary to put it into the hands of "the people." The American people, thus far, have been of a very different opinion. They have shown their political ingenuity by the establishment of institutions skillfully constructed to guard against hasty decisions by the people at large, and inconsiderate legislation by their representatives. The balance and limitation of powers is the one matter which the framers of American constitutions have most carefully regarded.[1] In order to introduce even a trial of the full Nationalist system, it would be necessary to give up all such limitations and break down all such restrictions.

The American will say to the "nationalist" that his notion of equality is fundamentally mistaken. Equality of political rights — equality of one man with another before the law — is the basic idea in the United States. But no notion could be farther from the mind of an enterprising, active, energetic, capable people like the Americans than the equal reward of every variety of capacity or performance. Of all peoples in the world, the American people would need to be most thoroughly transformed, and to lose its most characteristic traits, before it could even desire such an equality as is pictured in "Looking Backward." There is, of course, a superficial attractiveness in the earnest exposition of a society in which every man has work and sustenance assured him, so that there shall be no poverty and no suffering for man to endure. The practical American mind immediately asks, however, how far it is likely that the

---

[1] "The nation which will not adopt an equilibrium of power must adopt a despotism. There is no other alternative." John Adams, *Discourses on Davila.*

governmental and industrial system of the nationalistic ideal would secure these advantages; whether the institutions which have been sketched by the novelist as the most desirable apparatus to this end would be tolerated by a liberty-loving people; in short, whether the consequences which all experience leads us to attribute to the working of such institutions would not be, on the whole, far worse than the evils from which we suffer to-day. There is every probability that we should need to pay very dear for the socialistic whistle. In replying to such objections, Mr. Bellamy has the great advantage over all his critics that his scheme exists only on paper, and can therefore be modified with extreme ease: nothing need hinder him from confidently declaring that, under this entirely novel economic system, consequences would not ensue which could properly be deduced from the workings of human nature as it is to-day, and that every imaginable felicity will flow from the adoption of it. The test of Mr. Bellamy's rationality is not, however, the confidence of his prophecy of the unknown future, but his fairness in reporting the facts of the present and his wisdom in drawing out the lessons of experience. It is easy to perceive from any issue of "The New Nation" that his temper is entirely unjudicial, and that his doctrine is quite out of connection with political and economic science. When it comes to the question of "sizing up" Mr. Bellamy as an economist, very few Americans are likely to be long deceived. There is a painful lack of "intellectual seriousness" in him and his followers.

The ideal state of "Looking Backward" is a hard-and-fast bureaucracy, "a society of mandarins, medallists, and labor officers," as Dr. Schäffle says, "such as no Democrat could tolerate," the *personnel* of which, once instituted by a popular vote, would perpetuate itself in the closest routine until overthrown by a revolution. The power of appointment in each grade of the industrial army being in the officers of the grade above, the advantages of monarchical and of democratic rule would be equally absent. There is no institution which weighs more heavily on the Old World than the immense standing armies; they drain away the wealth and life of nations from the channels of true usefulness and check the progress of human civilization. The German flees to this country that, relieved of compulsory military service, he may be his own master during the best years of his life. But escape from the "industrial army" would be impossible for twenty-four years of middle life. Such an institution cannot be expected to appear soon in a country which has always repudiated the model on which Mr. Bellamy has constructed it. As a matter of fact, the author of "Looking Backward" is here, as too often elsewhere, the slave of fanciful analogies. In writing the book, he tells us, he had at first no thought "of attempting a serious contribution to the movement of social reform. The idea was of a mere literary fancy, a fairy-tale of social felicity." But he happened, in working out the details of this picture, to make an incidental use of the notion of an "industrial army" similar to the great military organizations of France and Germany. He came to recognize "in the modern military system, not merely a rhetorical analogy for a national industrial service, but its prototype, furnishing at once a complete working model for its organization, an arsenal of patriotic and national motives and arguments for its animation, and the unanswerable demonstration of its feasibility drawn from the actual experience of whole nations, organized and manœuvred as armies." Thus it was that Mr. Bellamy, in his own words, "stumbled over the destined corner-stone of the new social order;" he then completely recast the book in hand, to make it "the vehicle of a definite scheme of industrial reorganization." Mr. Bellamy's literary cleverness is amply demonstrated in the fullness with which he has developed the metaphor of the industrial army, — a figure of speech which seems to have carried him completely captive. Fondness for exposition by metaphor is no disqualification for literary effect, while it cannot be seriously regarded as one of the qualifications of a teacher of economic science. But, whether it be the "coach" of modern society, or the "industrial army," our author is not content until he has pursued his metaphor to the farthest limit of fancy. He then offers the developed trope as an equivalent to reality.

The American has usually been too prone to disregard the example of Europe, in matters where European experience might teach him useful lessons. Mr. Bellamy goes to the other extreme. In picturing the full development of the nationalist state, he adheres closely to the European type of socialism, and is regardless of any peculiarity, however important, in the American situation. He consigns to complete annihilation the separate commonwealths, such as New York or California, which now make up the American Union. In his Utopia the central government, the national power, is everything, — certain functions being delegated by it to the municipalities. There is no State government; there is no State pride; there is no local attachment to the differing institutions of Maine or Minnesota. The two hundred million Americans of the twentieth century are to recognize but one government. The centralization of power, which the wisest American statesmen have always dreaded, is carried to the utmost extreme. The capital importance of the political situation in the discussion of socialism in America seems to have escaped the attention of socialists in this country. Most of these are natives of lands in which the federal principle is not in force, and in which centralization of power is as easy as it is within the limits of Vermont or Illinois. When socialists of foreign birth become somewhat better acquainted with the political institutions of this country, they prophesy with less confidence. That an American author, however imaginative, should seriously suppose that within a hundred years the Federal principle will be utterly extinguished here, and every State line be abolished, is sufficiently remarkable. Evidently, he has as little hold on reality in the political sphere as in the economic. No American, possessing an ordinary amount of "horse-sense," dreams of the abolition of our State governments within a century: very few Americans have yet desired the virtual abolition of private property. When a novelist asserts that political liberty and individual rights will be safe under such centralization, he shows little trace of accepting the American formula as Chief-Justice Chase expressed it, — "An indestructible Union composed of indestructible States."

I am fully aware that the nationalists of the present day do not present "Looking Backward" as their practical programme for immediate action; they borrow most of this from other sources. The quotations here made, however, show plainly that the scheme laid out in the novel is the serious ideal of the one person in this country who is authority on the subject of "Nationalism." We are amply justified in looking beyond the particular measures which the nationalist advocates to-day to this ideal, and in estimating the practicability of the logically developed scheme. One great obstacle in the way of the adoption of such industrial Socialism in this country is the mere size of the country — divided now into forty-four States and four Territories, together equal in extent to four fifths of Europe. The enormous population of such a great country would, in all probability, be altogether unmanageable by the most ingeniously devised bureaucracy or industrial hierarchy. The people of the different States which make up the nation have strong local attachments; State pride is as strong, Mr. Charles Dudley Warner has lately told us, in the extreme Northwest as on the Atlantic coast. Statesmen at home and abroad unanimously eulogize the Federal idea as here carried out and declare the political freedom of America to be dependent on a vigorous life in the separate Commonwealths. On this rock American Socialism would inevitably founder should it ever come near. The corner-stone of our political freedom, the self-governing American State insures the destruction of every merely industrial Utopia. Some bold thinker may yet address himself, indeed, to imagining a scheme of socialism which will recognize in one Union the existence of fifty States, as distinct in the character of their inhabitants and the variety of their occupations as Massachusetts and Louisiana, or Pennsylvania and Oregon.

The practical difficulties, however, which the simple facts of geography and history and politics indicate will be easily overcome only on paper. The solution of the political problem, with which such writers as Matthew Arnold and Mr. Bryce credit America, does not warrant complete assurance that we shall solve the social and economic problems of the future. Nevertheless, it is in the highest degree improbable that Americans will attempt the settlement of the economic problem by abandoning, at the outset, the solution which they have given of the problem of political freedom.

The wonderful industrial and commercial evolution of this century has outrun the development of statute law in America as elsewhere. The development of legislation under a conservative democracy must be expected to lag considerably behind the full evolution of the commercial phenomena with which it is called upon to deal. The inventive talent and the business shrewdness of Americans have the advantage over the cumbersome machinery of Legislature and Congress in a progressive age. Immense private fortunes have resulted, for instance, from forwardness in building railroads and stringing telegraphs from ocean to ocean, with a main view to the benefit of the builders. The American people have always regarded with favor the enterprise which opens up new territory and facilitates intercourse between distant points. Its partiality for personal initiative leads it to endure many evils which gradually result from individuals improving new opportunities at the expense of the people; a limit is reached after a time, and the people call for stricter attention to the rights of the public. The modern democratic state has not yet mastered the question

of railroad legislation; but at no time has it been in
danger of destruction from railroad magnates. The
problem presented by the very significant development of "trusts" is no more threatening than the
corruption of legislatures by railway corporations has
been for years. Legal and moral compulsion have
sufficed to retain a measure of health in the body politic under all the menaces offered by the astounding
development of railways in the last fifty years: and
recent State and national legislation indicates that the
railway problem is gradually approaching solution.

The chief reason, apparently, which impelled Mr.
Bellamy, after he had completed his romance, to bring
within ten years the inevitable hour of the introduction of the "nationalist" system is the phenomenon
of the "trusts." But the highly rhetorical language
in which these supposed monstrosities were described,
and the confident prophecy of the immediate dissolu-
tion of the whole existing political and industrial system because of them, were poor substitutes for sugges-
tions of effective control. The panic about trusts
which the Nationalists did their utmost to encourage
four years ago was senseless. The elaboration of wise
measures concerning this natural development of modern business is a difficult matter, as all must concede;
but, even in these four years, progress has been made
in this direction. A very much less doubtful remedy
than the nationalization of all industries is near at
hand in such a revision of the tariff as would necessi-
tate the making of trusts world-wide. So extended,
they would have a much harder struggle for existence;
but if they should persist in some international form,
experience would probably teach new and more efficient measures of control or repression. At the pres-

ent, trusts in the United States are far less formidable to the philosophic mind than they were four years ago. In any case, the skies do not necessarily fall with the appearance of new phenomena in economics; and a nursery school of economists will not easily persuade the American people that they must on account of the new manifestation take such a leap in the dark as the plunge into nationalism would be.

Nationalism, considered as the thoroughgoing scheme of socialism and practical communism outlined in "Looking Backward," has been taken altogether too seriously by those who are not acquainted with the actual character of the movement.[1] Owing to Mr. Bellamy's literary reputation, to the fact that in Boston the nationalist clubs include a number of the younger journalists of the city, and to the good-natured interest which the American public always has in the movements of extremists, "nationalism" has received an amount of notice entirely out of proportion to its solidity. It has taken no hold on the "cultured and conservative class," for the conversion of which the novel is said to have been written. The press of the country as a rule treats Nationalism humorously as the latest Boston fad. The literary class, which gave it a large amount of gratuitous ad-

---

[1] One may be excused for sometimes thinking of Mr. Gilbert's Gondoliers, where they sing : —

> " For every one who feels inclined,
> Some post we undertake to find
> Congenial with his peace of mind,
> And all shall equal be.

> " This form of government we find
> The *beau ideal* of its kind —
> A despotism strict, combined
> With absolute equality."

vertising at first, has decidedly lost interest in its proposals. The *éclat* given to the movement by the novel to which it owes its inspiration, and by the friendship of the guild of letters for its talented author, has largely subsided. "Looking Backward" is very little likely to form the programme of an enduring political party. The entirely ineffective character of the movement so far as regards its distinctive aim — the nationalization of productive industries — is plain. The Labor Press derides it as the sentimental nostrum of people who are out of vital touch with workingmen; the followers of Mr. Henry George have no sympathy with it; practical men of affairs and teachers of economic science are not found in its clubs. It receives but a minor degree of encouragement from some liberal economists, who consider that the agitation will result in good, while they by no means accept its ideal.

The actual work which the nationalist clubs have thus far accomplished is on a line to which Mr. Bellamy did not even refer in his romance. The nationalists have recognized the entire impossibility of instituting the system in its logical completeness at once, and they have therefore taken up, as a practical programme, the advocacy of any movement which seems to them to tend in the direction of realizing their full hopes. Especially have they borrowed wholesale the proposals of such economists as Prof. Richard T. Ely in regard to public or semi-public monopolies. These proposals look to the considerable extension of the present functions of the municipality, the State, and the nation. Such measures as the manufacture of gas and electric light and the ownership of street railways by the cities, a national telegraph system, and even state ownership of railways, are on the list. A considerable number of American publicists are more or less friendly to various parts of this programme; but the names of such professors and students of economics have been entirely absent from the membership of the "nationalist clubs," for no spirit could well be more opposite to nationalism than the scientific spirit. Practically, then, the nationalist clubs are active agitators, in their fashion, for such measures of governmental extension as those just named, leaving largely out of sight for the time the measures which more logically justify the name of the movement.

In Massachusetts, where the movement has most vigor, the nationalists deserve credit for their exertions in aid of a permissive law, allowing towns and cities, under various restrictions, to supply their inhabitants with gas and electric light, as they can now supply water. This bill, which is obviously a simple recognition of the powers of a local government to undertake a new function, naturally suggested by the progress of civilization, was passed by the Massachusetts legislature with the general approval of the public. A number of towns have taken the preliminary steps required by the act, and some have actually gone into business under it; but the attitude of the great majority is still that of waiting for the practical results reached by these municipalities. The nationalists, very much elated by the passage of this act, — although very few members of the legislature who voted for it accept the nationalist programme, — took up, as their next proposal, the establishment of coal yards in Boston and other cities. The project was that the city should go into the coal business, buying in the largest quantities and selling at actual cost,

even in the smallest. There is a great difference, in
the eyes of the American citizen, between such a
measure, which is in fact a direct step toward the
nationalist ideal, and an act of the legislature which
simply permits towns to exercise a certain function,
analogous to those now exercised, if they desire so
to do. The establishment of a municipal coal yard
would be a direct entrance by the city into trade, not
in the line of Professor Ely's "natural monopolies."
The Supreme Court of Massachusetts gave its opinion that such a measure would be a perversion of
funds raised by taxation. The nationalists will do
well to withdraw the proposal and devote themselves
to agitating for a government telegraph, city street
railways, a national system of steam railways and
other measures, advocated by wiser heads. When
the question arises of a thorough and careful discussion of any one of these measures, in a scientific and
judicial spirit, the nationalists are found wanting:
the intellectual status of the Boston Club appears
from the fact that many of its members are enthusiastic adherents of theosophy, Esoteric Buddhism
and kindred humbugs. They favor indiscriminately
any and every proposal to confer fresh power upon the
government of city, State or Nation. The moderation and sense of proportion which mark the American
temper in practical affairs are conspicuous for their
absence in the clubs of the nationalists.

Any who would discuss the extension of municipal
or State control or ownership will be quite safe in
leaving out of account the very small contribution
which the nationalists have made to the understanding
of these problems. They have borrowed the proposals of abler and cooler minds, and have added little

or nothing to the strength of the arguments adduced. They are simply agitators whose logical aim, the nationalization of all industries, is fantastic. The economic ideal presented by their leader is entirely impracticable, in its characteristic features. The intellectual and moral ideal, also, indicated in "Looking Backward," must be pronounced in a high degree undesirable. The American citizen who sees clear and thinks straight is not attracted by it. He will prefer the present world, with its confessed shortcomings and its evident evils, as being, intellectually and spiritually, a richer and fairer world. The imagination of the American people may have been touched a few months by Mr. Bellamy's dream of equality. But whether he is a man of action or a man of thought, the American who is distinctively such feels no permanent attraction to a world where true individualism and all the virtues springing from it have been extirpated; where the private person is simply a cog in a vast industrial machine, and where a childish satisfaction in the fact of a well-filled stomach and a well-clothed back appears to be the temper that predominates over nobler satisfactions. He has never been a bigoted advocate of *laissez-faire;* he is not at all likely to be an irrational friend of wholesale Nationalism. The nationalists would make the most of the situation if, refraining from the dangerous political alliances which have so great a charm for them, they confined their exertions to organizations for the advocacy of such specific measures as municipal gasworks, electric-light systems, and street railways. Such associations would do a good service if they should present the rational arguments for such steps. Thus far, however, denunciation of what exists has been the prevailing fashion with the nationalist clubs; the character of the movement is so largely sentimental and its methods so extreme that it is a question whether the friends of practical reform measures owe anything of consequence, in the way of discussion or of action, to their members. In a later chapter, I shall indicate briefly the present standing of such proposals as those of Professor Ely, disengaging the discussion from the inappropriate name of "Nationalism" and the quite unnecessary connection with the nationalistic ideal of state ownership of the means of production.

The nationalist movement is thus seen to deserve little consideration by itself. Its methods are irrational, its spirit is sentimental, and the ideal which it holds up is neither desirable nor realizable. The preachers of such an ideal work confusion and obstruct true progress. The characteristic American spirit will carry out a very different programme of reforms, at once desirable and practicable, each one of which will be plainly seen to be a forward step in civilization. Such progress will not be at the expense of private initiative and personal efficiency. The price which it would be necessary, on the other hand, to pay, in the lowering of tone of individual character, for the comfort promised by the nationalist programme would be extreme. Such a step the American people are not likely to take until they have tried very many other measures.

CHAPTER VII.

CHRISTIAN SOCIALISM.

I. In England.

"Christian Socialism" is a term familiar to the readers of the biographies of Frederick Denison Maurice and Charles Kingsley. These great apostles of practical Christianity did not themselves invent the phrase, which goes back to Saint-Simon and his "Nouveau Christianisme."[1] Lamennais in France was the fervent preacher of a socialized Christianity a number of years before the founders of the Broad Church movement in England came together in 1849 to open the eyes of the distinctively "Christian" world to its duty towards the laboring classes. The leader of the Christian Socialist organization in Boston, which is one of the special subjects of this chapter, has declared that Christian Socialism "is not what it was in the days of Maurice and Kingsley:" but we shall best understand the later form, if we first consider the earlier form briefly.

The temper in which Maurice, Kingsley, Thomas Hughes, and Vansittart Neale undertook a "socialistic" propaganda in England is well defined in Proudhon's answer to the magistrate who asked him if he were not a socialist. "Certainly," was his reply.

[1] It was used first in our language in Robert Owen's *New Moral World*, Nov. 7, 1840, in a letter signed "Joseph Squiers, Coventry."

"Well, but what, then, is socialism?" "It is," answered Proudhon, "every aspiration towards the improvement of society." "But, in that case," said the magistrate, "we are all socialists." "That is precisely what I think," Proudhon responded. So the Prince of Wales and Sir W. V. Harcourt in the House of Commons declare to-day, "We are all socialists now." Kingsley and Maurice were not men of a scientific mind; and, when they took the name of "Christian Socialists," it was in the general sense that they wished to apply the gospel of human brotherhood more closely to actual life than they saw it applied in a self-seeking age mastered by greed for money.[1] In his famous sermon on the "Message of the Church to Laboring Men," preached in 1851, Kingsley, who usually came nearer to precise definition than Maurice, said: "All systems of society which favor the accumulation of capital in a few hands; which oust the masses from the soil which their forefathers possessed of old; which reduce them to the level of serfs and day-laborers living on wages and alms; which crush them down with debt, or in any wise degrade and enslave them, or deny them a permanent stake in the commonwealth, are contrary to the Kingdom of God, which Jesus proclaimed."

The burden of the social preaching of Maurice and Kingsley was that the Bible, especially the New Testament, is on the side of the working masses in their claim to be treated like fellow-men and brothers by the classes above them. "The Bible," said Kingsley,

[1] "That is the only title which will define our object and will commit us at once to the conflict we must engage in, sooner or later, with the unsocial Christians and the unchristian Socialists."

"not only dwells on the rights of property and the duties of labor, but, for once that it does that, it preaches ten times over *the duties of property and the rights of labor.*"

The chief practical aim of the Christian Socialists of the last generation in England was the encouragement of productive coöperation. The object of "The Christian Socialist," their organ, was stated to be to "diffuse the principles of coöperation by the practical application of Christianity to the purposes of trade and industry." Competition was denounced by Kingsley with all the vigor of which the English language was capable in his hands. Within a few years the Christian Socialists were instrumental in establishing forty-one societies for coöperative production. These, however, without an exception, failed to maintain themselves. The various newspaper organs of the body likewise passed away.[1]

Prof. R. T. Ely could write, with truth, ten years ago, "So far as there is to-day any active Christian Socialism in England, it is to be found in the Coöperative Union" of the distributive societies which have had such brilliant success. But it was coöperative production, not coöperative distribution, which the Christian Socialists endeavored to establish. They have been improperly credited with originating the latter system, which is due to the efforts of Robert Owen and his disciples, and which had become firmly established at Rochdale before 1848. Mr. Neale and

[1] The best accounts of Christian Socialism in England in the last generation are given by Rev. M. Kaufmann in his volume on the subject and by Prof. E. R. A. Seligman in an article on "Owen and the Christian Socialists," in the *Political Science Quarterly* for June, 1886.

Mr. Hughes, however, with other survivors of the Christian Socialist movement, were especially active in the formation in 1869 of the Coöperative Union, which has contributed so much to the spread of the stores in the last twenty years, and which holds an annual Congress. "We have managed to keep this great organization," wrote Mr. Hughes in 1882, "up to the principles of the Christian Socialists, — nominally, at any rate." The qualification is important, and it is especially significant in the light of the more recent history of the coöperative movement in England. Mr. Hughes, Mr. Neale, and the thinkers, in general, of this movement were engaged in a hard battle for a number of years to secure the practical recognition by the distributive societies — by the wholesale societies, in particular — of the principle of dividing a share of the realized profits of business with the workmen in the factories carried on by co-operators.

"The very success of distributive stores here," says a prominent English coöperator, "has tended to make our people look at everything from the standpoint of the consumer. We started distribution to accumulate capital, to employ ourselves in production; but, now we have got the capital, our eyes have become blinded to the real object of our founders' ambitions, and we commonly look at it as a means of producing goods as cheaply and advantageously as possible to the pockets of the consumers." The principle of the participation of the workmen in the profits of coöperative productive works was formally indorsed by the Coöperative Congresses of 1888 and 1889, through the exertions of Messrs. Neale, Hughes, and Holyoake, in particular. The Christian Socialism of 1848–1855 may be said, therefore, to have revived in no small degree in the coöperative distributive movement. The Union is now theoretically committed (so far as profit sharing is concerned) to a consistent and logical scheme of coöperative production, which it may some time work out in practice. The literature of the English coöperators has been written very largely, if not almost entirely, by the survivors of the Christian Socialist movement and their followers. From the "Manual for Coöperators," the work of Messrs. Neale and Hughes, the recognized standard, down to its many leaflets, the coöperative literature of England is true to these words of Reverend Mr. Kaufmann, the latest historian of Christian Socialism: "The method proposed is the method of association, and implies the gradual and peaceful conversion of competitive into coöperative industry. The organization of labor on coöperative principles is an essential element in every programme of Christian Socialism." The shining record of the distributive stores of Great Britain, and the briefer, but still encouraging, annals of the later coöperative productive establishments, prove that the "essential element" in the scheme of Maurice and Kingsley has been approved by time, despite the disappearance of the Christian Socialist movement itself. The report presented to the last Coöperative Congress at Rochdale gives the whole number of societies as 1,624, with 1,191,369 members, and a capital of £13,258,482. Included in these figures were 157 productive societies, having 25,017 members, and a share capital of £972,013.

Such has been the outcome in one way of the ideas dominant in the coöperative movement of Great Britain, — ideas thoroughly in harmony with the programme of the "Christian Socialists," when not directly derived from it. This practical socialism, it cannot be too emphatically recalled, is not state socialism. The English coöperators owe, and wish to owe, nothing to the State except a free field in which to work as societies recognized by law. Of socialism, in the full scientific sense of the word, they are entirely innocent. No idea could well be more remote from the minds of the English workingmen who have carried distributive coöperation to such brilliant results than the ownership of all productive property by the State, and the concentration of all capital in its hands. The name of "Socialists" can properly be applied to them only in the sense in which Kingsley and Maurice were such. First of all "Christians," these two men, like their associates, E. V. Neale and Thomas Hughes, were believers in social reform through the coöperation of individuals; any considerable measure of state control or ownership they never advocated. The Rev. Mr. Kaufmann, from whom I have quoted, is a clergyman of the Church of England who desires to see this kind of Christian Socialism more widely diffused in the Establishment. His words illustrate the spirit of those persons who would preserve to-day the essential characteristics of the movement begun by Kingsley and Maurice: "Its main object is to establish the kinship between the genius of Christianity and that 'passionate belief in the illimitable possibilities of human progress' which has been variously expressed in the schemes put forward at different times by those social idealists who now go under the general name of 'Socialists.' But the distinguishing mark of Christian Socialism is its firm faith in the power of Christian ethics to bring about a complete transformation of industrial economy. Hence its main efforts are directed toward bringing about a reconciliation of classes with the fuller development of the passive virtues of Christianity, and with it, ultimately, a regeneration of society as the result of a previous improvement in the individual. From the growth of the active virtues of Christianity among all, it expects important social reforms, founded upon Christian principle; and these are to remove the causes of social discontent, and so bring about social peace. In short, Christian Socialism works by means of spiritual *dynamics*, or religious influence, whereas Socialism proper (at least, in its most recent forms) aims at a mechanical reconstruction or governmental regulation of society on purely materialistic principles."

II. In the United States.

Christian Socialism in America is, indeed, a different matter from the movement we have been considering. Its likeness to the English organization formed forty-four years ago seems to reside more in the name than in the substance for which the name stands. The American clergymen of various denominations, especially those of the Episcopal Church, who have been thus far its most active promoters, are, more or less loosely, believers in pure Socialism as Dr. Schäffle defines it. The Boston organization, now in a state of suspended animation, ran an almost parallel course with the "First Nationalist Club" of the same city. "If there be any difference between the two," said "The Dawn," the monthly organ of the Christian Socialists, "it is simply that Nationalism emphasizes the present necessity of the spirit of nationality as a step towards universal federation, while Socialism does not. Fundamentally, however, they are but one, and are recognized as such by most." The names of the leading spirits in this Socialist propaganda were found on the roll of the Nationalist Club. The converse was not true, so that, while "Nationalism" professed entire friendliness towards Christian Socialism, as well it might, it was not at all committed to the specific measures of the latter movement. On all essential points, criticism directed against "Nationalism," as expounded in "Looking Backward," the Nationalist magazine, and "The New Nation," is applicable to Christian Socialism, which is more distinctively religious in its method and ecclesiastical in its *personnel.* The reason given for its existence was the need of rousing the Christian church to a sense of its shortcomings as a social power. "Nationalism" is a more secular movement, especially in its lay element, which includes many who would find themselves restless under clerical leadership, even the most liberal. The absence from Nationalism of a distinctively religious element is an unusual phenomenon in movements for social reform in the United States.

The London "Guild of St. Matthew," composed mostly of clergymen and laity belonging to the so-called "High Church," and now several years old, professes thoroughgoing Socialism. It is the model on which the Boston "Society of Christian Socialists" was framed.[1] A meeting was called by a few clergymen of the city, mostly members of the Nationalist Club, to consider the subject of forming another

[1] In the *Unitarian Review* for October, 1889, I have given a more detailed exposition of this Society.

organization, not hostile to it, but supplementary and auxiliary. The first meeting, of some twenty persons, in February, 1889, included Baptists, Episcopalians, Methodists, Congregationalists, Unitarians, Universalists, and representatives of "other Christian bodies." A Declaration of Principles was adopted April 15. This stated that "Our objects as Christian Socialists are: (1) To show that the aim of Socialism is embraced in the aim of Christianity: (2) To awaken members of Christian churches to the fact that the teachings of Jesus Christ lead directly to some specific form or forms of Socialism; that, therefore, the Church has a definite duty upon this matter, and must, in simple obedience to Christ, apply itself to the realization of the social principles of Christianity." A constitution was adopted April 23, and on May 7 an organization was perfected. The first president was the Rev. O. P. Gifford, pastor of the Warren Avenue Baptist Church. The vice-presidents were Mrs. Mary A. Livermore, the Rev. P. W. Sprague, and the Rev. Francis Bellamy. Mr. Sprague, author of a small volume on Christian Socialism, and the Rev. W. D. P. Bliss, the Secretary, the most active writer and speaker in the society, are Episcopalian clergymen; Mr. Bellamy, a cousin of the novelist, is a Baptist. A periodical, "The Dawn," was issued by the society, in various forms, beginning in May, 1889; Rev. Mr. Bliss is now the editor and proprietor of the weekly.

The aims and methods of the Christian Socialists have been the main subject of "The Dawn." They have been variously stated; but their best expression is found in the issue for August 15, 1889. I extract the more essential points. The main cause of present social ills is declared to be "the lack of Christianity in the social order." All special reforms needed run back to this one reform, "the Christianization of society into Brotherhood." All social, political, and industrial relations should be based on "the Fatherhood of God and the Brotherhood of man, in the spirit and according to the teachings of Jesus Christ." "Christ preached a social gospel; there is a social law of God. But men to-day forget this. . . . Business itself to-day is wrong. It rests upon a negation of the social law. Each man is for himself, each company for itself. It is based on competitive strife for profits. This is the exact opposite of Christianity. . . . To attempt, therefore, to apply Christianity to modern business is to attempt to be Christian in an unchristian way. It cannot be done. We must change the system. We must found business upon social law. Combination must take the place of competition; we must have a system in which business shall be carried on, not for private profits, but for the public good." The development of Christian Socialism is the need of the day; we must proceed one step at a time, "leaving to science and experience the exact form that society should adopt," yet moving on surely towards a fraternal democratic association which shall develop true individuality. Land and capital, and all means of industry, are "to be held and controlled in some way by the community as a whole, and operated for the benefit of the community equitably, in all its parts."

Such a declaration seemed to indicate an organization with a very vague outline, — something like a society for the propagation of virtue in general. "The Dawn," indeed, repeatedly declared itself not bound

to any specific measures; it held itself especially free
from advocacy of any measure as the "next step" on
which to concentrate the strength of the movement.
This method was evidently the method of clergymen
familiar with the broad and diffusive work of the
Christian church, who brought into a more specific
organization the general purpose and the comprehensive procedure of Christianity itself. The need of
another organization so general in its character is not
at once apparent to the outsider. If the Church,
however, is neglectful of its social duty, such a Society might well be instituted.

The methods advocated for accomplishing the above
aims were individual and political. The individual
should live up to his creed: he should get people to
read "Looking Backward," or similar literature, and
to subscribe for "The Dawn;" organize economic
classes; form Christian Socialist or Nationalist societies; and in every way, by word and deed, agitate for
the doing away of the system of every man for himself, and the bringing in of the system of combination
for the good of all. The "political" methods indicated were many; I give them all. "I. Stop letting
Capitalists and Saloon Keepers 'run' your politics.
Look out for the Caucus. II. Advocate gradual,
scientific Socialist Legislation. (a) Where not already done, adopt the Australian Ballot System. A
Free Ballot only will preserve Liberty. (b) Let the
State, city, or town provide Relief Works for the
unemployed. Set those unemployed, as far as possible, to building, under competent supervision, dwellings, or fittings for dwellings, according to the season,
to be sold to artisans at cost of production. If any
man has no trade that he can use, teach him one;

every man willing to work should have the opportunity. To see that he has this is the first necessity of Society. (c) Concentrate taxation more and more upon rental values of lands, moneys, and all natural resources, especially on lands held for speculation. Declare all mines hereafter opened the property of the Nation. (d) Enforce an Eight-Hour day; a Saturday Half Holiday; a Day of Rest for all. (e) Enfranchise woman; remove the poll tax; reform the Civil Service radically and thoroughly. (f) Institute free technical education; raise the school age; provide a midday meal for every scholar; supervise private schools. (g) Restrict the sale of liquors; do not license the saloon; suppress it when possible. (h) Extend governmental control over railroads, telegraphs, furnishing of light and heat, manufactories, etc., preparatory to their gradual municipalization or nationalization."

This was surely a comprehensive programme, and the more difficult to carry out, as "The Dawn" appeared to insist that movement must be made along the whole line at once, refusing to declare any one of these reforms "urgent," in order to devote the major part of its energies to the task of accomplishing it. The field was too broad for a society desirous of positive results. The Civil Service Reform societies in this country have had an immense work laid upon them, to accomplish their specific task. Yet Civil Service Reform is but one, though probably the most "urgent" of some twenty measures just enumerated. Woman suffrage, prohibition of the liquor traffic, the Australian ballot system, the eight-hour day, — the need of a new "Christian Socialist" organization to advocate these was not evident. Certainly, it could not be so efficient in promoting them as more limited societies, each solely devoted to one measure. Industrial education, the change in the school age, the supervision of private schools, — these, again, are matters which bodies of educators can more wisely determine. The midday meal for scholars is an amusing imitation — quite uncalled - for in America — of the practice of the School Board in the London slums. Relief works for the unemployed, with the provision of homes for artisans at cost, is the first distinctive and important measure of State Socialism advocated in this ample platform. It is coupled with the demand for a single-tax system and the extension of "governmental control over railroads, telegraphs, furnishing of light and heat, manufactories, etc., preparatory to their gradual municipalization or nationalization."

Detailed discussion is needless, here, of the long list of reforms proposed as subjects for legislation. They range from measures already adopted in the United States, like the Australian ballot system, now in force in thirty-five States, to the extreme ideal of the nationalization of all industries. Between these two extremes, of actual fact and an ideal at once undesirable and unrealizable under existing human nature, are enumerated measures of all degrees of rationality. Each one of them needs, and will probably receive, before adoption or rejection by the people, the legislatures, or Congress, a thorough discussion of its specific value and advisability. None of them will be forwarded by showing that it is necessarily associated with "Nationalism." Christian Socialists will prejudice several good causes if they can show a logical connection between them and scientific Socialism. But practical sagacity was not the forte of the body, if we may judge by the elastic platform and the refusal to press any specific measure as the most important matter to take in hand at once.

The secretary of the Boston society declared that, "born in Utopia, Christian Socialism is not to-day Utopian." This remark is very true, if applied to the practical doctrines of Maurice and Kingsley. But it is the reverse of a correct judgment, if applied, as the speaker intended, to the Christian Socialism of to-day. This latter is pure Socialism, professed and taught by clergymen who would convert the Christian church to the doctrine of Marx and Lassalle. In each issue, "The Dawn" printed a list of books recommended for reading. With few exceptions, this was made up of the most thoroughgoing socialist books and pamphlets. "Looking Backward" was praised as "the best picture yet drawn of the Socialistic State." Mr. Laurence Gronlund's works "are examples of the noblest spirit, views, and aims of modern Socialists." All argument going to prove that socialism, as professed by Karl Marx or Edward Bellamy, is economically impracticable and ethically undesirable, is entirely applicable to such "Christian Socialism." The ardor with which these clergymen and their associates undertook to recast human society deserved admiration for the Christian spirit of brotherhood displayed in it; but the movement could command slight respect as a programme for action in the real world.

The Christian Socialists of Boston were so remote from the practical temper of their English forerunners, that, to take a specific case, they rejected the teachings of forty years' experience, as declared by the survivors of the first movement, in respect to a very important point. These survivors are to be found to-day, without exception (certainly this is true of all the prominent men), among the heartiest advocates of the practical and approved method of coöperation known as "industrial partnership," or "profit sharing." "The Dawn," however, in its issue of June 15, 1889, made a detailed statement on the subject which placed the Christian Socialist movement it represented at odds with such English leaders as Thomas Hughes and E. Vansittart Neale, and even with a number of the most prominent men in this country, whose support it claimed for Christian Socialism. The profit-sharing system all these unite in commending — not as a final solution of all labor troubles, but as a most advisable "next step" in industrial reform — did not commend itself to those who had made up their minds to destroy competition, root and branch. They needed to ponder these words of a wiser Christian Socialist, Victor Aimé Huber: "Competition is one of the divine laws of social life and development, which, like every other law, requires the discipline of the Holy Spirit in the individual and in society, in Church and State, so as not to be abused by selfishness or poisoned by ignorance and folly."

A movement of later date than that which we have been considering is the "Christian Social Union," established in the early part of the year 1891; it has practically superseded the Boston society. The Union is an organization confined to members of the Episcopal Church, and taking for its model the English association with the same name, of which the Bishop of Durham is president. The head of the

American organization is Bishop F. D. Huntington of Central New York; the secretary is Prof. R. T. Ely; Rev. W. D. P. Bliss and Mr. Everett P. Wheeler are members of the executive committee. The objects of the Union are thus stated: "To claim for the Christian Law the ultimate authority to rule social practice; to study in common how to apply the moral truths and principles of Christianity to the social and economic difficulties of the present time; to present Christ in practical life as the Living Master and King, the enemy of wrong and selfishness, the power of righteousness and love." It has taken for its organ "The Economic Review," published by the Oxford University Branch. This Review has been distinguished by its ability and its hospitality to the friends and opponents alike of Socialism. Its general tone is very different from that of the one-sided organs of Socialism in this country. The Christian Social Union may be fairly regarded as a movement in the Episcopal Church in this country, of clergy and laity deeply interested in social reform who are not desirous either of taking the name Christian Socialist outright or of following the rather uncertain counsels of "The Dawn." It contemplates educational work chiefly and on this line it offers an example worthy of all imitation by other churches of America.[1]

[1] At the meeting of the Episcopal General Convention held in Baltimore in October last, Professor Ely explained the nature of the Union as "an institution within the Church, the aim of which is to promote social science. At present the society, believing that political problems are rapidly giving place to industrial problems, and that the solution of the social question is ultimately to be found in the person and the life of Christ, and assured that the application of the redemptive force of Christ to society can be no simple matter, owing to the manifold, in-

III. Christianity and Economics.

Of the great majority of the persons connected with the two movements just reviewed, the Christian Socialist Society and the Christian Social Union, it is entirely just to say, as a simple inference from current methods of instruction in theology and religion, that they are more accomplished in Christianity than in the sciences of economics and politics. In this time of social unrest, they can engage in no more profitable work than acquiring and extending a knowledge of these allied sciences. It is not only an acquaintance with the facts of these sciences that the members of these societies need, like all the rest of the world. A thorough respect for the scientific spirit and method is as indispensable in the sciences of man as in the sciences of physical nature. The humane heart should bè guided by an instructed head. The primary error which clergymen, untrained in the sciences of economics and politics, are especially prone to make is the intrusion of ethical considerations into the study. They do not realize that great

tricate, and immense problems raised by human society, makes its primary aim an educational one, seeking to know the actual economic and social facts in our country, to ascertain the nature of underlying principles, and to discover the methods which must be followed to bring about improved social conditions. The Social Union desires to aid all members of the Church to put into practice such truth as may be known on social and economic topics. It suggests the training of clergy and missionaries in social science, and seeks to stimulate clergy and laity in lines of progressive conservatism. . . . It marks out courses of reading, publishes leaflets on such topics as ' The Child Problem ' and 'Labor Disturbances,' and hopes to employ competent lecturers, publish a monthly bulletin, hold annual conventions to bring the local branches together, and offer prizes."

confusion must inevitably result from mingling, at the outset, two matters so diverse as the inquiry into what is and the inquiry into what ought to be. Questions of economic fact and economic law should be settled first, in entire independence of ethical considerations, so far as they are questions of fact and law in their own sphere. Ethics should occupy the second place in the study in order of time. If, to the wise moralist an undoubted economic fact or a plain economic law seems to need supplementing or modification in the interests of total human nature, he should still postpone consideration of what can and ought to be done, to the calmest deliberation on the actual fact and the supposed law. To propound at the very beginning a number of abstract moral notions, by which all inquiry is to be ruled, is destructive of sound conclusions. Such a conception, for instance, as that of "justice," — especially when it is taken to include, of necessity, a "right to employment" and an obligation on the part of "society" to secure every man a living, — is fatal to fruitful reasoning; the limits of "the just" can only be safely and profitably determined *after* an economic inquiry, conducted on strictly scientific principles, has been closed.[1]

[1] An excellent statement of the need and the manner of distinguishing economics and ethics will be found in Mr. J. N. Keyne's valuable book, *The Scope and Method of Political Economy.* He says, for instance : " It is universally agreed that in economics the positive investigation of facts is not an end in itself, but is to be used as the basis of a practical inquiry, in which ethical considerations are allowed their due weight. The question is not whether the positive inquiry shall complete as well as form the foundation of all economic discussion, but whether it shall be systematically combined with ethical and

Another consideration of the first importance in this connection is suggested by the association of the term "Christian" with "Socialism" or "Sociology." Before devoting a few pages to a question from which theology, as distinct from religion, should be rigorously excluded, however difficult the task may be, I may guard against a possible misunderstanding. The words which closed my volume on Profit Sharing, I here repeat, with no desire to modify them: "The Christian gospel has had a rebirth in more than one perplexed age. The labor difficulties of the troubled nineteenth century will find no more effectual solvent. Economics must be aided by ethics; the commercial spirit should be tempered by the Christian feeling of the brotherhood of man. The pure Christianity to which Leclaire gave expression in his last will and testament [1] is still the strongest force making for industrial and social progress."

We can hardly make too plain the truth that such a renascence of Christianity must be a rebirth of its spirit, not an attempt to apply the letter of the New Testament to modern civilization. The Christian

practical inquiries, or pursued in the first instance independently. The latter of these alternatives is to be preferred on grounds of scientific expediency. Our work will be done more thoroughly and both our theoretical and our practical conclusions will be more trustworthy if we are content to do one thing at a time." (Pages 46, 47.)

[1] "I believe in the God who has written in our hearts the law of duty, the law of progress, the law of sacrifice of one's self for others. I submit myself to his will, I bow before the mysteries of his power and of our destiny. I am the humble disciple of him who has told us to do to others what we would have others do to us, and to love our neighbor as ourselves : it is in this sense that I desire to remain a Christian to my last breath."

Social Union well declares that the one thing needed is "a zeal for the service of man in the spirit of Christ." But certain material assumptions are made by Christian Socialists, of all varieties, which cannot pass unquestioned by the thorough student of economic and social science. Let it be supposed that we can gather with some confidence from the New Testament (to be more precise, let us say from the first three Gospels), a consistent scheme of conduct for mankind with regard to the accumulation and the use of property, taught by Jesus of Nazareth. This being so, Christian Socialists appear to consider superfluous the further question whether or not we can or should accept this scheme as the working theory of modern life. Holding, as they do, certain more or less "orthodox" views of the inspiration of the Bible and of the person of Christ, as a being strictly divine or in some way superhuman, they naturally declare that: "In simple obedience to Christ" the Christian church must "apply itself to the realization of the social principles of Christianity." Here, however, as a simple fact, several questions are involved which are confused by the Christian Socialist. It is very essential to clearness of thought and to unity of action that we keep them apart, and give to each an answer unbiased by any species of bigotry, theological or anti-theological.

I. What did Jesus of Nazareth, the historical person, actually teach, in all probability, about the making of money, the holding of property and the disposition of wealth? What was his estimation of poverty and what counsels did he give concerning it? What did he say in detail, and what — a more important point — was the pervading spirit of his teachings in regard to all these matters, which we may call, for the sake of brevity, "the question of property?" What was the relative importance of his teachings in respect to property, in comparison with the whole content of his gospel? This inquiry is evidently one for impartial critics and exegetes to determine in the first place.

II. Supposing that this inquiry has been pursued as far as it can be with success, the second question arises: How far are these more or less plain words of Jesus in accord with the undoubted teaching of the science of our time concerning the facts and the laws of economics? How far are they in accord, also, with the anticipations professed by students of social science, guided entirely by extra-theological considerations, as to the probable future of civilized man?

III. It is, obviously, an interesting and entirely distinct inquiry: How far are these teachings of Jesus accepted and carried out in practice, not only by the great majority of people in the so-called Christian nations, but also and especially by the members of Christian churches who may fairly be considered to represent these churches?

IV. If we should find that the practice, not only of Christian nations, as a whole, but also of truly representative members of Christian churches diverges, more or less widely, from the teachings of Jesus carefully ascertained, where does the difficulty lie? Is it in an imperfect morality of Christendom to-day? Or does the difficulty lie in the fact that the view of human life under civilization which appears to be taken in the gospels is in some degree partial, and in need of supplement from the great body of subsequent experience?

When the Christian Socialist declares that his first

object is to "show that the aim of Socialism is embraced in the aim of Christianity," and that "the teachings of Jesus Christ lead directly to some specific form or forms of Socialism," I perceive, for myself, the large measure of justification for his words in the report of the teachings of Jesus given in the first three gospels. A species of communism was practiced by the first Christians in Jerusalem for an unknown time after the death of Jesus. Their Master had said, "Lay not up for yourselves treasures on earth." He had commanded them to sell all that they had and give to the poor. He not only declared that the poor are blessed; he had also denounced a woe upon the rich men of his time; for they had received their "consolation."[1] He had emphatically stated that it is easier for a camel to go through the eye of a needle than for a rich man to enter the Kingdom of Heaven. During his public ministry, Jesus, evidently, did not practice his craft, and trusted, for the support of himself and his immediate followers, to the well-known hospitality of the Orient. It was not at all strange, therefore, that his disciples, when bereft of a Master who had steadily disparaged the holding of property and had always laid emphasis on the life in common, should attempt to put his teaching into practice. Their strong expectation of his immediate "second coming" must have contributed in no small degree to their readiness to make the attempt, — an attempt, probably, of no long duration.

[1] It is probable that the words "in spirit" in Matthew v. 3 are an early gloss upon "the poor" given in Luke vi. 20 : the words in Luke are beyond dispute, unless we arrive, otherwise, at a conception of Jesus' thought with which they are incompatible, and ascribe them, therefore, to the influence of Essenism upon the evangelist.

In nearly every Christian century the sayings of Jesus to which I have alluded have been accepted by a few as positive commandments to be literally observed. The far greater majority have implicitly or explicitly regarded them as hyperbolical expressions, to be qualified in practice by the "common-sense" of the Christian believer. Beyond a doubt, the Christian Socialist is correct in emphasizing the extreme divergence between many of the precepts of Jesus in respect to acquiring and holding property and the actual practice of even the persons who best represent the Christian church to-day. We do not find the most exemplary Christian men and women of our time selling all their goods and giving them to the poor; we do not see them always lending to those who would borrow (this, of course, without interest), or uniformly giving to them that ask. This departure from the gospel teaching is not confined to "the world" in Christian countries; it marks the clergy and the devout laity as well. Beyond question, the general tone and temper of the teaching of Jesus in the gospels in regard to property and wealth is *not* the tone and temper which the Christian church of to-day manifests.

Thus answering the first and the third of our inquiries, with a single eye to truth, we discover the strength of the Christian Socialist's position. The weakness of his argument is not less apparent if we attempt to answer the second and the fourth inquiries with equal fairness. Professing, as the great majority of Christian people do, to accept the letter of the gospel as the rule of their lives, it is not strange that they should be greatly inclined to put these two questions entirely aside, or to answer them superficially and inconsistently. Perhaps the most common resort, in the face of the plain divergence between Christian theory and the practice of Christian people, is to assume that political economy is a wretched science without bowels of .compassion, that the teachings of Jesus are true to all the important facts of the case, and that "the sinfulness of human nature " is the sufficient reason for its actual disregard of his teachings. Economic science, it is true, in declaring the simple facts and laws of human life in respect to property, pictures a state of things quite out of harmony with that which Jesus commended. The economist, however, is not, in any degree, responsible for the facts or the laws in question; it is civilized man, and especially civilized man in Christian countries, who presents the phenomena of modern life which the economist simply investigates. The investigator is not at all blamable for the fact that what we may call the economic teaching of Jesus is practically rejected every day by the whole Christian world in its zealous pursuit and its interested use of money.

Firmly believing in the Christian principle of the brotherhood of man and in the power of the Christian spirit of love to clear the way for the effectual solution of many of the social troubles of our time, I am unable, in the face of the facts just stated, to rest in any conventional answer to our fourth inquiry. The response which I consider purely reasonable, and therefore in the end unavoidable (whatever may be its theological implications, with which I am in no way concerned here), is, briefly, to this effect: Jesus of Nazareth, as Emerson declared, is the one man in history who has fully appreciated the worth of the human soul: he stands at the head of the prophets of humanity; he has done more than any other to inspire and uplift the race. His fundamental spirit we may never forget but to our hurt, and we never practice it but to our advantage. The inspired prophet of the soul, however, should not be expected to discharge the very different function of the professor of economics. Of the poets (certainly Jesus belongs to their inspired company) we do not rightly ask guidance in politics. We do well to receive the message of the prophet as the transfiguring spirit of our lives; we wisely rejoice in the ideal which the poet brings before us, as the end toward which we should move.[1] Nevertheless, and with no need of apology, we are free, in reason and in right, to shape our practice according to the precepts of honorable statesmen, and well instructed teachers of economic science. We need not, we do not say, with the English bishop, that the Sermon on the Mount is impracticable: we simply assert our perfect right to take its spirit of human kindness as the rule to apply to our modern life, in accordance with the fullest enlightenment we can derive from science and experience.

The modern Christianity that claims to be moral and spiritual cannot be bound to the letter of the New Testament, in gospel or epistle, when this touches matters distinctively industrial or political. We should be repeating the error of those who defended human slavery from the Old Testament, did we exalt poverty and decry property because of various texts in the New. A literal adherence to the New Testament teachings, in every detail, would evi-

---

[1] " Blessings be with them, and eternal praise,
Who gave us nobler loves, and nobler cares ! "

dently lead to more than one procedure which modern men cannot but consider irrational. If we take, for instance, the words of the gospels in their plain meaning, Jesus believed that possession by evil spirits was the cause of what we call to-day epilepsy and insanity. Such a theory was in perfect harmony with the ideas of his time; but no physician of the present day in Christian countries practices medicine on this basis; his standing would be gone should he attempt it. The exorcist is, indeed, a regular functionary in the Roman Catholic Church, but medical science does not admit that he is a personage either necessary or helpful. Jesus, incited by the undoubted fact that wealth in his time was very largely the result of violence, eulogized the poor and condemned the rich; the tone of his teaching was hostile to the accumulation of property, and he commended indiscriminate almsgiving. In all reverence to him, we have a perfect right to inquire what the result would be, under modern conditions, if we obeyed his precepts to the letter, and endeavored to assume the same tone and temper in respect to wealth and poverty as characterizes the first three gospels. The most benevolent people in the Christian churches of our day organize the Associated Charities, largely in order to prevent those ruinous consequences to the moral character of the poor which are found to result from that indiscriminate giving to them that ask which is altogether incompatible with an enlightened spirit of love for man. No one is justified in pauperizing another human being in order to relieve his own feelings. A literal adherence to this particular gospel precept would cause a great decline in the morals of the poor; it would inevitably lead to an immense increase of poverty, one of the worst obstacles to the refinement of civilization. Philanthropic men and women need no defense, they are indeed the truest Christians after the spirit of Christ, who see the facts of modern life as they are, whose hearts are full of enthusiasm for humanity, but whose minds, of necessity, recognize that precepts suited to simple and rustic life in Judæa in the first century must be seriously modified to prevent the worst consequences in the nineteenth century, with all its complexities of condition. The first duty of the modern philanthropist is to avail himself of the experience of those who have discovered the best ways of dealing with the problem of poverty. The prophet of the moral law and the teacher of religious truth who eulogize poverty to-day are as far from wisdom as from kindness.

It is not necessary to go to the other extreme and eulogize wealth; this is sufficiently an object of desire to modern man to need no commendation. The philosopher, as well as the man of religion, will most carefully avoid adding strength to the desire of wealth, already strong enough, to say the least. Humanity is far greater than property; and property, public or private, has no right to be considered a sacred thing when the claims of humanity are in question. The most vigorous assertion of the supremacy of the spiritual and intellectual life over money-getting and property-holding is surely as much needed to-day as in any preceding generation. That Jesus of Nazareth, were he living under modern civilization, would side with competition against coöperation, with the rich, as such, against the poor, with the strong against the weak, is simply inconceivable to one who has the faintest sympathy with his spirit. This

spirit teaches us at once to turn an open ear to the
complaints of the working-classes of to-day, and to
lend a willing hand for the removal of all genuine
causes of complaint as fast as possible. Christianity
as a religion of human helpfulness and fellow-feeling
needs a wider extension into the industrial and commercial life of our time. It is the humane spirit of
Jesus Christ, his guiding principle of love to man
that we need to apply, more thoroughly and consistently, according to the light which science and experience supply.[1] The letter of the New Testament,
in gospel or epistle, does not establish the right of a
sentimental method to hinder human progress or perpetuate the sufferings of civilized man by throwing
false light upon them. It is not true, to-day, that
the poor are blessed simply because they are poor;
they are the last persons to have such a feeling themselves, and if they entertained it, there would be
a plain duty incumbent on the prosperous to dis-
abuse them of the sentiment! We feel sure to-day
that it is no harder for the rich whose property has
been rightfully acquired to enter the Kingdom of
God, than for the poor as a class, and even for many
who are neither rich nor poor.[2] Without entering
into disputed theological questions, it will be sufficient
to remark that, from the humanitarian standpoint,
— the only one open to science, — Jesus naturally
shared the views of his time concerning wealth.

[1] It is in this sense that the Ethical Culturist cries, "Back to
Jesus, then, back to his great ideal!" W. M. Salter in the *New
World*, December, 1892.

[2] Doctor Oliver Wendell Holmes has thus determined "the
spiritual standard of different classes : 1, the comfortably rich ;
2, the decently comfortable ; 3, the very rich, who are apt to be
irreligious ; 4, the very poor, who are apt to be immoral."

There was, of course, not even a trace of a science of political economy in that day; the attempt to construct such a science from the New Testament, labeling it "Christian," is thoroughly irrational.

The loose thinkers and active declaimers who denounce modern society by wholesale for what they consider its disregard of the words of Jesus should learn to distinguish things that differ. Their lax and shifting use of the word "socialism" is often accompanied by a use as lax and shifting of the words "Christian" and "Christianity." A profound delusion possesses those Christian Socialists who set forth the socialism of Karl Marx as the inevitable and just outcome of the gospel teaching. Their mental confusion disqualifies them altogether for leadership in rational reform. There is no conflict between the fundamental spirit of Jesus Christ and the acceptance of the undoubted teachings of economic science. Economics can never be rightly invaded by ethics; its undeniable province is the facts and laws of human nature that concern the pursuit and the expenditure of wealth. We have no choice about the intellectual acceptance of these truths. As rational beings, we must accept them, and then consider very carefully how far the free play of economic forces should be modified by moral and spiritual powers. Concerning this matter no one has a right to speak with authority who has not carefully studied economic science by itself, first of all, and who does not, from beginning to end, pay regard to human nature, as it actually is and as it is susceptible of modification for the better. The Christian Socialists are animated by generous impulses, but the excited spirit in which they deal with many of the most difficult phenomena of social life is not justifiable; the sentimental method which they follow is mistaken and altogether too likely to be fruitless, if not positively injurious. The renaissance of practical Christianity which all good men desire to see does not lie in the direction of a socialism founded on the letter of the New Testament, but in the spirit of its characteristic word, "Together."

My readers will bear in mind that the subject of this chapter is, specifically, the Christian Socialism of the last few years in the United States. I have avoided dwelling upon Christian Socialism in England, except in so far as it sheds light upon the same movement in this country, and I have altogether passed over the Christian Socialism of the Continent. That good effect which, in various degrees, accompanies every agitation for reform, and with which Nationalism has been credited, is also to be set down to the credit of Christian Socialism. There is, however, a much wiser method, and there are aims far more likely to be reached than those indicated by the confused logic, the copious rhetoric and the mistaken sentimentalism of the Christian Socialists of this country. In a later chapter I shall endeavor to point out a better way which pays respect to Christian Individualism. Here it may be said that this way is indicated by the earlier Christian Socialism of Maurice and Kingsley, who would have approved the programme of M. Charles Robert: "Economic Science enlightened by the Spirit of the Gospel."

CHAPTER VIII.

THE INDUSTRIAL FUTURE.

NATIONALISM and Christian Socialism put forth a long programme of fundamental changes in the industrial world which are expected to occur comparatively soon. The qualifications of the orators and writers of these two movements for the difficult office of the prophet we have not been able to rate high. Turning with pleasure from the necessary task of criticism of these agitations which must appear quite un-American to the careful thinker, both in their spirit and in most of their specific proposals, I would devote this chapter to a summary view of a few industrial changes which may more reasonably be expected. One who follows as far as may be the politic maxim which tells us not to prophesy unless we know will venture to mention only such changes as a near future may see effected, in a greater or less degree. What we know is a number of tendencies actively at work at the present day, which have had a certain amount of result, and for which it would appear quite safe to predict, in a general way, further results. As for naming the year or the day by which any of these changes will be accomplished, the wise man will prefer to be excused. The improvements which this chapter has in view are, furthermore, those which may properly be designated specifically "industrial," since they have an immediate reference to the working-classes and a less direct bearing upon the situation of other classes. At the same time, we have to remember that the American people are a nation of workers, and that no change in the so-called industrial world, directed to the benefit of the "working-classes," can be limited, either in thought or in practice, by lines which must be in the United States more or less arbitrary.

One of the prime features of the existing situation is the increasing organization of workmen on one side, and a corresponding development of organization among the employers of labor on the other. The day has long since gone by in which the desirability of labor organizations could seriously be discussed. Trade-unions, under whatever title, have thoroughly justified their own existence, in the United States as in England. Their great influence in raising wages, and otherwise improving the lot of the workingman, is now obvious. Nothing is *a priori* more naturally to be expected than exaggeration and abuse of their power by the trade-unions. Such excesses as every fair-minded man has deplored in this country within the last twenty years are the almost inevitable result of a consciousness of power far in excess of the consciousness of responsibility; this, under the usual conditions of human nature, is a later growth. But trade-unions as well as manufacturers' associations are finally subject to the control of public opinion. Public opinion in the United States has severely condemned the trade-unions for their course in the recent riotous and warlike proceedings at Homestead, Buffalo and the Tennessee coal-mines. The Knights of Labor, the Federation of Labor and other organizations of workingmen in this country must take home to themselves the lesson of moderation in the use of the power which they possess to injure the employer, for disturbance of the public peace and wide derangement of traffic and industry are too often associated with such injury.

All the labor unions put together are a small minority compared with the vast mass of disinterested people able to form an intelligent opinion as to the merits of labor disputes, very ready to express it when formed, and quite competent to recognize irrationality and tyranny, whether these are exemplified in the conduct of an association of employers or by a union of workingmen. The voice of the actual majority of the American people may not be the voice of God at any particular time, but it is apt to be disinterested with reference to disputes between employer and employed, and it is certainly able to enforce upon both parties its deliberate verdict concerning dissensions in the industrial world, — if not at once, then gradually and finally. As a chief article in his creed, the American has a boundless confidence in the essential reasonableness of human nature. He relies implicitly upon the presence of fundamental good nature and rationality in both parties to a disagreement. This confidence has been finally justified even in respect to the acutest labor troubles of the last twenty years, and nothing has happened to permanently weaken it. That "the Animosities are mortal but the Humanities live forever" is a saying nowhere more pertinent than here. We have not yet come to think so poorly of human nature as to suppose that either American employers or American workmen are incapable of reaching, or unwilling to reach, however gradually, a rational settlement of their controversies, in a spirit of reason and good-will. Difficulties of various kinds will inevitably arise until human nature is fundamentally altered. But the conciliation, if not the final settlement, of present troubles is attainable within a period which may be called moderate in length, when we consider the importance of the issues at stake. This fundamental feature of the American situation — the virtual omnipotence of the public opinion of a people among whom class distinctions are comparatively slight, while information is widely diffused — is one which the employer and the workman cannot too closely regard. This great body of well-informed and disinterested persons, who have a natural respect for the able employer and a natural sympathy with the industrious workman, can bring a pressure to bear upon labor troubles practically irresistible. They can visit the Philistine employer, endeavoring to exploit his workmen, with a condemnation of which even the most obdurate must feel the power. When labor makes war on labor; when members of a trade-union practice every manner of violence on the non-union workman who desires to work and mind his own business as a peaceable citizen, they may deceive a section of the public for a time with their catch-words, but the essential despotism of their procedure will soon be condemned by the public at large.[1] Under such opposition no strike will succeed. Here "that old common arbitrator, Time," who is supposed to end every human trouble, is simply an enlightened public opinion.

[1] " As long as the laborer has exactly his own way —
' It 's peace, and love, and brothers all, and do just what you like ;
But — it 's curse the blackleg, cut his throat, when he won't go out
    on strike,'
as Mr. Rudyard Kipling might express it." *The Spectator.*

As it is hardly probable that any future, near or remote, will be entirely free from labor difficulties, the first dictate of ordinary common-sense is the provision of some effective means for early conciliation and arbitration. The good judgment which leads people who have disputes, which might lead to protracted law-suits to resort to arbitration, is especially needed in the case of labor troubles, where a legal adjustment of the dispute is usually out of the question. The institution in the various industries of a city of local boards of arbitration after the style of the French *conseils des prud'hommes*, and especially of committees of conciliation in separate establishments, to take cognizance of all matters of dispute in the industry or the establishment, is in every way advisable. One of the most encouraging signs of the times in the United States is the creation by a number of commonwealths of State Boards of Arbitration and Conciliation, authorized by law to proffer their services to both parties to a strike, lockout or other labor difficulty. The record of what has been accomplished by the New York Board and the Massachusetts Board in the last half-dozen years demonstrates the extreme profit of such an agency appointed by the State for the early settlement of labor conflicts.[1]

[1] "In line with the experience of former years, the Board has found fresh reason to renew its confidence in the power of a free and candid public opinion applied to differences arising between employers and employed. With added experience and greater familiarity on the part of the business world with the methods and principles by which the action of the Board is regulated, the efficiency of the State Board as a conciliator has increased ; and, on the side of arbitration, it is a gratifying fact that in every such case, the advice offered and the price-lists recommended have been cheerfully accepted by all parties, with permanent

This record, and the long success of boards of conciliation and arbitration in the English hosiery and manufactured-iron trades, have recently led many persons to advocate compulsory arbitration. They would have the State establish Boards of Conciliation and Arbitration with full power to summon before them both parties to a labor dispute; to hear testimony from all concerned and to pass a verdict binding with all the force of law. The advocates of this measure have evidently failed to carry their observation or their reasoning far. Such compulsory arbitration would be fully equivalent to State regulation of wages and industry. We need only to inquire in what way and to what degree it is proposed to enforce the verdict upon the employer or the workman who finds it unfair, to discover the irrationality of the scheme. No one could seriously propose in a free country to oblige a workman to work continuously for wages which he deems too low, or to compel an employer of labor steadily to pay wages which, in his opinion, are too high. Few thinking persons would desire to confront either employer or workman with such a menace. The institution of compulsory arbitration in the sense of making the verdict of the board binding upon both parties, whether they have invited its mediation or not, is plainly out of the question in America.

The advisability of obliging a State Board of Arbitration to pay immediate attention to labor troubles, without waiting for an invitation from either party, but with ample powers to take testimony, is another matter. Such intervention has nothing in it necessarily offensive to the American spirit. The sole aim good results to the business affected." Annual Report of the Mass. Board for 1891.

would be the ascertainment of the actual facts by a disinterested third party, and the spreading of these facts before the people. When a State Board of Conciliation and Arbitration has been in existence long enough to command general confidence, and when it is supplemented, as in Massachusetts, by experts called in to give counsel in cases of particular difficulty, it is altogether likely that public opinion would come to favor the immediate intervention of such a board in any labor trouble, to the extent of hearing testimony and rendering an opinion not legally binding upon either party, in the absence of an express agreement by both parties to this effect.

Public opinion is already ripe in more than one quarter of the United States for such intervention in the direction where a strike or a lockout interferes in a high degree with the general welfare. A severe labor difficulty on a line of street cars, a steam railway or a line of steamers soon involves great inconvenience and loss to the public. The experience of this kind of labor troubles which we have had of late years has forcibly suggested the imperative need of preventive measures. One might well add to the common carriers just named the works which supply gas or electric light to the inhabitants of a city; but the stoppage of gas or electric light is an inconvenience which may be endured for a season without great injury. A strike on an important line of transportation, however, at once retards the whole industrial machinery and is injurious in an extreme degree, few persons being exempt from its more or less direct effects. This fact at once suggests that the terms of the labor contract between the railway, for instance, and its employees should be different from the form usually prevailing; that the employee on a railroad should be obliged by law to give notice, some time previous, of his intention to leave the service; and that arbitration should be applied to the case in a special manner. (It goes without saying that the legislature of every State should make it an act of felony on the part of an employee on a railway to desert a freight or passenger train in transit, to the great detriment of shippers of freight, or the risk of life of passengers.) The recommendations of the New York State Board of Mediation and Arbitration, several times renewed in the last few years, and especially emphasized with reference to the strike on the New York Central and Hudson River Railroad in August, 1890, and the strike at Buffalo in August, 1892, commend themselves with great force; the carrying of them into general practice will mark a great forward step in this direction.[1] The semi-military

[1] They are thus summarized by the Board : —

(1.) The service rendered by railroad corporations created by the State is a public service.

(2.) Entrance into such service should be by enlistment for a definite period, upon satisfactory examination as to mental and physical qualifications, with oath of fidelity to the people and to the corporation.

(3.) Resignation or dismissal from such service to be permitted for cause, to be stated in writing and filed with some designated authority, and to take effect after the lapse of a reasonable and fixed period.

(4.) Wages to be established at the time of entry, and changed only by mutual agreement, or decision by arbitration of a board chosen by the company and employees, or by a State board, or through the action of both, the latter serving as an appellate body. Other differences that may arise to be settled in like manner.

(5.) Promotions to be made upon a system that may be devised and agreeable to both parties.

organization of the railway service toward which these recommendations tend is highly advisable. In case of labor difficulties on a railway, the calling in of the State Board of Arbitration should be compulsory on the employees and officers, — the existing contract being continued until the Board has rendered its decision.

The probable result of a wise use of their power by trade-unions and of a gradual extension of arbitration will be a slow rise in wages, continuing that steady advance which such authorities as F. A. Walker and E. Chevallier have established. The desire to make the actual wage go as far as possible will lead all true friends of the workingman to remove unnecessary taxes, direct or indirect, which bear inequitably upon him. He needs to become a house-owner rather than a rent-payer; and this in many cases he can do by availing himself of the admirable system of Building and Loan Associations.[1] The workingman's house will, by preference, be located in a suburb of the city where his work lies. So far as this vital matter of healthy homes for people of moderate means is concerned, we may rationally hope that systems of cheap and rapid transit will soon put an end, with other

(6.) Any combination of two or more persons to embarrass or prevent the operation of a railroad in the service of the people, a misdemeanor ; and any obstruction of or violence towards a railroad serving the people, endangering the safety of life and property, a felony with punishment of adequate severity.

(7.) Establishment of a beneficiary fund for the relief of employees disabled by sickness or accident, and for the relief of their families in case of death, as is done upon the lines of a number of railroad corporations in other States.

[1] See Seymour Dexter's *Treatise on Coöperative Savings and Loan Associations,* — a complete guide to the formation and management of such organizations.

agencies, to the abominations of the tenement-house, and fundamentally improve the situation. When every considerable town or city has a fully developed system of electric railways running into the adjacent country in all directions, the ideal of a home for every family will be more nearly reached. But how needless in many places the tenement-house is, even in the absence of a system of electric railways, Philadelphia, that city of homes, has already shown.

The mention of electricity naturally leads to a few words concerning its bearing on the future of industry. Very probably this wonder-working force will greatly modify the existing factory system. The product mainly of the last hundred years, this system shows no sign of being an exception to the general law of change.[1] The late Dr. Werner Siemens, the famous electrician, declared that the tendency "of modern natural science is to bring the forces of Nature into the service of the individual workman, and thus give to his work an economic strength as opposed to the massed productions of the large factories." With other distinguished electricians, he looked forward to such improvements in the diffusion of electric power as will at least check the further building of immense factories where hundreds and thousands of operatives are crowded together. It is quite possible that, in accordance with the spiral nature of human progress, a considerable proportion of the industry of

[1] See, on this subject of the probable transience of present methods of production, the closing chapter of *The Modern Factory System* by R. W. C. Taylor, 1891. Mr. Taylor's speculations concerning the possible effects of electricity and other new motors on production and the entire industrial problem are of extreme interest. See, too, the article entitled "Something Electricity is Doing" in the *Century Magazine* for March, 1889.

the future may come to be carried on, as formerly, in private houses and in small shops widely diffused throughout the country districts. Power for the needful machinery may be derived from central stations, and improved methods of transportation be used in distributing the product of these small factories. In contradistinction to the socialist, the American, beyond all other men, puts his trust in science and invention for the improvement of existing conditions. Science, if we may so personify the human mind searching out the secrets of nature, has caused much of the difficulty of modern social problems by the application of steam-power to production and transportation. The power that has done the harm will provide the remedy, discovering and applying still greater forces. Electricity may remove the difficulties steam has brought, while in its turn it will doubtless bring other evils to accompany its marvelous advantages.

Within the last few months a great deal has been said in this country concerning the "sweating system." Like many other terms used in the current discussion of social subjects, the phrase receives the greatest variety of applications. Sometimes it is applied to cases in which a middleman between the manufacturer and the worker absorbs a wholly disproportionate share of the whole amount paid for an article produced under conditions of extreme hardship, difficulty and even inhumanity, due largely to the "sweater." At other times the term "sweating system" is used by sentimentalists to denote some of the ordinary and inevitable processes of distributing work from great centres among scattered workers, who would otherwise be quite unable to secure em-

ployment for themselves. In this case the middleman often receives only a fair return for his services
in distributing work among workers who cannot visit
the centre in person, and each person is supplied
more cheaply than he could procure the raw material
and return the completed product for himself. Yet,
in these cases, as in hundreds of other directions
in America, the middleman is a person whom it is
highly desirable that employers, producers and consumers should unite in abolishing as far as practicable.
Every encouragement should be given to the extension
of simple coöperative methods like those so successfully practiced in the "creameries." These will
secure for the producer or hand-worker that larger
share of the wholesale or retail price which modern
methods of transportation now make entirely feasible
for them.[1] No complaint of consequence is made in
the United States against the strictest practicable
regulation of factories and other places of labor,
in the interest of the health of the employees working
in them. Wherever the "sweating system" is actually in operation in foul, unwholesome shops or dwell-
ing-houses, there will be no reluctance in any part of
the United States over stringent sanitary control, by
the city or the State.

The recent legislation of numerous States proves
that employees in a manufactory will be protected by
laws imposing liability upon the proprietor of the factory for accidents, not the result of gross carelessness
on the part of the employee. On the other hand, a
recent effort by the Massachusetts legislature to for-

[1] See the very informing work by H. L. Myrick, *How to
Coöperate,* which is especially directed to the relief of farmers
from the extortions of middlemen.

bid the imposition of fines for carelessness in weaving has been properly set aside by the Supreme Court as an undue interference with private liberty. Abuses of the fining system by grasping overseers may occasionally occur, but they are not so frequent as to render it desirable to pass a law one effect of which would be the encouragement of gross carelessness on the part of the weaver.

The gradual diminution of the average hours of daily labor is a matter of vital importance in the progress of the working world. Under the nervous development of civilized mankind and the increasing "high pressure" under which modern men live, the shortening of the hours of work into which any element of nervous expenditure enters deserves the most careful consideration, to say the least. Beyond a doubt, the last hour of the usual ten-hour day is the least productive under common conditions. Only slight reflection upon the importance, in daily work of any kind, of the full attention and interest of the workman is needed to realize that in very many occupations one may easily accomplish in nine hours' work what he does now in ten hours. They who dispute this fail to consider that the workman has only so much working-force on the average to spend in the number of hours he labors, be they twelve or ten, and to recognize the importance of the moral element in the most ordinary day work. When we inquire as to the amount of shortening of the common ten-hour day which present industrial conditions will allow, undoubtedly a much stronger case can be made out for a nine-hour day than for an eight-hour day. The machinery used in most of the industrial processes of our civilization cannot, of course, turn out

as much product in nine hours as in ten; but even
here the carefulness and skill of the employee are
matters to which a time-limit finds application. In
such establishments as that of the N. O. Nelson
Company of St. Louis and the felt works of Dolgeville, N. Y., to mention no others, the working-day
has been shortened to nine hours, and the firms state
that they have substantially, if not completely, the
same amount of production with the nine-hour day
as with the former ten-hour day. In many handi-
crafts there is little reason to doubt that this would
be the usual result. The only shortening of the day's
work deserving serious consideration is one which
makes no reduction in the existing rate of wages; a
shorter day with a proportionate reduction in wages
will not even be discussed by any large number of
working-people here in America, unless, in some improbable way, the desire of the average American
workingman to live in comfort and get on in the
world is greatly weakened.

The case has not yet been made out for an eight-
hour day in many occupations, as likely to secure as
much product and to be otherwise as much for the
advantage of the employer and the employee as the
existing ten-hour day.[1] If we move gradually in
the direction of an eminently desirable shortening of
the hours of labor for all classes, we shall find numerous arguments in favor of a nine-hour day which,
simply as a matter of degree and proportion, lose
their strength when we attempt to apply them to an

[1] A careful and candid discussion of the usual arguments for
the eight hours limit will be found in the article on the "Eight
Hour Agitation," by Francis A. Walker, in the *Atlantic Monthly*
for June, 1890.

eight-hour day. Some persons will deem it a shallow and homely method of reasoning on this subject, but there is no slight weight, as respects the moral aspects of the question which are never to be left entirely out of sight, in the following considerations. In these United States the workman, under the ten-hour system, must reach his place of employment at seven o'clock in the morning; he then works steadily for five hours; he has one hour's intermission for dinner, and he then continues his work from one o'clock until six. Now if we add to these eleven hours the time taken to reach the factory or shop in the morning and the home in the evening, we perceive that the amount of acquaintance which the average workingman has with his family must be small; his children he may scarcely see during the week, except for an hour or two in the evening, and on Sunday. They whose daily labor begins an hour or two later in the morning and ends an hour or two earlier in the afternoon may estimate how much less home life, outside of Sunday, can signify to the workingman who takes out of every twenty-four hours ten hours of work, with an hour of intermission and at least another, on the average, for traveling to and from his place of labor. Here, as elsewhere, there is no general principle more safely to be applied to particular problems than the desirability, on the plainest principles of human nature, of extending privileges and opportunities which the well-to-do classes enjoy, as fast as possible, to those who now have to work harder and longer. To apply this principle in a very simple way: If the great body of working-people could quit work at five o'clock in the afternoon, thus reaching home at six o'clock in most cases, these men

and women would have before them the same hours
for the evening meal and the evening itself as other
people have who work on salaries or conduct business
of their own. They will have more opportunity
and, in all probability, more inclination than before
to spend the evening in home intercourse, social calls,
reading, and attending places of amusement, as others do. If in this way an hour can be taken from the
daily burden of work and given to home life, rest and
recreation, the gain is great. The next step in the
diminution of the hours of labor, after the nine-hour
day, should be the Saturday half-holiday. When the
question of shortening the hours of labor is handled
in a modest manner, eschewing unreliable generaliza-
tions as to the effect on the labor market or production in general, the plan should commend itself more
to the employer who remembers that his employees
have substantially the same desires and needs as himself. Very few employers of labor are free from an
obvious duty to experiment cautiously in this direction, in order to discover the actual results of a shortening of the ten-hour day to nine-and-a-half or nine
hours. At present, employers, as a rule, declare
that any shortening of the hours of labor would be
detrimental only. But there is already a large body
of experience in this general direction, including the
legislative reductions of hours in work in cotton and
woolen mills from twelve and eleven to ten hours,
and such voluntary reductions from ten hours to nine
hours as I have named, sufficient to make it plain
that the question is an open one for the sagacious
employer. He will prove his sagacity by careful experiments looking to a gradual reduction of hours
rather than by dogmatic declarations that any such

change would be ruinous to himself and undesirable for his employees. The last two generations have amply refuted similar prophets of evil! The general tendency in this nervous age, in which machinery plays so great a part in industry, is undeniably toward a diminution of working hours: it is a practical question of the length to which such a reduction can profitably be carried in any particular industry or establishment. How far such a reduction will ever go we may properly decline to prophesy. No such thing as a "normal work day" has yet been discovered, and one can have little sympathy with the "friends of labor" who apparently think that the less work mankind does the better. On the contrary, there is always more work needing to be done than there are competent workers to do it. A nine-hour day is plainly practicable now in many industries, with no decrease of the product.

The spread of voluntary life insurance from the salaried classes, who now chiefly practice it, to the upper grades, at least, of workers on wages is in every way desirable. The facilities for such insurance by thrifty work-people should be greatly enlarged, and American trade - unions would do well to imitate more the mutual benefit features of English labor organizations. In this direction, as in so many others, self-help on the part of workmen, either singly or in organizations, is far preferable to insurance by the State. The insurance of employees by firms and corporations, as at Dolgeville, N. Y., is one of the wisest measures for uniting the interests of both parties.

A great improvement in the condition of working people will be wrought by the extension of industrial education in the public schools and in privately endowed institutions like those with which the names of Auchmuty, Pierpont Morgan, Pratt, Williamson, Drexel and Armour are now honorably associated. The improvement will be gradual but sure, and the whole community will profit by this development of manual training.

More important than such matters as life insurance, bureaus of employment in every city, industrial education, fewer hours of labor, and boards of conciliation and arbitration, is the fundamental question of the best form of the labor contract. It is not probable that the industry of the future will be characterized by a single phase only of the relation of master and man. It is a very easy, in fact a dangerously easy proceeding to infer from the comparative success of the democratic system in politics that in the course of a few generations an "industrial democracy" will be completely established. Such solutions can easily be shown to be very defective. If the troublesome questions of human life could be at once utterly settled by such swift and simple reasoning from analogy, the lot of the thinker and of the man of action would be very different in this complicated world!

Coöperative production, — the system under which the workmen in an establishment contribute, or hire, the capital needed to carry on a manufacture; choose their own foremen and business managers, fixing the rate of salary for these and the allowance for wages for themselves; direct the conduct of the business according to a more or less democratic system; and divide among themselves, at the end of the year, the profits or losses of the twelve months gone by, — is a system most attractive to the logical thinker and to the philanthropic spirit. Equality is a word of magic sound in the industrial as in the political world; but the results of many a trial of it have been very different in the two worlds. When a body of workmen, controlling a considerable capital, come together to carry on a manufacture with the industrial processes of which they are well acquainted; when they recognize the prime necessity of securing for the exclusive control of the commercial department a man of marked business talent, to whom they will give large powers and a high salary, and whom they can and will implicitly trust, in good years and bad years alike; when they thus respect the aristocratic principle, which cannot safely be put by; when they refrain from suspicions and jealousies in case the enterprise is not immediately and constantly successful, — then the attempt at coöperative production on a large scale is likely to have permanent success. How severe a demand, financially, intellectually and morally, is thus made upon a body of workmen any observant person may realize, in some faint degree, if he will look around him among people supposed to be in a higher state of culture than the ordinary hand-worker, and perceive how difficult attempts at coöperation, even for certain limited and specific objects, are often found to be among such persons. The coöperation necessary in the case of the workman is one that is to last month after month and year after year; it will be unsuccessful unless there is complete fidelity on the part of all the men to the common welfare, a fidelity easily weakened by a single example of betrayal of trust or even of unwillingness to do one's part in the actual work. It is hard enough to get a large number of men to work steadily together for a common purpose under the spur of the plainest self-interest. How much more difficult must it be to keep them together when the very first conditions are the difficult virtues of self-denial and mutual trust and a frank confession that here, at least, one man is *not* as good as another. Citizens of a republican country like our own, who do not thoroughly realize the inevitable limitations of political freedom, furnish poor material for a so-called "industrial democracy," the continuance of which would demand an ungrudging recognition of natural aristocracy in the control.

The cases in which the difficulties of coöperative production have been successfully overcome are still comparatively few in this country; the "History of Coöperation in the United States" gives the best accessible account of many of these. The successes have been on a small scale for the most part, and, unfortunately, the history of so promising a movement as that of the Somerset Foundry Company in Massachusetts shows that years of prosperity are not proof against disaster arising from purely moral causes, — suspicion and jealousy among the workers. In the English "Coöperative News," Mr. Benjamin Jones, a person of high authority in the coöperative distributive movement, has been publishing for months a series of "Short Papers on Coöperative Production." He has given details of the history of a large number of coöperative productive enterprises in Great Britain which have come to grief within the last fifty or sixty years. Making allowance in the case of the writers in the "History of Coöperation in the United States," for a possible bias in favor of the scheme, and in the case of Mr. Jones of a possible bias against it, we may conclude with confidence from the exhibit made

in these two works that the chances of success in cooperative production, in any but modest enterprises,
are slight. The scheme seems to make too severe a
moral and intellectual demand upon the workman, —
a demand which would scarcely be met by other sorts
and conditions of men generally supposed to be better
trained than the average wage-earner.

The hopes of John Stuart Mill with respect to
coöperative production have been shown by time to
have been too sanguine. The permanent acceptance
of the ordinary and unmodified wages system is not,
however, the only alternative. Referring the reader
to the chapter on "The Wages System in its Various
Forms," in my work on profit sharing, for a vindi-
cation of this system against various crude thinkers,
I repeat the expression of my belief that it needs a
gradual modification in the direction of equality and
democracy. Mr. David F. Schloss has thrown much
light upon numerous approved variations of the pure
wages system in his recent valuable volume. Having, myself, given considerable time to the study of a
modification of the wages system which seems to me
more important than most of those ably expounded
by Mr. Schloss, I will turn from the general sugges-
tions of this chapter to a reconsideration of a special
problem. Other modifications of the simple day-wage
or piece-wage system, such as the offering of prizes
for extra quality of work, or for economy in production; the payment of a percentage on sales in addition
to salary or wages; "progressive wages;" and the
premium system in all its varieties, including "gain-
sharing," have undoubtedly a large field for their
profitable application. For the general principle of
profit sharing, as well, a case has been fully made

out. The extent to which the principle is applicable is the matter now to be tested by experience.

An important argument for the wider extension of profit sharing, thoroughly approved in a number of instances, is its value as a training school for coöperative production. Numerous years' experience as an employee in a profit-sharing house supplies precisely that tuition in the knowledge and the virtues of business needed by the average workman. Great commercial establishments like the Maison Leclaire, the Godin foundry, the Coöperative Paper Works of Angoulême and the Bon Marché, have enforced upon large bodies of people in a leading handicraft, in two prominent manufactures and in a great distributive concern the truth that success in trade and production demands more than the strict application of the democratic principle. These four concerns are virtually coöperative; certainly, they secure to the employees and stockholders the substantial benefits of purely coöperative productive enterprises, while they are still, logically, profit-sharing establishments. There has been a process of development in them, out of profit sharing on the basis of the ordinary wages system into profit sharing on a basis of modified coöperation. In this slowness of growth and in the education which it implies reside the strength and the promise of permanence of these houses.

The unmodified wages system compensating the employee according to his hours or the actual amount of work accomplished; various modifications of it like "progressive wages;" profit sharing, inclining to coöperative production; and coöperative production itself, though in a less degree than the preceding methods, are the probable forms of the labor contract in the near future. There is no necessity for attempting to predict the proportion in which these systems will divide the industrial field among them ten years or a hundred years hence. It seems to me probable, however, that, with a steady progress in intellectual enlightenment and moral ability, such modifications of the wages system as profit sharing will be widely extended, and that they will lead, in the course of time, to a much larger practice of coöperative production proper than we now see.

CHAPTER IX.

INDUSTRIAL PARTNERSHIP.

I. What Profit Sharing Means.

The position to which a careful study of the record
of the system of dividing the profits leads many I
have thus stated: "Profit Sharing, the division of
realized profits between the capitalist, the employer
and the employee, in addition to regular interest,
salary and wages, is the most equitable and generally
satisfactory method of remunerating the three industrial agents." [1] Subsequent observation and reflection have strengthened my belief in the soundness of
this view. Profit Sharing has attracted much attention in the last four years; there has been a substantial increase in the number of firms practicing it, and
a considerable public opinion in favor of it has been
developed. It is by no means a cure-all, even for
troubles specifically industrial; much less is it a panacea for the many distresses of our time not due to
industrial causes. To aid the movement toward a
rational evolution of the wages system, I would here
supplement the exposition and the argument of my
detailed work on the subject. The present chapter
considers with some fullness two or three leading objections made to the method, and states compactly the
advance which profit sharing has made in the last

[1] *Profit Sharing*, p. 412 ; 1889.

four years; both sections largely take for granted the facts and the arguments I have heretofore presented.

Profit Sharing should be defined by the addition of the words "between employer and employee." Mr. Sedley Taylor obscured a proper distinction when he qualified the division as one "between capital and labor." It is not the capitalist as such, but the employer who contracts with the employee; even when the two functions are united in the same person, as they often are, they should be kept logically distinct. Profit Sharing, thus defined, is a step forward, both natural and necessary, in "the evolution of the wages system." But the most forcible, as it is also the most common objection to this development derives its apparent strength from a very obvious criticism suggested by the name. Profit and loss are the Siamese twins of business. If one is mentioned, the other immediately presents itself to the mind. Hence arises the usual objection to the scheme of profit sharing that it does not include the sharing of losses by the employee. Because loss is not associated with profit in the name of the method, it does not, however, follow that no provision has actually been made to remedy the superficial inequity which it requires no keenness of mind to observe. If we consider the matter with a little care, we shall see that the standard systems of profit sharing do not suffer from this objection, the whole force of which lies in its immediate plausibility.

One point only need be remembered to change the vigor of the criticism in question into weakness: the workingman should be treated as fairly as the manager. The employer may fail, in a certain year, of that recompense in profits to which his business talent seems to entitle him. He draws a salary in proportion to the importance of the place. If trade is flourishing, he generally receives also a share of the profits. If the venture is for the time unsuccessful, he will redouble, if possible, his pains and skill. The capitalist does not require him after a bad year to pay back a part of the large salary which he has been receiving. If the manager fails to obtain a good profit over and above wages, salary and interest, and even the payment of interest becomes uncertain, his salary, which stands as the usual just recompense of his skill and power, will be cut down. He is not supposed to do less now than in successful years; he is quite likely to do more. He loses in bad years, however, the difference between his normal salary and the lower amount which he actually receives; but out of this reduced salary he is not expected to take a portion toward making good any loss of interest to the capitalist, in the year past.

The employee contributes to the joint undertaking hand-labor qualified by a varying amount of intelligence. For this hand-labor he receives, under the common wages system, a fixed return by the day or the week. He can expect nothing beyond this in the shape of a share in the net profits, however slight, after all expenses for interest, salaries, wages, reserve, depreciation, and repairs have been met. Let us now suppose that his employer admits him to a share in the profits, — a share determined in all its conditions by the employer, and moderate in size as it is based on a calculation of the probabilities of a series of years, good and bad. Under the stimulus of this promised bonus, the workman is expected to increase the efficiency of his labor, as regards quantity and quality of his product, economy, carefulness and good order. He does so; and he thus makes an extra contribution to the business, as compared with the common workman. At the end of the year, if it has been prosperous, he receives the bonus. This is not a sheer gift from the employer; it is a fair return, warranted by the nature of the industrial contract and by the state of trade, for the workman's increased contribution to the joint undertaking.

The gain of the year, however, depends not only upon good work by the employee, but very largely — it may be chiefly — on skill in the commercial management. With this management, no system of industrial partnership allows the workman to meddle; he is not permitted to go to the accounts when he likes, or in any least degree to prescribe the business policy. In his own place, as a producer or distributor, he is asked to do his best. If he has common human nature in him, he will be roused by the prospect of a dividend on his wages. Ample experience shows that the average workman will make his extra contribution in good years, and in bad years, too, toward the success of the firm. Like the employer, he will be punctual, careful, economical, and in every way diligent in a time of depression, as well as in a time of prosperity. Every year the employee in a true industrial partnership is a successful maker of profit, when compared with the ordinary wage-earner, so far as his own department and his own power and responsibility are concerned. In no year is he rightly held responsible for losses entirely beyond his control: he does, he can do, nothing toward incurring losses except through bad workmanship; if he is a poor workman, he should, of course, be dropped from the industrial partnership.

If the year has brought no profit to the concern, and no loss, the employee, who has put forth extra effort, receives no return for it in the shape of a bonus. He draws his wages as the manager takes his salary, both sums being the return which it is desirable shall suffer from no retroactive demands. In these indifferent years the manager fails of that extra reward for the service he gives in excess of a fair return for the fixed salary which is supposed to correspond to the average state of prosperity in the business. In like manner, the employee fails of a return for the extraordinary manual service he has rendered, — that amount of effort by which he has surpassed the common achievement of workers in his industry.

If times go from bad to worse, both salaries and wages must be reduced. But the manager will not be assessed on his past year's salary to make up losses to the capitalist. No more should the workman be called upon to pay back a part of his wages to make good the salary of the manager, or the interest of the capitalist. It would seem to be clear that in a profit-sharing establishment the efficient workman shares losses in bad years, even before his wages are reduced. Furthermore, no wise firm, whether giving its employees a share in realized profits or not, neglects to lay up a reserve fund out of the profits of good years, to meet the probable losses of bad times. An annual payment to such a reserve fund takes precedence of a dividend in excess of interest, salary and wages. To the formation of such a fund, the employee in a profit-sharing house evidently contributes as well as the manager; if there were no such reserve, the bonus to the employee and the net profit to the employer would be larger. The workman thus adds in prosperous times to a fund expressly intended to meet the losses of adverse years; in these latter years he suffers a loss of that bonus which rewards his unusual exertion as compared with that of the simple wage-earner.

It will be further asserted, however, and very properly, that the capitalist is exposed to the risk of losing his capital, in whole or in part, as well as his interest, owing to the incapacity or the misfortunes of the employer. The employer, too, who has prospered a number of years and laid up a fortune, small or great, may come to times when he must break in upon this accumulation in order to pay the interest to the capitalist which he has not realized from his business. If, then, the workman is not called upon to pay back any share of his wages, which he has saved up, is there not an obvious inequity, despite all that has thus far been urged in his defense? The answer is plain. There would be an injustice if the workmen received as much of the whole profit as the employer or the capitalist. But, in fact, no profit-sharing establishment places the three parties on an equality. A portion of the profits ranging from five or ten per cent. up to twenty or twenty-five goes to the employees. This method of division is justified by the fact that they are free from the great risks which the manager and the capitalist incur. An equal division could only be defended did the workmen incur similar risks. The actual inequality of the shares of profit corresponds to the inequality of the risks run by the three parties.

Provision is made, then, for the sharing of money losses in the profit-sharing house through a reserve fund. If we bear in mind the whole output of effort, we see how real a loss is also borne by the workman in bad years, through the failure of a bonus and the usual reduction of wages. Those who consider that the objection in question finally disposes of the whole matter practice a curiously cheap-and-easy style of argument. They make a remarkable reflection upon the mental abilities of the three hundred firms now practicing the system if they suppose it has never occurred to these firms. The fact that so many establishments have adopted profit sharing, when the objection must have offered itself at the outset, is a plain intimation of its fallacious character.

Let us approach from another side the fact for which the term Profit Sharing stands. Man has no greater helper than words, and often he has no worse enemy. When they present themselves to him as fully equal to the expression of reality, they lead him far astray. Profit sharing is, in fact, but one prominent feature of a certain system of associating employer and employee. "Industrial partnership" is a term which includes this feature, and numerous others. It is the more comprehensive and the more characteristic phrase. The advocates of "profit sharing" do not need to seek the advantage of a name less open to obvious retort; but it is said to be a test of a sound thought that it will bear a change of clothing. If advocates and opponents will, then, carefully consider the implications of "Industrial Partnership," the principle of profit sharing will be better appreciated. Both words need to be emphasized. The association is industrial, not strictly commercial. To excite and maintain, nevertheless, a real feeling of *partnership* in the mind of the workingman, the profit-sharing system is put in operation. If this friendly feeling show itself in a sincere interest in the success of the concern, and in greater economy, carefulness and zeal on the part of the employee, then the method in any given year is successful, profit or no profit. The central difficulty in the existing labor situation comes from the loss of the feeling of association in a common cause which characterized the relations of master and man in the simple and limited industries of former times. The farmer working his own land, with his minor sons to help him, is an instance of perhaps the closest kind of interested coöperation. When his farm requires the work also of two or three "hired men," he probably continues in the field, superintending and working side by side with them. The shoemaker in the little shops which used to be so common by the Massachusetts roadside sat on the bench in the same room with his small company of workmen. In these two industries — to go no farther for instances — the association of employer and employee was close and familiar. Labor troubles were infrequent in such an atmosphere. But in these days of great shoe factories, using the most elaborate machinery and employing hundreds of men, the productive industry and the commercial handling of the product are sharply separated. The factory and the counting-room know each other, at most, only by sight. The space which separates a great shoe factory in Milford from the selling office in Boston is but a feeble index of the personal separation between the actual maker of the shoes on the machine and the partners in the firm. The field is thus opened wide for every kind of misunderstanding, suspicion and dislike. The record of recent industry shows how well this opportunity is improved. The actual attitude of the two parties in too many instances is one of ill-concealed hostility.

The former feeling of partnership has vanished in the stupendous development of modern industrial civilization. Master and man too often talk of each other as if they were entirely distinct species, with the fewest possible points of sympathy or contact. It is this profound alienation between those who hire labor on a large scale and their employees that strikes the rest of the world as the most lamentable feature in the modern industrial system. The employer is too wont to think of his men as so many machines, or, at the best, as creatures largely irrational. The workman regards the owner of the vast establishment where he works as a selfish tyrant, chiefly bent on reducing wages to the lowest possible point. The masters combine against the men, and the men combine against the masters. Workingmen dream of a happy day when all industry shall be purely coöperative, and the employing class be abolished. The capitalist dreams of the time when improved machinery shall have reduced the need of hand-labor to a minimum. Meanwhile, the right and natural combination of the employer and his men in each industrial establishment is left out of sight.

It is not possible, of course, to call back the simple arrangements of primitive industry. Mediæval guilds have perished, too, with the men that formed them. The scale of modern industry no longer permits the large employer to know his men personally. The fundamental question, however, is not to be put by: Is not the old spirit of association capable of revival in some new form? Mankind has gone on swiftly in these later times, in a marvelous development of manufacture and commerce. Carried along by its tremendous material sweep, we have had little time or thought to spend upon that most important matter, the adjustment of the new material conditions according to the laws of morality and humanity.[1] The morally "unreasoning progress of the world" has brought us to the days of lockouts, black-lists, strikes, and boycotts, — in one word, to industrial war. When we pause and reflect on the means of reconciliation of the hostile classes, we may be very sure that the problem is largely a moral one; but at the same time, the moral solution must be grounded on some readjustment of the material interests involved. Fine words butter no parsnips, and to little purpose do grasping employers repeat that the interests of labor and capital are one. "Which one?" we well may ask, as in the case of a matrimonial contract! The answer that the common capitalist practically makes is evident.

Beside other characteristics which forcibly recommend it to the American Spirit, profit sharing has this plain mark, that it is a thoroughly conservative movement. It attempts to recall, as far as is possible

---

[1] "We have profoundly forgotten everywhere that cash-payment is not the sole relation of human beings ; we think, nothing doubting, that it absolves and liquidates all engagements of man. . . . One thing I do know : never on this earth was the relation of man to man long carried on by cash-payment alone. Cash never yet paid one man fully his deserts to another, nor could it, nor can it, now or henceforth to the end of the world. In brief, we shall have to dismiss the Cash-Gospel rigorously into its own place : we shall have to know that there is some infinitely deeper Gospel, subsidiary, explanatory, and daily and hourly corrective to the Cash one; or else that the Cash one itself and all others are fast traveling." Carlyle.

under the changed conditions of modern industry, the old sentiment of partnership felt when the shoe manufacturer in his small shop worked in close proximity with his few employees, or when the farmer hired men on shares, or the catch of the fishing schooner was apportioned among the crew. We can no longer divide the actual products of most industries among the workers. But we can modify the wages system, and strengthen it at a weak point, by adding to fixed wages a variable bonus, dependent on the workman's zeal.

Standing in no attitude of hostility to employers, and rejecting totally the notion that they are to be superseded altogether by coöperation or by the State, I am firmly of the opinion that they should take forward steps in the reasoning, conscious evolution of the wages system. Such a step as profit sharing is in the direct line of their own interest. As M. Charles Secrétan has said: "Whether we regret it or rejoice over it, the fact remains that society cannot be fossilized; the alternative is not, as some would fain believe, between the enfranchisement of the masses or the perpetuity of their serfdom and vassalage, but between enfranchisement and the universal bondage with which a state socialism threatens us." He continues: "Socialism knows perfectly well that coöperation is its deadliest foe, while the dissatisfied are its abettors. Two ways, and only two, lie open before us, — to revolt against the reign of liberty by coercion and violence, or to support it by reforms freely effected. We advocate the latter course. We advise masters to give their employers a share in their profits. We recommend to the wage-earning class coöperative stores, with a view to collective saving and to the combination of producers."

The best kind of socialism is the kind which employers have it fully in their power to inaugurate and develop, — partnership with their workmen. This evidently should not be a *commercial* partnership. The workmen have not a large capital to contribute. As a body, in any given establishment, they have not the acquaintance with the conditions of trade which would make their advice of value to the counting-room. Of commercial skill they are naturally destitute, and their interference with the books or the plans of the partners, who combine their capital and their skill in the firm, would be ruinous. The confusion by workmen of the two kinds of partnership, industrial and commercial, is one cause of the failure of most coöperative productive establishments. The same confusion, by business men, is the source of the chief objection to profit sharing, — that it does not carry along with it "loss sharing" out of wages paid. When the distinction is clearly made and firmly held, coöperative workmen will leave the commercial conduct of their factory to a manager, with large powers and a high salary; and employers will cease to ask that workmen shall share losses which are due to the commercial department.

Profit sharing rests for its justification upon the fact that in the industrial department of a business the workmen will probably increase the quantity of the product, improve its quality, take better care of implements, economize materials, diminish the cost of superintendence, and end most of the labor troubles, in view of a promised bonus. The existing evidence going to prove this fact is now accessible to every employer. No one claims that profit sharing gives the workmen skill in buying raw material or in selling the finished product.

The limit to which the industrial partnership should go is thus easily discernible. If the workmen in a productive establishment actually make the gains just indicated in quantity, quality, economy and good order, then they actually earn a bonus in addition to wages. If the employer chooses, he can make the bonus payable in every year when this gain over the usual cost of manufacture is realized, without regard to the results in the commercial department. The Yale and Towne Manufacturing Company of Stamford, Conn., practice such a system, devised by Mr. Henry R. Towne, to which he gives the name of "Gain Sharing." [1] The essence of the method "consists in ascertaining the present labor cost of a given product, and in dividing equitably with those engaged in producing it the gain or benefit accruing from increased efficiency or economy on their part." The industrial department being thus entirely separated from the commercial, a bonus to labor might be earned, and would have to be paid, in years when the commercial department showed a loss. So far as the workmen are concerned, they have done all they could to help the firm by diminishing the actual cost of manufacture. One part of the gain in production has gone to them, and the other falls to the firm. Both parties, therefore, are so far gainers by the industrial partnership.

Professional advocates of "the cause of labor" (whose own exertions are chiefly vocal) will denounce even this kind of association, under which the employees would get a bonus in every year in which the

---

[1] I have elsewhere described it briefly (*Profit Sharing,* p. 326); and it may be found in detail in the tenth volume of the *Transactions of the American Society of Mechanical Engineers.*

actual cost of production is diminished by them, simply because the employer also profits by the decrease. Advantage to all the parties concerned is, however, of the very essence of partnership of any kind. It would be a curious procedure, in a world where enlightened self-interest must play an important rôle in human affairs, did we ask the employing class to adopt a new system which will inure to the benefit of the workmen only. The sounder position is that every step of genuine progress is a benefit to all who take it. The workman who objects to a ten per cent. bonus on his wages, because his employer's gain has also increased from the improvement in the quality of labor, is fit for a lunatic asylum. It is not the industrious workmen who make this irrational objection to the betterment of their own condition, but those persons who imagine that a benefit to one class should always be accompanied by an injury to another, and who would be seriously disturbed by seeing employer and employee prospering together in a real partnership!

The method called "gain sharing" is more favorable to the workmen than the less strictly logical system of profit sharing, or industrial partnership, under which the payment of a bonus to labor is conditioned on the commercial prosperity of the firm. This brief consideration of it may, however, help to enlighten those who rest in the argument for loss sharing as finally disposing of the case for profit sharing. If gains are made in one department by workmen, and losses are incurred in another with which they have nothing to do, it is not reasonable that they should be called upon to share these losses out of their wages, if they have also received no bonus on account of the gain they have made in production. They take the risks of labor and they improve its quality and quantity. If they do this, it is highly irrational to ask them to share also the risks of capital and management. The irrationality would vanish did the workmen own shares, have free access to the books, and a voice in the control of the business. But the undesirability of these features, taken altogether, is to nobody more clear than to the advocates of loss sharing out of wages.

The question, not for carpers, but for practical men, is, How far shall the partnership between master and men go? It should obviously be confined to the industrial department, and stop short of a voice in the management, an inspection of the accounts, and a responsibility for losses. These three things stand together. If we establish the third, we must also admit the first two; if we deny the advisability of the first two, we must also reject the third as inequitable. When all the zeal of the employees and all the talent of the counting-room have been ineffectual to avoid losses in the market under adverse circumstances, the commercial partners properly bear all the money loss of the year past. The workman was invited to do his best, like one really interested; and he was promised a share in the profits, if any should be made. He took the risk and did his part, under the sensible limitations and conditions imposed by the firm. His responsibility must, in reason and equity, be measured by the power allowed him. Give the body of workmen, in a shoe factory or a flour mill, where they think of practicing profit sharing, the right to examine the books at any time; give them a powerful voice in shaping the business policy; let them command when to buy and where to sell; — then we can reasonably and equitably ask them at the end of a bad year to bear a share of the money loss, out of the wages and the bonuses previously received. However such an arrangement might work, it is not the actual or historical system of profit sharing, or industrial partnership; it is an entirely different method.

Gain sharing is probably too logical an arrangement for the mass of employers; they would be unwilling to pay a bonus to labor in years in which the business as a whole, including the productive and the commercial departments, showed no profit or even a positive loss. The practical effect of the majority of profit-sharing systems in operation to-day is that the workman takes the risk that the commercial department will do as well as the industrial department of the manufactory. The workmen have it fully in their power to make a reduction from the present average cost of production in an iron foundry or a cotton mill; if they do not accomplish this, then profit sharing would be recommended to little purpose. Making their contribution to the success of the business as a whole, they must then depend upon the business ability of the firm for the payment of any bonus. But this dependence is probably the best arrangement generally open to the producer. Having industrial ability, he allies himself with men of commercial talent. If the firm cannot succeed in selling goods at a profit, much less would a combination of simple producers be able to do it. The workman to-day depends for his wages even, in the long run, upon the shrewdness and the perseverance of his employer. It would probably be best, in the great majority of cases where profit sharing is introduced, that he should depend for his bonus also upon the same conditions. He then casts in his lot as a producer with the manager of the buying and selling department, and there is no separation in interests between the two departments, however logically desirable such a separation may seem to some to be.

Thus considered, the objection most commonly raised against profit sharing, that it does not involve loss sharing, will be seen to be a boomerang in the hands of its users. The workman in an industrial partnership shares profits only when the whole establishment makes a profit, to making which he has contributed in his department. He fails to receive a bonus, and thus shares losses, when he has actually done his part toward making a dividend, but the firm has not done as well, because success with them is not so simple a matter. Objection might be made with more consistency from the workman's side than from the employer's side. But when we take both parties into full consideration, and remember that it is a real partnership they seek, in which one department should not expect to profit when the other is losing, the equity of profit sharing becomes manifest. The strictly limited and well-defined scheme of profit sharing is plainly different from productive coöperation as well as from the pure wages system. The limitations which belong to its very nature are entirely disregarded by the critic who asks, " Why should the workman share profits, and not share losses also? " The objection must be deemed superficial and wide of the mark, when we consider, as we have done, that the partnership into which the employer himself invites the men is industrial, not commercial; that he surrenders in no manner or degree his absolute control over affairs; that he is just as much of an autocrat as he was before; that he keeps his books entirely free from troublesome inspection; that he himself fixes the percentage of the bonus on wages, after he has calculated the average profit of a series of years, good, bad and indifferent; that he is to pay this bonus in prosperous times only, when it has actually been realized; and that he is not to pay it in any year until a proper contribution has been made to a substantial reserve fund.

It is very evident that the strain comes upon the method of industrial partnership in years when the men have been doing well in the productive department, and have actually, on their side, made their due contribution toward realizing a good profit (in comparison with what they would have done under the simple wages method), and then learn that they will receive no bonus because the commercial department, for which they are in no respect responsible, as they have no power in it, shows a loss. The test of the workmen comes when they are thus disappointed of a bonus for which they had hoped. But is not the bad year a time of strain for all, under the pure wages system as well, when a reduction of wages is among the first remedies proposed? The critics of industrial partnership, who prefer the ease of prophecy to the more difficult labor of studying facts of record, tell us that the workman at such a time will sulk, will "kick," will strike, will, in short, make all manner of trouble, because he is so stupid that he cannot understand for himself the reasons given why no profit was made that year, and so suspicious that he will not take the word of the most honorable employer, or the expert accountant, to the effect that no bonus has been realized. The record does not justify such a wholesale judgment. For instance, the Geneva firm of Billon & Isaac, makers of parts of music-boxes, divided among their men, for the five years 1871–75, an average bonus of 21 per cent. on wages. In 1876, on account of the approaching Russo-Turkish War, the bonus fell to 4 per cent., and in the next year it went out of sight. "The crisis served to prove," said M. Billon, "that in bad years, as in good, we stood better with our employees than those firms which have not applied the principle of participation." For the six years following, the bonus averaged 12 per cent.; and for the three years 1884–86, there was none. "But our workmen continue to work courageously in hope of better times." One of the workmen said: "When there is no bonus, why, there is none; but we have still the satisfaction of knowing that we and our employers have done our best." The great Pillsbury flour mills of Minneapolis paid in 1883 – 85 three dividends to labor, amounting to \$125,000, or 33 per cent. on wages. For the next two years, owing to the great decline in wheat, no profits could be divided. The employees received the news "in the best possible spirit." Such are two samples of the testimony going to show that the workman under profit sharing, abroad and at home, is not the foolish person our prophets declare he will invariably be in bad times. A worthy missionary to New Zealand was in the habit of dispensing blankets among the Maoris who attended his meetings. Noticing that one native came too frequently for these comfortable garments, he mentioned the fact. "No more blankets?" responded the Maori; "well, then no more Hallelujah!" and he departed, not to return.

We cannot expect the workmen to be in a hallelujah frame of mind when the year's account allows no bonus: even their employers are not apt to rejoice greatly over such a state of affairs. But the critics of industrial partnership who prophesy that the workmen will at once depart from their sound mind forget the difference between an intelligent artisan and a naked Maori. The sharing of profits is, we must again remember, but one feature, however important and agreeable, of the system of industrial partnership. From the very nature of the method, the sharing of losses in bad times by the workman, *out of his savings*, would be irrational and unjust: he loses, and properly loses, only the bonus which he has actually earned. The principal objection to profit sharing, we see, is made by those who pay little attention to its necessary limitations.

Instituted by a business man of uncommon sagacity, the method of industrial partnership has received the very general approval of the political economists, from John Stuart Mill down to Prof. Alfred Marshall. They advise a wide and thorough trial of the plan, that its practical utility and its limitations may be determined by actual experience. This is my own position as an amateur. The principle is flexible and admits of a great variety of forms and applications. . So long as the one aim is kept in view, of arousing the essential feeling of a common interest in the prosperity of a house, it matters not what special complexion the method may take, as it is applied to the needs of the cotton mill, the iron foundry, the newspaper establishment, or the great retail store. There is a percentage of failure in the trials of the plan, from all kinds of causes, but the usual result is that the participating workman produces more, or improves the quality of his product, is careful of the tools he handles and the machinery he runs, is saving of the materials, superintends and is superintended by his fellow-workmen, and almost without exception refrains from strikes.

Profit sharing should not by the least instructed person be confounded with any of the social panaceas so abundant to-day, to some of which we have been attending. The Socialist, the Nationalist, the Christian Socialist, the Single-Tax advocate, — all these, as a rule, look down with lofty contempt upon a plan that would only result in promoting a kindly feeling of partnership between employer and employee, in the general improvement of the quality of work, and in a modest dividend to labor as a common practice. It is so much easier, finer, and more pleasing to reconstruct the entire modern world on paper, dismissing with an epigram, a poem, or an allegory, such minor, troublesome factors in the situation as human nature and economic law. Industrial partnership has this great advantage over the socialisms of the day, and even over the more sober scheme of productive coöperation: it pays due respect to the two great principles of modern society which must find a *modus vivendi*, — Democracy and Aristocracy. The varied, perpetual and innumerable labor troubles of our time mean fundamentally this one thing, — that the democratic spirit has invaded the industrial world. The majority are in revolt there against the aristocratic régime formerly unquestioned. Universal suffrage and political democracy have forcibly suggested, not to workingmen only but also to many of the more prosperous classes, a false analogy between government and industry. If the one can be carried on by counting hands, then why not the other? Why should there not be industrial democracy as well as political democracy? Why should not the factory and the counting-room be conducted on republican principles? Why not, indeed, except for the one fact that human nature has not been developed on the line of uniformity of mind and equality of talent! Fight against it as we may, there is a natural aristocracy of the best in character and ability, the true *aristoi.* "Men prate," indeed, as Lowell says, —

> " Of all heads to an equal grade cashiered,
> On level with the dullest, and expect
> A wondrous cure-all in equality; "

but "Enduring Nature, force conservative," is "indifferent to our noisy whims." An equal suffrage, indeed, — the wisest man to count for no more at the polls than the most foolish, the best to have only one vote like the worst! With the help of the common schools, and much more of Providence, we have managed to escape ruin more than once, at an enormous cost of money, and more than money, in a nation conducted on this democratic principle. Such reverence do we pay to political equality, and the end we have attained is worth all the cost!

But will one act in private business as if men had equal knowledge, faculty, talent, genius or force of character? Will one try to conduct the iron foundry as he would a caucus, or manage the printing-house after the style of the town-meeting? In fact, in this America, where a career is so open to talent, our political equality is matched with a strict aristocracy in business. Ability on top, the leaders to the front, if a railway is to serve the public well, or the

cotton and woolen mills are to clothe men cheaply!
No talent is rarer than the ability to conduct successfully a great industry with the autocratic power
that is for the good of all. The most rampant American in politics has the practical sense to confess,
admire, and follow "business faculty" when he sees
it. "One man is as good as another" is only true in
the industrial world with Patrick's wise amendment,
"Faith, and a good deal better." The profit-sharing
system leaves undisturbed this natural aristocracy,
which we find fully developed in our republic. It
respects the plain superiority of head over hand, as
good for both. It preserves all the motives to enterprise in the employer which now rule him and call
out his full power. But it respects these same motives
in the wage-earner, and gives him, too, a reason for
playing his part like a man, in a true partnership.
When Edme-Jean Leclaire was dividing his first
bonus to labor in 1843, Thomas Carlyle was thus
writing: "A question arises here: Whether in some
ulterior, perhaps some not far distant stage of this
'chivalry of labor' your master-worker may not find
it possible and needful to grant his workers permanent *interest* in his enterprise and theirs? So that it
become in practical result what in essential fact and
justice it ever is, — a joint enterprise; all men, from
the chief master down to the lowest overseer and
operative, economically as well as loyally concerned
for it; — which question I do not answer. The answer near or else far is perhaps, Yes; — and yet one
knows the difficulties. Despotism is essential in most
enterprises. I am told they do not tolerate 'freedom
of debate' on board a Seventy-four! Republican
senate and plebiscita would not answer well in cotton

mills, and yet observe there too, freedom, not no-
mad's or ape's freedom, but man's freedom; this is
indispensable. We must have it and will have it!
Reconcile despotism with freedom: — well, is that
such a mystery? Do you not already know the way?
It is to make your despotism just. Rigorous as
destiny, but just, too, as destiny and its laws. The
laws of God: all men obey these, and have no freedom at all but in obeying them. The way is already
known, part of the way, — and courage and some
other qualities are needed for walking on it." [1]

The problem thus set by Carlyle, the man of
thought, — the union of aristocracy and democracy in
industry, — was worked out by Leclaire, the man of
action! The difficulty of reconciling the natural and
necessary aristocracy of the ablest brains in business
with the true democratic sentiment that rests on the
great and inspiring thought of our common humanity
and brotherhood is solved in no small degree by the
system of industrial partnership. On the justice
which it does to these two great facts and sentiments
of our nature I base my confidence in its steady diffusion, content to leave to time and experience the determination of the extent of its usefulness.

Profit sharing has this great recommendation to
the employer: it is entirely in his own hands. He
must begin it. He may form and reform it, to suit
his industry; and he can continue it or end it, as he
is satisfied, or not, with the results. This being so,

[1] *Past and Present*, Bk. IV. ch. v. Dr. Gerhart von Schulze-
Gaevernitz has not overestimated the political and social influence of the Censor of the Age : he gives two hundred pages of
exposition to Carlyle in his valuable work on England entitled
Zum Socialen Frieden.

there is now no good reason why he should not at
least understand its principles and make himself acquainted with its record. It is full time that the
employing class, as a whole, should do something
more toward the fundamental and rational settlement
of labor troubles than simply to resist organizations
of workingmen conscious of their power, but not yet
wise enough to use that power fairly. We rightly
condemn the obvious excesses of the Knights of Labor; but even-handed justice will inquire what the
aristocracy of the industrial world are doing to make
the Knights of Labor superfluous. Let the salt of
this world prove its saltness by its refreshing and
saving power! To the thinker, before whose bar
every man of action must in the end appear, to justify
himself and his works, an employer content with simply opposing the follies of "organized labor" has lost
his savor. Only a change of head and a change of
heart will save him from condemnation by that public
opinion to which master and men are alike subject.
The duty of the employer to-day is plain, to take wise
forward steps and do his share in the evolution of
modern industry. Such a step is the industrial partnership, which keeps the workman in sight all through
the whole business year, puts into his vocabulary the
inspiring word "profit," and rewards his zealous pains
with a dividend measured by his wages. Such a step
has paid, in every sense, in the great majority of
actual instances. It pays, since in the industrial
world, as everywhere else in human concerns, "All
are needed by each one."

II. Recent Progress in Profit Sharing.

The recent establishment in the United States of the Association for the Promotion of Profit Sharing, which now publishes a small quarterly periodical called "Employer and Employed," renders unnecessary in this place a detailed account of the considerable progress of Industrial Partnership in the last four years. Of the periodical just named, two numbers have been issued containing among other matters the constitution and the list of members of the American Association; lists of profit - sharing firms in England and France; reviews of the situation in France, England and Germany; a full report of the last annual meeting of the N. O. Nelson Manufacturing Company at Leclaire, Ill.,[1] and an abstract of Mr. T. W. Bushill's evidence before the Royal Labor

[1] The resolutions passed by the employees on this occasion should not be omitted here : —

"*Resolved*, That we record our increased confidence in and appreciation of the business principle and business practice of coöperation.

"*Resolved*, That, since seven years of experience under the system has resulted not only in the prosperity and exceptional growth of our company, but in an actual distribution of the benefits among the men at the bench as well as among the capitalists, we commend the plan as a harmonizer of the interests and views of both classes, and as a powerful agent for the solution of the old and stubborn problem presented by the antagonism between capitalists and laborers.

"*Resolved*, That, since it has brought us to shorter working days, for the standard day, with the added benefit of an interest in the company's profits, and an opportunity not elsewhere enjoyed for investing our savings where there is a direct relation between the profits on our investment and the quantity and quality of the work we do, we observe with pleasure the disposition of railroad men, and other large handlers of capital, to adopt

Commission. In its successive issues "Employer and Employed" gives detailed reports of the more notable instances of profit sharing in America and Europe, and reviews the important literature concerning the movement. It is distinctively the "organ" of the Association, of which the President is the United States Commissioner of Labor, Carroll D. Wright, — the two Vice-Presidents being Francis A. Walker and N. O. Nelson, and the Secretary-Treasurer, N. P. Gilman, while the executive committee consists of Messrs. R. Fulton Cutting and Alfred Dolge of New York, Henry R. Towne of Stamford, Conn., and George A. Chace of Fall River, Mass., and Prof. F. H. Giddings of Bryn Mawr, Pa. The Association has been established for the purpose of supplying information concerning profit sharing and various other improvements on the wages system, for the benefit of inquiring employers, and in order to advance in several other ways the knowledge and the practice of the system of industrial partnership.

The literature of profit sharing has been increased since January, 1889, by several valuable works, the more important of which are "Methods of Industrial Remuneration," by D. F. Schloss; "Profit-Sharing

the method that has so much of humanity and so much of common-sense to commend it."

Such a judgment pronounced by employees who have had seven years' experience of profit sharing, applied in good faith and constantly developed with an eye to the welfare of master and man, is the best reply to the objections raised by business men who know nothing of the scheme in actual practice, and by critics of two extreme schools, the adherents of the old-style "orthodox" political economy, who look without interest upon schemes of a coöperative nature, and writers of a socialistic bias.

Precedents," by Henry G. Rawson; "The Distribution of the Produce," by James C. Smith, and the French "Guide Pratique pour l'Application de la Participation aux Bénéfices," by Albert Trombert, with an introduction by M. Charles Robert. Articles touching more or less fully upon profit sharing have been comparatively numerous of late in the reviews, and a much larger share of attention has been given to the movement than formerly by the daily and weekly press. In the widespread discussion of remedies for social confusions, and especially for labor troubles, profit sharing had, indeed, received but little notice up to the appearance of Mr. Sedley Taylor's small volume in 1884. My own larger work on the subject coincided in the year of its appearance with the first exhibit of profit sharing at a great exposition, — the Paris Exposition being especially distinguished by its department of social economy, including coöperative production and profit sharing. The exhibit has been kept together as the nucleus of a permanent museum. At the approaching Columbian Exposition in Chicago, one of the series of congresses of the World's Auxiliary will be devoted to industrial partnership.

An increasing tendency is visible in the continued discussion of the labor question to regard with favor such moderate measures as profit sharing. The socialists of America who prefer to take gigantic strides and leaps in theory rather than short steps of actual progress on the path of industrial reform have little to say in favor of the system, which, for the most part, they consider a delusion and a snare, against which the workingman should be on his guard. Others regard it as a very short step toward the socialist régime, too short, indeed, to excite much of their sympathy. To the great body of intelligent people, however, who finally determine public opinion in this country, the sober and conservative profit-sharing movement has been steadily commending itself. At present there is a widely diffused and strengthening body of opinion favorable to the system, in many parts of the United States.

The list of cases of profit sharing in this country which I gave in March, 1889, included 37 firms and corporations. Several of these, as Mr. Schloss and others have properly remarked, were not strictly instances of profit sharing. Among the 37 cases, there have been several instances of discontinuance of the system for various reasons. On the other hand, there has been a considerable increase in the number of houses applying the system; at a very moderate estimate these now amount to 100, at least, at the present time. Among the more important new instances may be named the Bourne Cotton Mills at Fall River, Mass., and the De Vinne Press in New York. Premature publicity is an obvious hindrance to successful profit sharing; for this reason no detailed list of the American houses has recently been published. A firm contemplating the introduction of profit sharing can now easily obtain full information on the subject; after making up its mind to give the system a trial of several years' duration, it should cultivate privacy. Further observation has strengthened my judgment that American profit-sharing firms will do wisely to withhold a part of the bonus for deposit in a savings bank or pension fund, or, best of all, for investment in the stock of the company.

In 1889 I observed that a renewal of experiments

in industrial partnership might be expected in England, after the considerable period of discouragement due to the failure of the noted Briggs colliery case. The last four years have amply confirmed this anticipation. Profit sharing has made a greater advance, in this period, in England than in any other country. According to the list prepared by Messrs. Bushill and Schloss, in September, 1892, there were in Great Britain 4 industrial partnerships, with 400 employees, and 71 profit-sharing firms, with some 15,000 employees. (The compilers of the list adhere to the definition of profit sharing adopted at the International Congress at Paris, in July, 1889, — "An agreement spontaneously entered into by which the workman or employee receives a share of profits determined in advance.") They add that "there are many other firms which give their employees in addition to their wages a bonus the amount of which is not fixed beforehand." Among the more noteworthy firms on this British list are, Brooke, Bond & Co., London, wholesale "tea blenders," with 154 employees; Clarke, Nickolls & Coombs, London, confectionery manufacturers, with 1,000 work - people; the Colombo Iron Works of Ceylon, having their offices in London, with 500 employees; Hazell, Watson & Viney, London, printers, employing 1,200 hands; the New Welsh Slate Company, quarry owners at Festiniog, with 260 hands; the South Metropolitan Gas Company of London, employing about 2,000 men; the London, Deptford and Greenwich Tramways Company, with 104 employees; and W. D. & H. O. Wills of Bristol, tobacco manufacturers, with 1,100 hands.

As a result of a debate on the subject in the House

of Commons in the spring of 1890, a report on profit sharing was presented to the Board of Trade early in 1891, by Mr. J. Lowry Whittle of the Patent Office. This public document (Eyre & Spottiswoode, 4½*d*.) includes little information that is new, but Mr. Whittle thus concludes: "Divested of the eloquence of advocates, the case for profit sharing comes to this, that in a very large number of industries, where employer and employed are on terms of mutual respect, an intelligent painstaking employer will find in this system a contrivance which, although requiring much personal care at first, will ultimately work, automatically, to continue and extend good relations between him and his workmen, to guard against possible mischiefs in the future, and in the long run to materially increase his own profits and his people's well-being."

The most recent list gives 115 profit-sharing firms in France. The French Participation Society continues to aid the movement by the publication of its quarterly bulletin; it still holds to its conservative attitude toward governmental encouragement of profit sharing, which it does not favor beyond the giving preference in public contracts to the houses which allot a share of the profits to their employees. The seriousness with which most French firms take up the system and the patience with which they give it a trial of reasonable length contrasts favorably with too many experiments in the United States.

By the law of May 22, 1888, a government monopoly of the manufacture of tobacco was introduced in Portugal. At the same time, profit sharing was instituted in the four tobacco manufactories then existing; the results in improving the condition of the

employees have been very favorable. These receive
5.1 per cent. of any excess of net product over 3,500
contos reis; all classes of employees participate, and
the working day is eight hours in length.

The last four years have seen no considerable
change in the situation of profit sharing in Germany.
The "Guide Pratique" enumerates 20 cases in Germany and 3 in Austria-Hungary; among the later
instances the most notable is that of the Dollfus-Mieg
Company, the great manufacturing corporation of
Mühlhausen, long famous for its lively interest in the
welfare of its employees.[1]

The "Guide Pratique" further enumerates 5 cases
of profit sharing in Belgium; 4 in Denmark, Sweden
and Norway; 2 in Spain; 6 in Holland; 4 in Italy,
and 1 in Russia.

The total number of business houses now practicing some system of profit sharing is, without doubt,
considerably over 300. These figures indicate the
existence of an economic phenomenon of no small
importance, which deserves the careful study of the
economist. The experience of these 300 firms in the
coming years will doubtless supply many practical lessons of value; but it is hardly probable that the student, who has carefully and candidly studied the record already made up, will need to alter his conclusions
fundamentally. Profit sharing, beyond a reasonable
doubt, is to be one of the forms which the labor contract of the near future will take, in a considerable
number of cases. The weaknesses which numerous

[1] Herr Leopold Katscher has made a condensed translation
into German of my work on Profit Sharing under the title *Die
Teilung des Geschäftsgewinns zwischen Unternehmern und Anges-
tellten.* Leipzig, 1891.

theorists prophesy will be discovered in the system, when once it becomes generally prevalent, still remain to be seen. Thus far, the strength of the appeal which the system makes to ordinary human nature is manifest by the very large percentage of cases where it has been successful.

CHAPTER X.

THE FUNCTIONS OF THE STATE.

WE have considered some of the more important specifically industrial changes to be expected in the near future, which affect chiefly the "working classes." The state socialist passes lightly over such developments of advancing civilization and calls for drastic legislation to reach the desired end immediately. One fault, however, cannot be found with the German state socialist which may well be laid at the door of his American brother, — a disregard of the relations of economic progress and political development. If, from his programme, the German struck off the numerous political reforms demanded, he would doubtless lose much of his interest in it. To the Englishman and the American the political privileges asked-for have long been familiar. The irrationality of German socialism in their eyes resides entirely in its purely economic proposals, of which experience under a republican government has shown the impracticability. The American socialist commits a great mistake if he supposes that the economic reforms demanded by state socialism could be accomplished without great changes in political institutions and general social relations. These would affect all classes and are not distinctively parts of the "labor problem."

Without going into details, it will be sufficient here to note some guiding principles, and to make a few applications to present conditions. The American is not prone to suppose that the limit of the functions of the State has been definitively fixed for all time. He is ready to learn from experience the changes which new conditions require of a republic for securing the welfare of the whole people; but he will not commit the fault of emphasizing more than the German the importance of economic and industrial, compared with political and general social changes. He will not form a purely mythological conception of the State as a power omniscient, omnipotent and morally perfect, the intervention of which needs only to be secured to remedy every social evil.[1] As George William Curtis said in his last address before the Civil Service Reform League, "the American Republic, greatest and best of all republics, has no more power than the Roman Republic by its name alone to secure freedom and wise progress. It is but an instrument, and its beneficent efficiency depends upon the intelligence, character, and conscience of the people who wield it, and upon the wisdom and skill with which it is kept in repair and adjusted to the changing conditions of its operation."

Every general consideration of reason leads the American to expect a steady enlargement of the

---

[1] M. de Laveleye in his last work *Le Gouvernement dans la Démocratie* did well to reject the common fallacy that "society" is an "organism" in the sense of having a life and individuality of its own. Originating in the tendency to personification and the phrase "the social body," he says, this conception "is only a metaphor, and in the social sciences above all we should repeat with Paul Louis Courier, 'From metaphor and from the Evil One, good Lord, deliver us!' . . . Society is only the *ensemble* of relations between the individuals who compose it. Relations are not enough to constitute a person." (Book I. ch. ix.)

sphere and functions of the State, an evolution into something higher, more complex and far-reaching than the present form of government. But this should be a real and unforced evolution, in response to the actual needs of each generation, and determined, not by theoretical considerations and the persistent meddling of the doctrinaire, but by spontaneous social changes, often unexpected by the wisest. The American will attend to the special guarantees for the security of freedom and justice which the great size of our territory and the immense population subject to a central government make requisite. Lincoln's question means far more now than when he uttered it: "Must a government be of necessity too strong for the liberties of its own people, or too weak to maintain its own existence? Is there in all republics this inherent weakness?" One important matter here is the simple size of the governmental machine. The latest report of the Civil Service Commission gives the number of employees in the postal service of the United States in 1891 as 112,800; the number of other employees as 70,688. There has been, says the Commission, "a very startling growth in the number of government employees compared with the growth of population. . . . This growth of a service which can be used for political ends is a rapidly increasing menace to republican government." The existing situation, resulting from the long domination of the spoils system in American politics, offers many reasons for delaying any considerable enlargement of the powers committed to the city council, the State government, Congress, or the national executive. The wise reformer will agree with Mr. Curtis that our first duty is "to restrict still further the executive power as exercised by party; . . . the superstition of divine right has passed from the king to the party, and the old conviction of the law in the monarchy, that the king can do no wrong, has become the practical faith of great multitudes in this country in regard to party. Armed with the arbitrary power of patriotism, party overbears the very expression of the popular will. It makes the whole civil service a drilled and disciplined army whose living depends upon carrying elections at any cost for the party which controls it."

Some reformers, indeed, propose that city councils should assume complete control of street railways, for instance, believing that the whole people will then be so vitally interested in sound politics that a purer city government will at once be the consequence. This notion, however, is purely *a priori*, and it conflicts with experience. If the State is to do anything more for the public than it now does in America, the existing agencies must be first thoroughly purified. In no respect has the lack of a "political sense" been more evident among American socialists and semi-socialists than in their disregard of this necessity. The extension and perfecting of the Australian ballot system and the passage of stringent laws against the illegitimate use of money in elections are parallel steps with the reform in the Civil Service which the statesman sees to be urgent. The vigor of the strong opposition to these reforms would be much increased by multiplying the possibilities of corruption through the extension of the powers of the city council, for example, over gas-works and street railways. No little progress in the direction of civil service reform needs to be made before the American city can safely assume such powers as Birmingham, Manchester and Glasgow exercise with such good effect apparently. The question would remain whether under American conditions a close following of the methods pursued by these cities would be practicable; the chief difficulty, aside from the much wider basis of suffrage in our cities, would disappear with the disappearance of the corruption now disgracefully common.

The assumption by the American city of the manufacture of artificial light, for public uses and for sale to the citizens, is one of the early extensions of the powers now generally exercised which we are safest in predicting. At present, only three considerable cities, — Philadelphia, Richmond, Va., and Wheeling, W. Va., — with seven much smaller cities in the South and West, own and carry on gas-works. Prof. E. W. Bemis, of the Chicago University, has ably stated the facts and the arguments for municipal ownership of gas in the United States.[1] It is probable, however, that the establishment of an electric-light plant will be for some time to come a wiser proceeding for the American municipality than the assumption of the manufacture of gas. The difficulties of administration and the exposure to corruption are here much less. No fewer than 125 towns and cities now manufacture their own electric light, and their experience, thus far, is more favorable, financially and otherwise, than is the case with municipal gas-works. The analogy of municipal water-works, a system widely prevalent in the United States, appears to am-

[1] See his monograph on the subject in the publications of the American Economic Association, vol. vi., Nos. 4 and 5, and a supplementary article entitled, "Recent Results of Municipal Gas Making in the United States," in *The Review of Reviews* for February, 1893.

ply justify the ownership and management of gas-works and electric-light plants by the city. The practical obstacle in the way is the corruption to be feared under the existing civil service system; if this were thoroughly reformed, there seems little reason to suppose at the worst that municipal gas-works and electric-light plants would be operated so wastefully as to charge more than private companies.

The ownership and management of street railways by the city is, on the other hand, a step which there seems little reason for advocating in any near future in the United States. If we regard the practical limitation of efficiency in the usual municipal government, we shall be the less inclined to favor municipal ownership and control of street railways when the municipality has already assumed the conduct of gas-works and electric-light plants. In every direction, whether of city, State, or nation, a particular enlargement of the functions already discharged is plainly a question not of absolute right, but of practical proportion, a matter of more or less need, — not a matter of absolute wisdom or folly, or of pure right or wrong. A point is reached, sooner or later, in any of these directions, where individual ownership or control of a certain business, more or less affecting the public interest, is plainly superior to ownership or control by the city, State or nation, with its inevitable disadvantages. Long before this point is reached, there are many cases in which it is matter for argument whether the State or the individual is capable of working with the more efficiency and satisfaction to the public. In these cases the American instinct will decide that the State should make out a very strong case before disturbing individual control, whatever its evils, for these may well be capable of effectual regulation.

The question of extending the present functions of the American State should, for clearness' sake, be kept apart from proposals for enlarging the powers of municipalities. As a matter of fact, the American socialist rarely advocates any considerable extension of the powers of a specific State like Illinois or Alabama; his eyes are fixed on the National rather than the State power. He would nationalize the issue of money and banking; he would have national ownership and operation of railroads, telegraphs and telephones, and he would nationalize the land also. It is in a very different spirit and with far more wisdom that Massachusetts has taken up the policy of state control of corporations and industry within her borders. The policy of supervision and regulation by commissions in the interest of the people has here received a thorough trial with the happiest results. The experience of Massachusetts, beginning with the establishment of a Board of Bank Commissioners in 1851, has down to the present time proved to the satisfaction of the people that they have found the right road on which they need only to walk wisely and persistently to reach every attainable result. The Board of Railroad Commissioners, for example, established in 1869, relies almost entirely upon the force of public opinion to carry out its decisions, when these call for certain acts on the part of railroad companies; "indeed, the board is the best protection that the railroad companies have against hasty and unwise action by the legislature."[1]

[1] Mr. George K. Holmes in *The Political Science Quarterly* for September, 1890. Mr. Holmes' paper on "State Control of Corporations and Industry in Massachusetts" is a very able statement of the results of the system, and it is to be commended

The method of control by commissions, State and National, will probably need to be applied strictly to Trusts. After what has already been said on this matter, in connection with Nationalism (p. 215), I will simply refer the reader to the best discussions in recent economic literature of the very important problem of these great industrial combinations. President E. B. Andrews thus concludes his excellent presentation of "Trusts according to Official Investigations" in the "Quarterly Journal of Economics" for January, 1889: "Those who suppose that trusts, however organized, whatever their field, are as a rule going to tumble of their own weight, have not, we believe, duly studied the changed conditions under which the most modern industry is carried on." Prof. J. W. Jenks gave an able treatment of "The Whiskey Trust" in the "Political Science Quarterly" for June, 1889. His later article in the "Economic

emphatically to the attention of advocates of State ownership of railways and other industries. Mr. Holmes does not overstate the case when he declares that "the ascertainment and publication of facts have been the means by which Massachusetts has solved the problem of regulating corporations and monopolies. . . . The general conclusion warranted, then, is that, by extending the sphere of the State in the way of regulation, inspection and publication of facts, and in maintaining at least the natural monopolies, the evils arising from corporations and from the private ownership of the means of production and transportation may be prevented by discretionary administrative officers. The problem of these evils, to which many writers are giving extreme or visionary answers, has been substantially solved by the political experience of Massachusetts." Massachusetts, it may well be added, has had all the experience the people seem to desire in the direction of unprofitable State ownership of railways, in the cases of the Hoosac tunnel and the Hartford and Erie R. R., from both of which it has retired.

Journal" for December, 1892, on "Trusts in the United States," is a very full statement of all the essential facts, and an impartial consideration of the causes leading to the origin of these associations. He says: "Enough has been shown, in reference to the good influence of the Trust, to make it clear that it would be injurious to the industrial prosperity of the country if the great combinations of capital were to be entirely suppressed. . . . Since Trusts are clearly the normal outgrowth of present industrial conditions, any law or interpretation of law that attempts to suppress them must fail." Professor Jenks, however, like President Andrews, if in a less degree, favors "proper supervision" by the State.

The national government needs to proceed far more cautiously than the municipality or the various commonwealths of the Union in the direction of state socialism. The sound policy of regulation and control of the railways in their interstate relations by commissions has been adopted by Congress, and a good beginning made. Further steps in this direction are undoubtedly as practicable as they are desirable, so long as the duties of the interstate commission are confined to matters where the authority of the separate State commissions is not, and cannot be, adequate. The notion of a federal system of railways, owned by the nation and under the control of Congress, is in a high degree irrational. The recent experience of the French Republic with the Panama Canal is a faint indication of what might be expected in the United States under a system of national railways.

In respect to a much more manageable undertaking, a national telegraph system, what we have to

consider foremost is not the specific ability of the
United States to do a certain thing by itself, but the
question whether, with its already large load of responsibilities and duties, the nation may advisably go
on to assume other functions. The United States
government conducts with tolerable efficiency the important business of carrying the mails. While the
system by no means deserves the eulogy which it
receives from the undiscriminating, it is plainly an
advantage, on the whole, to the entire country that
the mails should be under control of the general government, — especially as they are, in fact, transported
by railways and stages owned by individuals. Some
of the palpable deficiencies of the government mail
system are largely supplied by a telegraph system
privately owned. The case is not sufficiently made
out for government ownership of the latter if we show
that the government could send messages at least as
cheaply as they are sent at present, without incurring
a deficit. The further question must be considered,
whether the service rendered at any price by the government would be as prompt and efficient as that now
supplied by the great corporation which owns most
of the telegraph lines in the country. If the government both carried letters and sent dispatches, with a
monopoly of the entire field, there would be no such
easy corrective, as at present, of its probable shortcomings. In general, it is altogether likely that
regulation, by governmental authority, of telegraph
companies, railway companies, trusts, and every other
variety of business corporations, is much to be preferred to governmental ownership. There will be
ample time to consider thoroughly the plan of ownership when the policy of control has been proved to

be insufficient; this point is yet far from being reached in this country.

Americans must experiment and gain wisdom from experience for America. For if we have a body of undeniable facts in European experience predominating in favor of the government telegraph or railway, a second question at once arises: Are the conditions sufficiently similar here to make it safe to follow this European model? "What do we care for abroad?" was the ingenuous remark of an American Congressman, when the long experience of Europe in regard to cheap money was brought forward in opposition to some "wildcat" scheme of his own. His error was plain enough. Human nature, and gold or silver dollars and paper substitutes for them, are fundamentally the same in their working in Europe and in America. There is no Ohio political economy worthy of respect from intelligent men; there is no Nevada science of finance better adapted to American soil than the knowledge painfully acquired by the greatest commercial nations of the Old World, most of all by the people from whom we have sprung. Such chauvinism has probably seen its most glorious day of spread-eagle and buncombe. But its opposite, a spurious cosmopolitanism, based on a plentiful lack of thought, is very common among the social reformers of the day who cry "Thorough!" They would enthusiastically adopt the English telegraph system, the Swiss referendum, the German national railway, the Hungarian zone-system, and the Australian eight-hour law. On one hand are the snug little island of Great Britain and the cantons of Switzerland, — a country half as large as Maine, — the German imperialism, the Hungarian notions of comfort and convenience in railway travel, and the peculiar Australian population and opportunity. On the other hand, here is a vast domain of federated States, inhabited by a people impatient of control, active in the boundless field open to private enterprise, and now sobering down under a sense of leadership among the nations such as Australia has not known. Before such immense differences in physical circumstance, political constitution, and national temper, we must beware of a superficial cosmopolitanism as well as of a shallow chauvinism. European experience is a part of the total record which we have thoroughly to consider; but any direct imitation of transatlantic methods would be irrational under such a different sky.

They choose, therefore, a hard path in social reform who elaborate a system based in part upon the foreign record of fact, but much more largely upon the pure theorizing of French and German writers, and present each practical matter (such as the municipal electric light) as only one portion of a thorough, comprehensive State Socialism. This system, they cease not to declare, is to be preached and agitated, with vigor and rigor, all along the line, until Collectivism is triumphant and private ownership of the means of production is extinguished. If there were anything of the temper of statesmanship among American Socialists, they would carefully avoid exciting opposition to a particular, definite and limited social improvement by thus proclaiming it an integral part of a doctrinaire system of the widest sweep.

A reform of the first order of urgency in America is that of methods of taxation. Able writers like Prof. R. T. Ely, in his volume on "Taxation in American

States and Cities," and Prof. E. R. A. Seligman, in his various essays in the "Political Science Quarterly" and elsewhere, have exposed none too severely the absurdities and inequities of our present system.[1] The changes which have been made in the last few years in New York, Pennsylvania and Massachusetts — to mention no other States — indicate some of the first steps toward a consistent and scientific method. The main principles of just taxation are familiar to all students of economics, — such as equality of sacrifice, a short list of things taxable, and a land tax as the basis of all other taxes. Soon it will be obvious to many that an exemption of real estate from taxation by the State is desirable in the interest of the local government; that franchises for such monopolies as gas-works, water-works, electric lighting and street railways should be sold to the highest bidder; that personal property should be entirely released from taxation; that an income tax of a moderate amount should be devised; and that taxes on corporations, and on inheritances, direct and collateral, should be imposed. The last two taxes would yield a large proportion of the revenue needed by the State, if not by the city. Beyond question, a large part of the discontent of the present day is due to the unequal incidence of taxation, the result of following methods fully antiquated and seen to be irrational.

The indirect taxation which is the result of the tariff system, high or low, the impartial observer cannot fail to declare should be so adjusted as to avoid favoring any business interest or class of people to the detriment of other interests or classes. The em-

[1] Prof. C. F. Bastable's new treatise on "Public Finance" should be read by every American legislator.

phatic verdict of experience of modern times is to the
effect that the best tariff is that which imposes moderate duties on a few articles. Just as long as an extended list of high protective duties prevails, so long
will every inducement be present for the influencing of
legislators by special interests in illicit ways. Ballot
reform, election reform and civil service reform are
all intimately connected with a tariff reform which
shall remove, so far as practical conditions of government allow, the motives for influencing legislation by
interested individuals or classes. These four reforms,
thoroughly carried out, will remove the ground from
under any "people's party," committed to irrational
ideas of currency and finance. The eight hundred
thousand votes to be credited to the "Populists" in
the late presidential election by no means guarantee
the continuance of the organization or the success of
its principles. Its members will learn that we are
suffering much more at present from an excess than
from a deficiency of legislation of a socialistic tendency. No action of Congress in recent years has
deserved more condemnation than its extravagance in
the bestowal of military pensions; the result has been
appropriations large enough to support a great standing army, and a distinct weakening of honorable unwillingness to receive aid from the government on the
part of persons not in need of it. Many who would
scorn to "come on the town" now receive pensions
from the national government.

Plainly, the future of the American State is not to
be something new and strange, but a steady growth
from what has already prevailed for a hundred years.
We must first seek the purification of existing methods and institutions; then will come their extension,

with good effect, to wider fields. As I have more than once declared, the American mind is very free from practical bias toward the individualism of Herbert Spencer or the socialism of Karl Marx. Exceedingly remote from all our thinking and feeling has been the notion which so many are fond of repeating as the ripe wisdom of all time, that "the State is only a machine for the protection of life and property." Without going to school to Greece and Rome, the instinct of the American people has led them forward on paths familiar to those two nations. The greatest political treatise of antiquity began with a fundamental statement which the American would thoroughly accept. "Every State is a community of some kind, and every community is established with a view to some good; for mankind always act in order to obtain that which they think good. But, if all the communities aim at some good, the State or political community, which is the highest of all, and which embraces all the rest, aims, and in a greater degree than any other, at the highest good." Thus, says Dr. Jowett commenting on this passage in Aristotle, "the ancients taught a nobler lesson, that ethics and politics are inseparable."[1]

Whatever the problems of the present or of the time to come may be, it is not probable that the political sense and the "animated moderation" which have characterized the American people in times past will fail them hereafter. A people which has gone through such a titanic struggle as the Civil War and settled the enormous problem of negro slavery in the South,

[1] So Edmund Burke declared that the citizens of a State form "a partnership in all science, in all art, in every virtue, in all perfection."

may well be pardoned if it looks forward not boast-
fully but serenely to the future and its difficulties.
The problems of America will undoubtedly be much
more like those which harass modern Europe; undoubtedly, as the years go by, the lessons of the Old
World will become of more and more practical value
to the New. But Americans may be pardoned for
believing that theories like socialism, which owe much
of their inspiration to the success of democratic institutions here, will find their solution in America rather
than in Europe. Lowell wrote after our civil war:

> " Earth's biggest country 's got her soul,
> And risen up earth's greatest nation."

This being so, it will not be strange if socialism, like
some other fundamental questions of the modern
world, receives its decisive answer from the American
Spirit.

CHAPTER XI.

THE HIGHER INDIVIDUALISM.

WE have noted the assumption, common in socialistic literature, that individualism implies the selfishness of the person who holds it as a political and
economic doctrine, while the socialist, on the contrary, is a person of generous temper, with broad
and deep sympathies. As a matter of fact, however,
there are two individualisms in the moral sphere, to
be sharply distinguished.

There is a Lower Individualism, which is simply
private selfishness. It has nothing to do with theories
of the right relation of the State and the citizen; it
has no concern for the common weal; it will cheerfully think, if not say, "The public be damned," if,
in the interesting process, its own pockets are replen-
ished; it is purely the mind of the flesh, the spirit of
the brute, the survival of the barbarian under a civilization supposed to be rational and Christian. It is
the same old enemy with which morality and religion
have always had to contend. Naturally, however,
when it pretends to put forth an idea, this will be on
the side of a thoroughly competitive system, — "each
man for himself:" it will practice coöperation only
within its own family, firm or "trust." This doctrine, if it can be so called, is as absurd scientifically
as it is wrong morally.

A Higher Individualism is possible and has long

been actual with at least a few of each generation of mankind. It respects every person as having something of infinite worth in him, and would begin to improve the world by elevating the single spirit, counting no advance permanent that is not based on reformed and cultivated individuals. This method fully deserves the epithet "Christian," derived from "the only soul in history who has appreciated the worth of a man." The teaching of Jesus was profoundly individualistic in its imperative address to the private conscience. Such a spiritual doctrine does not find its natural alliance with a mechanical Socialism. This, with most of its expounders, is materialistic to the core. The Christian spirit is in full harmony with a rationalized Individualism in social life. So inspired, individualism includes voluntary coöperation, the method of modern civilization; and the ideal towards which it tends is Fraternalism, not Paternalism. The inquiry is extremely pertinent: "Have we yet even discovered the resources of an individualism which is not synonymous with selfishness but welcomes and fosters public spirit?" Few wise persons will answer this question in the affirmative.

If we consider briefly a few of the reforms demanded to-day by sober thinkers, we shall see how slight, as compared with the revolutionary processes of Socialism, is the effort needed to carry them out, if a few strong persons will work on the plane of the Higher Individualism. No evil in our cities appeals more forcibly to the kind-hearted than the crowded tenement-houses, such as those at the North End in Boston or in "Cherry Hill" in New York. Vice finds a hot-bed in the conditions of brute-like living which here abound, and many diseases become endemic. Every one who has a particle of philanthropy in him cries out that these evils should be made to cease from off the earth. The end is clear; but what means shall we use? The socialist will dilate upon what Glasgow and Liverpool have done, and urge that Boston and New York at once purchase whole squares, pull down the noisome houses of to-day, and erect, instead, clean and convenient tenements, to be let at low rates. This, however, would be too much like journeying from Chicago to Minneapolis *via* Paris, the Suez Canal and Japan. The Chicagoan would thus reach Minneapolis in time, indeed, if money and patience held out. But a more direct way would be first to discover what persons are responsible, as owners or lessors of these foul habitations; and then to bring home to them as individuals the distress and the crime which they occasion, while drawing profit from such inhuman conditions. Many of these persons sin as much through ignorance as through hardness of heart. One may preach to them their simple duty to keep their houses clean and un-crowded with far more hope of success than he could preach municipal socialism to the citizens, or the city government, of Boston or New York.

If these owners or lessors of bad tenement-houses remain indifferent, and will do nothing, the lash of public opinion should fall upon them. But if this should be of no effect, the men and women who are taught by the Higher Individualism that we *are* our brothers' keepers, to a great degree, can then follow the example of Mrs. Lincoln in Boston. Let them singly, or in small associations, buy or lease one or more city houses in the poorer districts, and care for them in person, or through kindly and capable agents.

A large part of the tenement-house problem is manageable under this simple plan. No kind of charitable work by the well-to-do surpasses in effectiveness this business system, which asks moderate rents for decent tenements, and returns a fair interest on the capital invested to the owner or lessor of the house. Where this plan is not expedient, the Peabody trustees in London, the Improved Dwelling-House Associations in Boston and New York, and such individuals as Mr. A. T. White in Brooklyn have demonstrated the eminent success of a more difficult method. Mr. J. A. Riis, a good authority, believes thoroughly in the compatibility of "philanthropy and five per cent.," — the one as the beginning, the other as the result. "Model tenement building," he says, "has not been attempted in New York on anything like as large a scale as in many other cities; and it is, perhaps, owing to this, in a measure, that a belief prevails that it cannot succeed here. This is a wrong notion entirely."

The tenement-house problem in our American cities is thus fully within the control of a comparatively few persons. In view of the enormous fortunes of our later day, George Peabody's gift of $2,500,000 for the London poor seems small; many persons in these United States could easily surpass his munificence. Yet the sum he gave now affords healthful and pleasant homes at low rent for more than twenty thousand people; and the capital has doubled, thus doubling the resources of the trustees. Very few of the very rich or the moderately rich in the United States would need to be converted to a higher individualism than they now practice, to make this tenement-house problem a thing of the past, so far as money can do it.

City governments, of course, should practice vigorous measures of inspection and sanitation. But the evil can first be checked, and then gradually diminished by the simple methods indicated. A Christian Individualism would at least try to make more conscientious men and women out of the owners of tenement-houses, and not hasten to throw the responsibility entirely upon an impersonal city government. Such private philanthropies as the Fresh Air Fund, the Country Week, and the Children's Aid Society are highly approved agencies for lightening the evils of tenement life.

The labor problem in some of its most difficult phases is within the control of individual employers who have a touch of true philanthropy in their make-up. At present, the firms least disturbed by strikes and other industrial commotions are those which bear in mind that their employees are not machines but men and women, very susceptible to good-will plainly exhibited, and animated by an ambition to make something of themselves if the way is open. The example of employers like the Fairbanks Company of St. Johnsbury, Vt., the Ludlow Company in Massachusetts, the Cheneys of South Manchester, Conn., the Warners of Bridgeport, Conn., the Ferris Brothers of Newark, N. J., and the Illinois Steel Works at Joliet is one which might easily be copied by hundreds of large employers of labor throughout the country; they could thus attain similar happy results in their relations with their men. It is only the will that is lacking. The gospel and the law which should be vigorously declared to employers of labor as a class is not that the whole state of things which renders them possible is to be abolished, and that their great

ability for business is henceforth to count for nothing;
but rather that their present individualism is on a low
plane; that they do not steadily show themselves such
leaders as they might well be; that they fail to rise
to the level of their opportunity; and that their wealth
has grown faster than their disposition or ability to
make the best use of it.

Far-sighted men of business can do much to gradually shape the present wages system into a better
method, which shall distribute the profits of industry
more evenly among all the workers with head and
hand. The ideal in industry is coöperative production. This means that the most capable men will be
satisfied with large salaries for management, and that
the profits of business will be divided among all the
fellow-workers. Very few employers or workmen are
yet educated up to the moral and intellectual level
on which alone such coöperation is likely to be successful. Some method more in harmony, perhaps,
with all the facts, which shall give hand-workers a
gradually increasing part of the profits, is the obvious
educational agency for bringing both the employer
and the employee up to the coöperative standpoint.
Profit sharing has no more distinctive mark than its
appeal to the individual reason and its complete reliance on private initiative. No one should force the
employer to divide his profits with his men. His
conversion is wisely left to those two efficient apostles
of civilization, Reason and Philanthropy. The system will be more widely practiced as a higher type of
character in the industrial world becomes more common. Men like Leclaire, Godin, Laroche-Joubert,
Boucicaut, Van Marken, Bushill, Hazard, Dolge and
Nelson show what is meant here by a well-developed
individualism.

The captains of industry would fight State Socialism to the uttermost, but the one power to which they
will not offer successful resistance is the widening
and deepening conviction of their duty to be as great
in using as in gaining wealth. Let the men of wealth
do as Mr. Carnegie advises, if they prefer to leave
unmodified the general industrial system under which
they have made their fortunes. Let them look about,
each man in his town or city, to find what he can do
in the way of endowing schools of various kinds;
building libraries and stocking them with books;
assisting promising young men and women through
college; establishing hospitals; supporting homes for
the destitute; laying out parks and play-grounds; or
in a hundred other charities and philanthropies which
will be sure to do more good than harm. Let them
establish trade - schools, like Messrs. Pratt, Drexel
and Armour. Let them endow music, like Mr. Higginson of Boston, or theology, like the Scottish Lord
Gifford: let them open new avenues of wise philanthropy by endowing newspapers that shall be clean,
able and independent of party, or periodicals of too
high a grade for a small subscription list to support.
Let them aid research in natural and in social science.
Let them help in the publication of books needed only
by the few, and in the support of men of mind engaged in investigations likely to be of use to many,
but only hindered by the lack of means. In numerous
important directions they can create a demand for
the best things of life by bringing the supply first.
There is always room in sound philanthropy for all
the money that can be spared. The rich man should
seek the close alliance of the man of science and the
man of sagacious humanity, who can do him no greater

service than to show him where to employ his surplus fortune for the public good. They should often insist that, for his own happiness, he give himself and his service with his money. "If to the ethics of labor among us is added the ethics of wealth, if the rich can only take their proper part in the organic life of the American world, then the times provide an opportunity such as never was offered before for the uses of wealth. Never before was the call to service so persuasive to wealth, or the science of service so clear, or the happiness of service so sure." [1] Beyond calculation is the good that could be effected in securing social comfort and progress by the rich who will simply continue and strengthen the present happy fashion of employing a considerable share of their wealth for the common benefit. Every man who follows the laudable custom of giving while he is able to direct his gift aright, and see its good results, is a practical apostle of peace and good-will among men.

It would be but a partial view to suppose that a Higher Individualism is needed only by the rich and the employers of labor. Men who are not politicians in search of votes may plainly report what their eyes see and their judgment tells them concerning their fellow-men who depend upon hand-labor for support. As in every other part of the human world, sheer unwillingness to work and earn their living is here the characteristic of not a few. In the great "army of the unemployed" — to use a favorite phrase of the day — there is material for whole regiments who dread nothing more and desire nothing less than the offer of work, — such work as millions of undeclamatory men are doing, year in and year out, in silent faithfulness.

[1] Professor F. G. Peabody on "The Problem of Rich Men."

These "unemployed" prefer to agitate for a new earth, where indolence shall take precedence, and every industrious person be obliged to support at least one of the talking brethren. A "sweating system" that would make these gentlemen of leisure perspire profusely in honest labor would be an unmixed good. A standing, or sitting, multitude of happy-go-lucky incapables, the survivals of barbarism, are found in every civilized state. They lack the elements of power which have brought or will surely bring comfort to other men. They are weak, untrusty, shiftless, thriftless, and destitute of ambition. The one discontent that they ought to feel most sharply — discontent with their ignoble selves — is quite absent from their minds. Such persons, with no saving salt of individuality, are not few in the most advanced countries. It is the eternal privilege of these foolish ones to be governed by the wise, as Carlyle said. If any of them happily take a turn and mend, — go to work, save and prosper, — they lose their interest in the reconstruction of society for the benefit of the lazy. They have not thus become a part of anything that needs to be reformed, — through their hard work, through their savings, through their ownership of a house, through their foundation of a comfortable home. They have simply followed the old and difficult path of personal regeneration. From being "of no account," they have become somebodies: they are now individuals of potency, on a much higher level than before. The method of human civilization was plainly determined long ago, — the method which requires personal ambition and effort. The capable majority will never abandon this plan or reconstitute society in favor of those who make no vigorous effort for themselves. A helping hand always for those unable to help themselves, for those who do their utmost and fail, — this no true man or woman will think of withholding or refusing. But the strong were never born simply to support the weak. Least of all were they born to copy the methods which have made the weak miserable!

One of the great enemies of a true individualism among workingmen is, too often, the tyranny of the trade-union which would then seem to be organized expressly to discourage ambition, repress personal initiative and bring in the kingdom of the mediocre in all its dullness and flatness. Trade-union regulations concerning the amount and quality of work allowed to be done, the number of apprentices and the general relations of master and men not rarely fill disinterested persons with astonishment. A labor "machine" often appears to have as full swing in these unions as the political machine we all know. Idle declamation and cheap demagoguery are probably as difficult to suppress in the labor-union as in the town-meeting. The sensible workingman, although convinced that the trade-union has been of great service in raising wages and improving his general condition, may well hesitate about frequenting assemblies where the voice of moderation is too seldom heard, and where his own efforts would be as vain as those of the independent citizen at a primary. Not more organization alone, but more rational individualism as well, is the need of the workingman to-day.

For all classes no other word better expresses the spirit of the desirable Higher Individualism than "coöperation." In the socialistic state there would be no voluntary coöperation; there would be no room for the spontaneous formation of associations to carry out plans of philanthropy or reform: the State would overshadow and blight every such attempt; the individual would be pauperized, and the government magnified continually. The enlightened individualism of the man who hastens to ally himself with every other man who has the same general aim in politics, in reform, in charity, in culture, in religion, — the individualism which zealously practices the method of voluntary coöperation, — is to-day a very great and happily increasing power. "The real battle of our time is in the direction of union and of organization, and it is in this direction that hope now lies. The new gospel is not that of leaving every one to help himself, any more than it is that of helping every one: it is that of helping every one to help himself." [1] The "independent" in politics, in reform, and in religion must have backbone enough to leave a party or a church with which he is not in sympathy; but he is just as much an individual when he joins others who are like-minded, to establish with them a new party or a new church. Only through such coöperation can the individual truly find his whole self; only thus will those egotisms be surmounted which obstruct his growth into a nobler personality. Free coöperation is the method of the highest civilization, a method impossible under scientific socialism which would cut at the very root of voluntary association. Where the individual withers and the State is all in all, coöperation would become simply mechanical: it would lose the heart and soul which once made it life-giving to all who engage in it.

[1] *Introduction to Social Philosophy*, by John S. Mackenzie, p. 115.

The message of "Christian Socialism" should be heard with respect, how much soever its apostles may strain their message beyond the facts of the Christianity of the New Testament and those of modern life. But the Christian Individualism is at least as worthy of attention which aims at the building up of each human soul after the method of Jesus. Least of all teachers did the Prophet of Nazareth rely upon external agencies to develop and perfect the inward man. A system that insists predominantly upon governmental machinery as the means, and material prosperity as the end, must be at issue with modern Christianity so far as this has kept the secret of Jesus and heeded his precepts. To find one's soul is still the main object in human life, and we help each other most effectually when we thus help ourselves. We have been well told that the method of Jesus is inwardness, and his secret self-renouncement, — both working in and through an element of mildness. A true church of the Christian spirit must offend the scientific socialist, for it has long since anticipated all that is charitable in his method: it will disparage the machinery he admires, and it will exalt the soul, of which he says little in his zeal for provisions and clothing. Christianity has unwisely interfered at times with the healthful working of natural law for human society, but Socialism would trangress far more, and deserve severe rebuke from the idealist.

Dr. Edwin Hatch has declared that the basis of modern Christian society is not Christian but Roman and Stoical. If this be the fact, we may perceive how many elements are needed in building up the spiritual fabric of civilization and culture. No religion of humanity will be kept sound and free from sentimentalism without a stoical infusion of deep respect for the eternal laws of God. "That serene Power," says Emerson, "interposes the check upon the caprices and officiousness of our wills. Its charity is not our charity. One of its agents is our will; but that which expresses itself in our will is stronger than our will. We are very forward to help it, but it will not be accelerated. It resists our meddling, eleemosynary contrivances. . . . We legislate against forestalling and monopoly; we have a common granary for the poor. But the selfishness which hoards the corn for high prices is the preventive of famine, and the law of self-preservation is surer policy than any legislation can be. We concoct eleemosynary systems, and it turns out that our charity increases pauperism." An individualist and stoic of the low type would not go on to say, with Emerson, that "none is accomplished so long as any are incomplete: the happiness of one cannot consist with the misery of any other."

The follies of Socialism excuse no one for lack of the Higher Individualism. The gospel of membership one in another is still the saving truth. "No man liveth to himself," says Christian Socialism: "Bear ye one another's burdens, and so fulfil the law of Christ." Christian Individualism declares "Each man shall bear his own burden." The reconciliation of all such apparent oppositions is found in human life, which is large enough to need and absorb all the Higher Individualism and all the Spiritual Socialism we can bring to it. To him who joins the scientific temper, that desires to know the facts and respect the laws of human life, to the Christian spirit which would humanize, as far as possible, the sterner con-

ditions and the more destructive forces, — to such a
man a bigoted individualism of practice or theory is
nothing, and a sentimental socialism is nothing. A
new creation, a higher order of mankind, developed
through the advance of knowledge, the progress of
art and the discipline of the spirit, is everything.
In apostolic words we may say, "As many as shall
"walk by this rule, peace be on them;" for they are
"the Israel of God."

CHAPTER XII.

SOCIAL SPIRIT.

No phenomenon of the closing years of the nineteenth century is more promising for the moral and
intellectual future of the race than the earnest discussion of socialism. The Higher Individualism implies
a deepening interest in methods that have long been
followed for the upraising of the poor and the ignorant, and in new methods logically consistent with
these. A sign of the prosperity of civilized man, —
for only those who are successful can be asked to
spend much time in improving the lot of others, —
the active social spirit of our day denotes the greater
humanizing of mankind, and the larger extent to which
practical Christianity is leavening our modern life.
Conscious and deliberate effort by the educated and
the well-to-do to improve, more quickly than has before been found possible, the lot of the less fortunate
and the less capable is a power sure of continuance
and increased efficiency. It is, nevertheless, to be
kept in subjection to reason. When, carried away by
generous feeling or by the whirl of self-conceit, many
go so far as to assure us that improvement in the lot
of the "destitute classes" is the one thing needful for
the salvation of civilized man, we must demur. The
one thing needful, the one thing indispensable, for
the very uplifting of the "destitute classes" themselves is that the progress of civilization continue to

be at least as rapid as it has been in times gone by. If any more considerable improvement in the lot of the poor and the ignorant is to be made, it must be due to a large increase in the speed and vigor of the civilizing process. This cannot be effected unless every road be made plain and smooth before all the individual talent and force of character that modern man possesses. If civilized society should so far lose that sense of proportion in which reason essentially consists as to make its chief object the alleviation of the poverty of the poor, instead of the increase of the wealth of the whole community, it would dig a pit into which both rich and poor would speedily tumble.

The method of civilization, long since substantially determined by centuries of experience, requires certain intellectual qualities, such as sober acceptance of the actual facts of man's environment, trust in human nature as it is, and readiness to follow the lead of unusual talent or character. There is, probably, some kind of reason for the existence of the idle classes in the fashionable world, whose one motive seems to be anxiety for a new amusement more expensive than the last. Leaving these drones and butterflies out of view, and fixing our thought upon the men who in the world of trade, commerce and finance actually lead the industrial development of these United States, — the railway captains, the great manufacturers and the far-seeing bankers; considering, in another direction, those who write the histories, the essays, the biographies, — yes, even the poems and novels of the day; considering, too, the men who devote themselves to the fine arts of painting, sculpture, and architecture; reviewing in our minds the very large number who sustain the cause of religion and philanthropy in a thousand different ways, giving their time, their money, and themselves to humane pursuits; considering, once more, the lonely astronomer in his observatory, the scientist in his laboratory, and every like devotee of pure knowledge; — we see activities and tendencies as worthy of encouragement and fostering as the comfort of the thousands upon thousands of Nature's less than average workmanship. No gospel needs to be preached in this luxurious age more vigorously than the gospel of the "dignity of labor" (a phrase unhappily falling into disrepute among hand-workers themselves). But there is extreme need, also, that the hand should not dream of exalting itself above the head. Modern civilization is not due to mere distension of muscle; it is primarily the fruit of the intense action of the human brain, and the great mass of mankind can follow no surer path of welfare than that of high respect for the patient inventor, the busy manufacturer, and the master of commerce or finance, who may seem to be working purely for their own good, but whose efforts can never benefit themselves without producing an improvement in the lot of their fellow-men.

It is obvious to the clear-sighted, as Dr. Schäffle has insisted,[1] that in our humane concern for the wel-

[1] "An active endeavor to improve the condition of the industrial proletariat is a praiseworthy undertaking of the highest order, but it has not so imperious and overweening a significance that the whole historic development of society should be shattered, and everything else be set at stake because of it. If we bear this in mind, we shall find a complete justification for many things in the existing state of society which are in themselves offensive, and which would not be admissible in the ideal construction of the best systems of Production and Distribution in the abstract. The economic system of any people has to be

fare of those now lagging in the rear of civilization there is danger of exaggerating their importance beyond all proportion. The human race has always had more than a desirable number of the incapable, and the intellectually and morally deficient. In the few millions of years which, the scientists kindly tell us, remain for this round earth, it is not probable that all such persons will be improved out of existence. Poverty, ignorance and inefficiency are relative terms, and until human nature, in its endless variety and complexity, has been entirely remade after one pattern, we must expect infinite variety in the circumstances and conditions of individuals. It is of prime importance in modern life that the moral and intellectual leaders of human progress should be encouraged to continue their leadership in every possible way. Most of all is this needful in democratic countries. It is a matter of vital consequence, not only to the poor but also to the classes that are now well-to-do and successful, that all the resources of talent should be employed to alleviate and brighten our human lot. To this end, every plain dictate of Nature — Nature, the most severe and unrelenting of aristocrats, who pays little heed to "petulant schemes" of equality and uniformity to which sentimentalists would postpone "Time's slow proof" — should be obeyed. None are more deeply concerned than the masses that such obedience be ready and complete.

in harmony with all other sides of the national life, of which, indeed, it is the regulated and orderly system of support and nourishment. It must be subservient to the imperious needs of Religion, Politics, Law, Education, Art, and family life, both socially and for individuals." *The Impossibility of Social Democracy*, p. 113.

No more ingenious scheme, however, than scientific socialism has ever been imagined by the perverse intellect of partial thinkers for diminishing the progress of civilization. The philosophic thinker is repelled by the exaggerated emphasis which they place on the material comfort of the least successful part of the human race. The palace of the multi-millionaire, whose conscience does not forbid his assailing legislators with every argument in his power, is not, indeed, a spectacle to afford comfort to the enlightened observer of contemporary life; but a proposal to strike a dead level for all men between the palace and the poorhouse would not, therefore, be agreeable to him. The palace is an incident in general progress; the phalanstery would be an accompaniment of widespread stagnation. The full-fledged socialist, in America and elsewhere, commonly indulges in unmitigated denunciation of all the rich. He improves upon the motto of Terence so far that nothing human is alien to him, except the man of wealth. Now if we remember the relativity of the notion of wealth and consider that, as a simple fact, the vast majority of the rich people of this country at least have acquired their fortunes by honest and legitimate effort, and that their wealth, in a rough way, corresponds to the amount of actual capacity which they have shown; if we consider, still further, that in acquiring this wealth they have contributed greatly, and of necessity, to the welfare of thousands upon thousands of their fellow-men, we shall incline to a more rational socialism that has some sympathy with the honest rich as well as with the honest poor.

The great body of the American people are neither rich nor poor. They are not exposed to the temptations or disadvantages of extreme wealth or extreme poverty. They are capitalists, to the extent of knowing in some degree what the possession of private property means. They are all the more highly developed human beings because of this possession of capital, — for capital, rightly interpreted, means power and opportunity. With this mass of people the solution of every industrial and social problem finally rests in this country. They are not making an outcry, or clamoring for the discontinuance of many existing institutions. They feel, quite strongly enough, a discontent with their own lot; but their condition renders them quite incapable of such indiscriminate denunciation of the rich as the socialist usually falls into. They are only too ready to perceive the advantages, rather than the disadvantages, of wealth, as compared with that modest competence which leaves personal exertion of a regular character essential. These American citizens, possessed of American ambition, have no desire to level things down to their own standard of comfort; on the contrary, they are determined to level up their own lot to the highest attainable point. Just so fast and so far as this great class, neither rich nor poor, receives the cultivation and refinement of the higher education (and it desires nothing more ardently than the best educational opportunities), will the material and moral problems of advanced civilization obtain satisfactory solution. No socialism, we may be sure, will commend itself to them which virtually denounces leadership by the men who have fully shown their capacity. Where, indeed, is the religion or the philosophy which has ever led men to trust themselves long to guidance by the incompetent?

The fundamental antecedent to any form of rational social betterment must be a willingness on the part of the individual to think upon the lot of other men with a lively and sympathetic interest. Experience shows that a certain degree of material comfort is almost indispensable, with the great mass of mankind, for the manifestation of any considerable degree of such interest. When the simple effort to obtain bread for the day or the year requires the full strength and ability of the individual, there is little room for altruism and small chance of one's putting himself, imaginatively, in the other man's place. So great is the number, however, of the well-to-do in our country, as compared with the number of the positively indigent, that the appeal to the comfortable and prosperous classes to interest themselves, individually and coöperatively, in the welfare of their weaker brethren is, as it should be, incessant. It may be impossible to improve civilization in that extreme geometrical proportion which the eager philanthropist often imagines. None the less do we need to combat steadfastly the native tendency of the prosperous man to be satisfied with himself. He is only too prone to consider the comfort of others as of little consequence if that large self which includes his family is luxuriously appareled, royally housed, and gratified with the obsequiousness mankind is ever ready to exhibit to wealth. But here we have to deal, not with any transient or superficial phenomenon of a passing year or generation, but with that "old Adam," as the theologians once delighted to call it, of selfishness. Yet while the preacher denounces "self" and "sin" as equivalent, the man of science and even the man of philosophy more contentedly recognize that human nature is as it is, and must be taken as it is, and that, in all probability, the theologian, the philanthropist and the preacher would fail miserably in making it over, even according to the highest and brightest ideal in their earnest minds. Condescension and superciliousness toward actual human nature, groping its way toward something better and higher, are out of place. Human nature, as the main feature in the social situation, must be recognized without praise or blame. Its multiformity and complexity forbid the acceptance of the depressing pictures of a monotonous future which socialism has thus far presented.

The scientific temper, both as respects calmness in observation and sobriety in expectation, is one of the factors on which we may safely rely for the rationalization of socialism and individualism alike. The cool and deliberate spirit which, first of all, inquires carefully into the facts of the situation, whether in the world of physics or in the world of human nature, and then infers the lines on which movement may be initiated with profit, in conformity with the past evolution, is an excellent corrective of the temper of the ordinary socialist. He almost invariably gives a very one-sided and unjust picture of our industrial civilization; he contemplates with a jaundiced eye all the unpromising phenomena of the present, despising the happier mood which a fuller view would authorize. The man of scientific spirit will think better of the existing situation, as he compares it with the past; at the same time, he will have a more moderate conception of the possibilities of progress in the immediate future, — the only future concerning which he cares to occupy himself much. He offers us a far brighter prospect of probable achievement in this near future than the socialist. It is curious, indeed, in this century of discovery and invention that the socialist should put so largely to one side the possibilities of social improvement which we may rationally expect from the progress of applied science and inventive skill. He is strangely biased by his propensity to rely upon legislation as an instrument of progress. Surely, one need consider but briefly the history of the last hundred years, to see how small a part legislation has played in the tremendous development of modern society, compared with science, invention and discovery. The merest allusion to the great steps in the amazing scientific and industrial development will here suffice. We may confidently trust ourselves for much of our salvation to further advance in man's mastery over the powers of nature. The first step in such mastery has ever been a submission of the mind to the facts of a universe of law and order. The plainest note of the socialistic agitation of our time is, on the contrary, an obstinate desire to impose on our complicated society — the result of thousands of years of evolution — an ideal scheme, not even thought out with theoretical consistency, and never yet presented in such a practical form as to assure careful thinkers that it would keep in running order for a year in any civilized nation. In the very different prophetic strain to which old Experience hath attained, one may feel safe in anticipating that, however the pace may be accelerated, the future development of civilization will be essentially on the same lines which it has followed in the last hundred years.

One must risk the charge of cant in the discussion of social reform by saying that, after all, the difficulty with the men and women of to-day, rich or poor, is moral rather than economic.[1]   More than once, of late years, it has been declared with great reason, that if men and women were morally fit for socialism, — morally good enough to give such a scheme a chance to work, — there would be no need of setting up the socialistic state, because every advantage which it promises would have been already secured, through the moral elevation of the men and women who would have to constitute that state.   The assertion is quite unanswerable, as a calculation of the probabilities, moral and economic.   We cannot be sure that any socialistic scheme ever yet outlined would succeed in practice.   Socialists who admit this, believe in the necessity for a long preliminary period, largely given to a preparation of the heart and conscience.   But it is altogether probable that, in the course of such a preparation, the full benefits of the fanciful industrial and political scheme would be anticipated.   Despite its enthusiasm for equality in comfort and possessions among the citizens of the ideal State, socialism lays little stress upon morals.   The monotonous emphasis of its advocates is upon the material side of life, and upon legislation rather than upon that slow moral ad-

[1] " It has been reserved for this generation to propagate the absurdity that the want of money is the root of all evil ; all the wisest teachers of mankind have hitherto been disposed to think differently, and criminal statistics are far from demonstrating that they are wrong. . . . A mere increase of material prosperity generates as many evils as it destroys; it may diminish offenses against property, but it augments offenses against the person, and multiplies drunkenness to an alarming extent. While it is an undoubted fact that material wretchedness has a debasing effect, both morally and physically, it is also equally true that the same results are sometimes found to flow from an increase of economic well-being." W. D. Morrison in *Crime and its Causes.*

vancement which in fact conditions all lasting material progress. There is no small force in the declaration that "Socialism is individualism run mad." The saying implies that a scheme is irrational which holds that the main matter is the greatest amount of material comfort for the individual.

Human society has not been ruled by such a law. Whoever is responsible for the fact, — God, or Nature, or mankind, — the advance of the race in knowledge, wisdom and righteousness has been the far more exigent standard. Thousands of individuals may suffer and even perish in the tremendous struggle for existence, following the unseen but imperative leading of the power that makes for knowledge, wisdom and righteousness, — we can only say, "So it has been, and so it must be." There is a Calvinism based on natural science and human history which we may not decline to receive. Let us temper the severities and cruelties of our lot with all the charity and kindness that we can muster; we cannot deny these. Yet not man but God declares the lines on which humanity must advance. "A god it is who fixed the goal;" a god it is who decrees the way. The one right and reasonable attitude of man is to bend his mind to patient study of the facts and laws of a God-ordained universe, seeking to derive strength and mastery by submission to the forces of nature and of the spirit, very sure that social betterment lies on the difficult line of obedience and righteousness, not over the flowery paths of the assertion, comfort and indulgence of the lower self.

They have a very inadequate view of the scope of human nature who suppose that any social ideal can take the place of religion, or remove the motives of

human hope entirely from the hereafter and the elsewhere, and plant them in a future, near or remote,
upon this earth. The absence of religion from socialism is not sufficiently explained by the opposition of
the Christian church, naturally a conservative power,
to hasty projects of social reform. However much
the Christian church has erred in the past through
the extreme conservatism of the religious sentiment
and other causes, it has been a profoundly social
rather than individualistic force. Undoubtedly its
ideal for human life has been greatly modified, and
every trace of the asceticism of the church of the
Middle Ages will disappear: altogether undesirable is
the monastic conception of existence in the eyes of the
man of the nineteenth century. On the other hand,
the ideal of socialism must appear materialistic even
to men engrossed in the furthering of a civilization
that tends strongly toward the comfort of the flesh
and profusion of luxury. There are deeper wants in
human nature than those of which socialism makes so
much account, — moral and spiritual appetites which
it scarcely notices. With all its faults and follies on
its head, the Christian church is yet more true to the
undying aspirations of the human soul than the socialistic scheme. The Socialism of to-day, as a whole, is
destitute of moral enthusiasm, and its apostles show
little religious conviction that they must rise "to do
the task He set to each, who shapes us to His ends
and not our own."

The words "Kingdom of God" still express a com-
manding truth for social reformers. In constant
progress toward the ideal they denote, purified by
wider knowledge and deeper insight, stand the hope
and the salvation of mankind. Complete attainment

and full satisfaction are impossible, but devotion to
the cause of humanity is ever a duty and shall come
to be more and more a joy. Continuous social reform in the name of the Most High God of the actual
universe is the religious commandment for our age.
All the moral earnestness, all the self-forgetting devotion, all the self-sacrificing enthusiasm for humanity
that we can draw from any source, — we need them
in the strenuous and unremitting task! Each generation must do its part. No generation, present or to
come, may rationally think for a moment that the
labor is finished and the duty done. Every generation
will find a sure support in the inexhaustible inspira-
tions of a religion of humanity.

CHAPTER XIII.

THE WAY TO UTOPIA.

UTOPIA was first made known by "Sir Thomas
Moore Knight sometyme Lord Chauncelor of England, a man of singular vertue and of a cleare un-
spotted conscience, (as wittnesseth Erasmus) more
pure and white then the whitest snow, and of such an
angelicall witt, as England, he sayth, never had the
like before, nor never shall againe, universally, as
well in the lawes of our Realme, as in all other
sciences right well studied." His report of that bliss-
ful country has been pronounced the only work of literary genius of the age in England, and it has not
lost its charm in three hundred and seventy-seven
years. Ralph Robinson, who most happily translated
it from the original Latin into the English of Edward
VI., was justified in entitling the book "a frutefull,
pleasaunt and wittie worke of the best state of a publique weale, and of the new yle, called Utopia."

Concerning the wit of the "Utopia," there can be
no question, in the later as in the earlier sense of the
word. More was a man of infinite humor, joined
to an unaffected piety. He could ascend with a
smile the shaking scaffold, from which the smallest
time-serving would have saved him, saying, "I pray
you, I pray you, Mr. Lievetenaunt, see mee safe upp,
and for my cominge downe lett mee shift for my
selfe." "After his prayers sayed, hee turned to the

executioner, and with a cheerful Countenaunce spake unto him, 'Pluck upp thie spirittes, man, and be not affrayed to doe thine office, my neck is very short. Take heede, therefore, thou scute not awrie for savinge thine honestie.'" The humor which did not forsake him before the headsman's axe plays incessantly over the pages of his narrative of the travels of Raphaell Hythlodaye. The mariner thus surnamed ("skilled in non-sense") had "sailed indeede, not as the mariner Palinure, but as the experte and prudent prince Ulisses; yea, rather as the auncient and sage philosopher Plato." He had toiled over leagues of tropical desert, until his eyes beheld the very pleasant land "Nusquama," or "Utopia," which, being interpreted, is "Nowhere." Amaurote ("the dimly seen") is its chief city, by which flows the Anyder ("waterless" river). The Utopians have for allies the Nephelogetes ("cloud-dwellers"), and for enemies the Alaopolitans ("citizens of Blind Man's Town").

Sir Thomas was not a professional reformer of the type the world has come to know well, who, with all his virtues, has had the gift of humor denied him by the immortal gods, and whose stubborn skull is more impenetrable by a jest than the traditional Scotchman's. An ornament of the New Learning of his day, cultured, accomplished, traveled, a statesman, philosopher, scholar, man of faith, and soul of honor, Sir Thomas More was not built on the narrow scale of most of the idealists who would reconstruct society. He has expressed himself in every degree of seriousness and playfulness in his famous book. Nobly indignant when he describes the conspiracy of the rich against the poor in Henry Seventh's reign, he uses pleasant satire and easy banter again and again in his

exposition of the Utopian laws and customs. The
"Utopia" is a masterpiece of wit, written by a man
who knew the world, and sent forth this book, inspired by Colet and Erasmus, not as a sure prophecy
of the form civilization must take in a thousand years
or less, but as a quickener of human sympathy and a
stimulus to thought and to faith in man.

More's fine fancy and playful humor have made his
plea for human brotherhood immortal. His far-seeing eye anticipated more than one of the greatest conquests of the modern spirit. Free public education
for both sexes; the liberty of every man to worship
God according to his own conviction; peace between
nations; humanity in penal laws; healthful dwellings; well-appointed hospitals; abundant recreation;
shorter hours of labor for all classes, — in these great
matters, his Utopia has been a model to our most advanced civilization. Still we lag in the rear of the
"philosophical city" in more than one point wherein
Time may yet justify Sir Thomas' sagacity, his principles being as sound, apparently, as in the matters
just named, and the difficulties no more insuperable.
Not yet is the intellectual life as much an object of desire and attainment as in that thoughtful land. For,
before the six hours' work which is sufficient to procure comfort for all, "it is a solempne custome there
to have lectures daylye in the morning, where to be
presente they onely be constrained that be namely
[especially] chosen and appoynted to learninge. How-
beit a greate multitude of every sort of people, both
men and women, go to heare lectures, some one and
some another, as everye mans nature is inclined."
Thus do the Utopians show that though "when nede
requireth," they are "liable to abide and suffer much

bodelie laboure; els they be not greatly desirous and fond of it; but in the exercise and studie of the mind they be never wery. . . . For whie, in the institution of that weale publique, this end is onelye and chiefely pretended [put forward] and mynded, that what time may possibly be spared from the necessary occupacions and affayres of the commen wealth, all that the citizeins should withdraw from the bodely service to the free libertye of the mind and garnisshinge of the same. For herein they suppose the felicitye of this liffe to consiste."

Not yet has religion risen among very many to the faith of "the moste and the wysest parte " of the Utopians. These "beleve that there is a certayne godlie powre unknowen, everlastinge, incomprehensible, inexplicable, farre above the capacitie and retche of mans witte, dispersed throughoute all the worlde, not in bignes, but in vertue and power. Him they call the father of al. To him alone they attribute the beginninges, the encreasinges, the procedinges, the chaunges and the endes of al thinges. Neither they geve any divine honours to any other then to him."

In Utopia is no want. All classes dressing alike; laboring the same number of hours or to equal fatigue; all skilled in agriculture, and knowing a trade beside; housed in homes that are wholesome and well provided with gardens; changing their residences every ten years, and alternating between city and country, according to need; taking their meals, thirty families together, in a common hall; condemning the criminal to temporary bondage on the meaner labors, yet liking rather to reward virtue than to punish vice, and believing reformation the end of all punishment; making divorce difficult "bycause they know this to be

the next way to break love betwene man and wyfe, to
be in easye hope of a new mariage;" holding "warre
or battel as a thing very beastly, — and yet to no
kinde of beastes in so muche use as to man," — and,
therefore, to be detested and abhorred, — it is not
strange that the happy Utopians "have but few
lawes," and that they "utterlie exclude and banishe
all attorneis, proctours, and sergeauntes at the lawe."
In this favored country there are not two kinds of
justice, — "the one meete for the inferior sorte of
the people, goynge afote and crepynge lowe by the
grounde and bounde down on every side with many
bandes; . . . the other a princelye vertue which like
as it is of much higher majestie, then the other pore
justice, so also it is of much more libertie, as to the
which nothing is unlawfull that it lusteth after."

The Utopians "imbrace chieflie the pleasures of
the mind. . . . The chiefe parte of them they thinke
doth come of the exercise of vertue and conscience of
good life." What modern clergyman, hearing of these
things, does not sympathize with that "vertuous and
godly man, a professour of divinitie," whom Sir
Thomas, in his introductory epistle, pleasantly represents as being "excedynge desierous to go unto
Utopia, . . . to the intente he maye further and increase oure religion, whiche is there alreadye luckelye
begonne, . . . yea, and that he himselfe may be made
bishoppe of Utopia!"

Unfortunately, neither Sir Thomas More nor his
"righte welbeloved" Peter Giles was mindful in season to inquire of Raphaell "in what part of the newe
world Utopia is situate." When that far-traveled
man was, of his own accord, touching upon this matter of topography, "one of Master Mores servauntes

came to him and whispered in his eare," and another
of the company, "by reason of cold taken . . . a
shippeborde, coughed out so loude that he toke " from
Peter's hearing "certen of his wordes." In an actual, very un-Utopian world, Sir Thomas More, that
son of truth and courtesy, came to the block, and
Henry VIII. went forward unrebuked on his primrose
path of consecutive Mormonism. Hythlodaye took
his voyage to Utopia again, to return no more. Who,
then, can supply the defect, and instruct us "not
onely in the longitude or true meridian of the ylande,
but also in the just latitude thereof, that is to say in
the sublevation or height of the pole in that region "?
Where lies that realm of justice and mutual kindness?
Surely, it is not now in America, where More's sailor
would seem to have located it; for we have not heard
of it here, in the Northern or the Southern country.

Thoughts of the millennial state now occupy many
minds, — even those that have been more wont to
inquire the road to Arcady than the way to Utopia.
The poet and the novelist turn socialist. Destitute
of Sir Thomas More's qualifications for the journey,
they lack his modesty as well. "As I cannot agree
and consent," so he wrote at the close of Hythlodaye's
narative, "to all thinges that he saide, beyng els without doubt a man singularly well learned, and also in
all worldelye matters exactly and profoundly experienced, so must I nedes confesse and graunt that many
thinges be in the Utopian weale publique whiche in
our cities I maye rather wishe for then hope after."
This is the utterance of a true philosophic spirit, filled
with sincere love for mankind, but not destitute of
historic sense, a clear judgment of probability, and
the gift of humor. Without these qualities, the seek-

ers after Utopia err widely, and come to fantastic and unhuman lands. The confidence of such ill-equipped explorers is too often in inverse proportion to their outfit.

The building of ideal commonwealths is, indeed, the favorite pastime (if indeed it has not become an industry) to-day of many a hasty prophet who will not so far compliment our existing social and industrial order as to seriously try to understand it. Some of these bards could not pass an examination in the Constitution of the United States. Six or twelve months are quite sufficient time for them to run up the pretty gingerbread-work of the walls of their Utopia, to pave the streets with candy, and set fountains of sweetened honey running in all the public squares. The expense of the journey to the pasteboard city is made very low, and every man may command a copy of an infallible guide-book. The way is so broad, we are assured, that the greatest multitude could not extravagate therefrom. All the hard peas, in the shape of commandments of personal character, are carefully boiled by the leaders of these crusades before they place them in their followers' shoes. Pullman cars will soon be ready for them, when the ties and rails are laid in the shape of laws of legislature and Congress and Parliament; then the blessed city will easily be reached by express train.

"Is this Jerusalem?" the little children in Peter the Hermit's crusade were wont to ask each evening, after a few days' march, as they sighted a new town. "No, poor children," as Matthew Arnold wrote, "not this town, nor the next, nor yet the next, is Jerusalem. Jerusalem is far off, and it needs time and strength and much endurance to reach it. Seas and mountains, labor and peril, hunger and thirst, disease and death, are between Jerusalem and you." Altering but a few words, we may proceed with the quotation: "So, when one marks the ferment and stir of life among State Socialists of every degree at this moment, and sees them impelled to take possession of the world, and to assert themselves and their own actual spirit, one is disposed to exclaim to them: '*Jerusalem is not yet.* Your present spirit is not Jerusalem, is not the goal you have to reach, the place you may be satisfied in.'"

But where lies the road to Utopia, which strong men, not ashamed to confess their love for the ideal, may take with modest confidence, and follow to profit? We may learn somewhat if we consider how far Sir Thomas More's chart has been found, after four hundred years' experience, to be a correct prophecy of human progress. The intervening centuries have so far justified his faith that we may well believe him to have been on the wrong track when he attempted several directions wherein civilization has departed from his Utopia. We have established religious toleration; we have extended free education; we have abolished slavery; we have obliterated the inhuman laws that hung a man for theft as for murder; we are trying to make the reformation of the criminal classes the chief end in punishment; we have erected representative governments; we have reduced the hours of the laboring day, by custom or by law; and we have restrained the short-sighted selfishness of employers. These reforms, to name no others, which Sir Thomas anticipated in principle, if not in detail, have passed through their Utopian phase, to become incorporate in modern civilization. Many another reform remains to be accomplished, at which the Philistine of to-day can only fling the contemptuous epithet "Utopian." The stupidity of mankind has chosen this adjective especially to mark the fantastic, the chimerical, and the utterly impracticable: but there are many very sober works of the human mind, with which the most orthodox branch of the great Philistine sect finds no fault as irrational, that have a far larger proportion of error to truth than More's great imagination. Mankind is most of all obtuse in recognizing the characteristic note and tone of genius, especially when it is so fine and playful as in the romance of Nowhere.

Sir Thomas, with that rare candor of his, would be quick to confess, could he see this present world, that in many respects it has far surpassed his Utopia, and is more wonderful than his strangest dream. Could he have even fancied a nation of which, thanks to natural science and inventive talent, this can be said, that its whole capital in 1830 was not equal to the sum spent in 1880 simply on gathering in the crops? Yet this is what Mr. David A. Wells has to say of the United States in his report of "recent economic changes." Considering this marvelous fact and many others like unto it, and observing that human society has grown more multiform and complicated with the centuries rather than more simple and uniform, Sir Thomas would cheerfully acknowledge that, in more than one great feature, he had wrongly sketched Utopia. He would amiably admonish those who imitate the faults in his pattern, rather than draw inspiration from his principles.

The way to Utopia does not lie on the dead level of uniformity. Nature, for whom we should feel much more respect than for the whole company of

builders of imaginary commonwealths, from Plato to
our own day, has certainly not made all mankind from
one mould. Any scheme of society, let it issue from
the wisest brain, that builds the ideal state on the
principle of monotony is immeasurably less natural
than the present diversity, in itself intellectually pleasing and morally desirable. The modern spirit properly rejoices in variety; the mind and the conscience
have no surer stimulant than the sight of degrees of
attainment and excellence. The Utopian fashion of
garments, which is one "throughoute all the ilande
(savyng that there is a difference betwene the mans
garmente and the womans, betwene the maried and
the unmaried)" and which "continueth for evermore
unchaunged," grates as much on the sense of beauty
in variety as an "industrial army" does upon the love
of free movement. Whatever one may rightly say of
the shortcomings or the vices of existing civilization,
it corresponds in some degree to the infinite variety
of human capacities and endowments. Builders of
Utopia will build in vain, if they can offer no more
attractive prospect than that presented by the false
notion of the desirability of uniformity. "Semely
and comely to the eye, no lette to the movynge and
weldynge of the bodye, also fytte both for wynter
and summer:" — Sir Thomas may thus eulogize the
garments of the Utopians, but streets full of their
wearers would surely be an abomination to the human
sense of beauty, and a disgust forever to the eye compelled to view a world turned Shaker.

As in dress, so in respect to free play and easy
movement among the individuals that make up society, — uniformity is barbarous, increasing variety
and complexity are an integral part of civilization.

The mechanism of an army, which carries captive the dreamer's imagination, revolts wiser minds when they think of its dead monotony and the crushing weight it lays upon individuality. A life of the strictest regimentation for twenty-four years of early manhood, — what an existence to offer every child of this century, rich in its fair variety! Men and women, indeed, weary of the sharp struggle for bread, go and live among the most successful communists the modern earth has known; they take the Shaker garb and walk for months the placid round of the Shaker discipline. But intellectual torpor falls upon them in this unnatural microcosm; the mind rebels against a scheme that works to the preternatural production of stupidity, and the proselytes flee back to a world which has at least one virtue — it is alive.

If modern life, freely developed, had a plain tendency to uniformity of talent, character, and achievement among men, the socialist would have a justification for his arbitrary leveling of all remaining diversities. If the equality rational men should strive after is an equality of fortune and furniture, then the builders of Utopia have been right, and the development of civilization has been disastrous. But here, as in many other directions, all mankind is wiser than any individual man. Our existing civilization in its finest development has not asserted the principle of equal *reward*, but the principle of equal *opportunity* for every man and woman. An open career for talent: then let the ablest win the prizes, showing forth the genius that is in them, the benefit of which cannot possibly be confined to themselves alone. Impose upon the strong and successful the Christian duty of providing hospitals for the wounded

and defeated in life's warfare; but do not ask them
to forsake the field, and let the battle with ignorance
and poverty be lost, while they nurse the idiot and
the infirm! Uniformity of lot is one false guide-post
pointing to Utopia, equality of reward is another.
This kind of socialism has been built from above
downward. Beginning with a very "high priori"
notion in his own limited mind, the socialist lets this
house down from the clouds. He is disgusted with
the dirty earth when his airy construction reaches it,
and calls it every manner of bad name. The common
breezes of human reason and feeling blow upon that
house, and lo! where is it? There is not the slightest reason why one should apologize for human nature
to the socialistic theorist. The fault is in his own
biased mind, his own narrow view.

Actual human nature, as it has developed during
tens of thousands of years of life here on this solid
earth, is, in all probability, a better piece of work
than any amount of human wit could have made it.
Its greatest apparent vices lie close to its most approved virtues. Selfishness is not far removed from
a just self-respect; and self-denial would be impossible, were there no strong forces of individualism in
us, needing not extirpation but restraint. In attack-
ing private property the socialists make their worst
blunder; if successful, they would lead mankind fa-
tally astray from the right path to Utopia. A large
part of the human race is even yet destitute of that
invigorating and edifying moral discipline which private ownership implies and demands. The virtues of
carefulness, foresight, and self-restraint which the
accumulation of a modest competence requires; the
virtues of truth and honesty and regard for other

men's rights which the law of *meum et tuum* inculcates, — are very fundamental in the manhood developed by long ages of civilization. A new moral
type would need to be evolved, if human nature were
exposed to the relaxing influences of a socialistic
régime wherein the plainest duties of to-day — such
as thrift, foresight and respect for the property rights
of others — would have no reason for existence.

The history of institutions indicates the parallel
growth of the monogamous family and the right of
private property. The believers in free love and free
lust naturally gravitate to the socialistic party. The
burden of proof lies upon the socialist to show that
the virtual extinction of private possessions and the
inevitable weakening of certain virtues now essential
to civilized society would not probably bring about
sexual communism. Private property and the monogamous family — this latter the greatest conquest,
Goethe said, which mankind has yet made over the
savage — have their roots deep in the same soil of
thought and sentiment. Neither has yet been disturbed but to the great injury of the other.

Utopia, if we may trust the experience of all the
later centuries, does not lie in the direction of the
political oligarchy or bureaucracy which socialistic
schemes necessarily imply. Nothing is more infantile
in recent socialism than the innocence with which it
would set aside the hard-won triumphs of the democratic sentiment, and all the careful systems of checks
and balances which statesmen of the highest sagacity
have seen to be necessary to the preservation of political freedom. The American socialist waves his
magic staff in air, and President, Senate, Supreme
Court, disappear. State lines, State rights, and

State responsibilities vanish; and for the security of the individual against dictators or oligarchies we have only the confident assurance that all the precedents of tyranny will be reversed in the millennial time. Social chaos quickly followed by Cæsar would be the far more likely succession.

Let us introduce a little modesty into our prophecies; let us pay moderate regard to human nature as it is, and not ask it to transform itself in fifty years or less; let us cease to lay out the road to Utopia at a right angle to the line which human progress has thus far followed. What, after all, do we desire for every man but the opportunities of ample and pleasurable life which many men now have, thanks to ability, industry, perseverance, thrift, self-denial, and self-help, on the part of generation after generation? Human progress were a weak thing, could not its *speed* be accelerated somewhat, and the moral and material happiness of the majority be multiplied at a rate beyond that of the past. But human progress were just as much a vain thing if its *method* could be changed at once, and moral tone be safely taken from it by the substitution of reliance upon the State for reliance upon individual faculty and personal virtue. There was never a more purely mythological creation than "The State" of the American socialist, — omnipresent, omniscient, omnipotent. What the actual State is, with its limited functions, we have only to use our eyes to see. The national civil service was long abandoned as loot to political workers. The American municipality in most cases has not even kept its streets clean. Only a small portion of the Kingdom of Heaven cometh through legislation. The Kingdom comes slowly, far behind the hot pace of our desires,

through hard work of hand and head, and that stern-
est of experiences, the moral discipline of the will.
To the working classes of to-day the advocate of
Utopia has, for instance, no more imperative message
to deliver than the commandment of abstinence from
drink and tobacco. The sums that could thus be
saved in the United States would plant a hundred
thousand happy families every year in homes of their
own, far more to be desired than the choicest corner
lots in an impracticable Boston of the year 2000 A. D. !

Industry, thrift and temperance, — these be very
rude and homely virtues, ye right worshipful doc-
tors and illustrious grand masters of socialism, by the
side of your airy castles of indolence and affluence
erected by act of Congress. But, homely and rude
as they are, they have done many a good work: they
have procured for mankind a long list of solid comforts, and their power has not been exhausted, while
your fantastic commonwealths have risen and disappeared by the dozen. One must yet sympathize very
heartily with the disgust the working-classes feel for
those who come from homes of luxury to preach temperance and thrift in the intervals of their devotion
to the claims of fashion. There are many kinds of intemperance, and these preachers are often forcible
examples of some of the worst.

A number of steps in the direction of Utopia have
been indicated in this volume. It is a perpetual journey, and not all of these steps together will bring us
to complete felicity. Nevertheless each step will
bring us farther on the way. We may wisely hope
and trust that better conditions and shorter hours of
labor will gradually prevail; that a more equal division will be made of the profits of industry; that a

closer coöperation will be accomplished of the capitalist, the employer and the workman; that sounder systems of taxation will equalize the burden and the ability of the tax-payer; that every family will come to own a home; that education will multiply its pervasive powers through every social grade; that accumulated wealth will be more and more freely used to strengthen and adorn the public life; that science, art and invention will irresistibly combine their offices to humanize and beautify the common lot. To a thousand agencies of good we must look for our progressive deliverance from the evils that beset us.

There is no highway to Utopia, though the approaches be many. Utopia itself is a magical city that rises from its foundations and moves onward as we advance. Little respect for it could we have if it did not thus elude our hands, — as little, possibly, as we should feel for an unprogressive heaven, after a few days' residence! None the less should our march be steadfast toward it over the solid ground of Nature. The ever-becoming "philosophical city," in constant flux from good to better, cannot reach a final best. Our imperfect civilization is in many respects wonderful beyond the scope of Sir Thomas More's highest imagination. So in all probability will our fondest dream be put to shame by the future reality. But that reality will come the sooner because of our dreaming, much more because of our striving; for Utopia is a city

> "Built of tears and sacred flames,
> And virtue reaching to its aims ;
> Built of furtherance and pursuing,
> Not of spent deeds, but of doing."

SELECT BIBLIOGRAPHY.

This list is intended to give but a few titles of the best recent books, mostly issued since 1888, on topics touched by this volume : a brief list of valuable articles in the periodicals is added. "The Reader's Guide in Economic, Social and Political Science," edited by R. R. Bowker and George Iles (G. P. Putnam's Sons. 1891), will be found very serviceable by all students.

Contemporary Socialism. By John Rae, M. A. Second edition, revised and enlarged. Charles Scribner's Sons. New York, 1891.

Socialism New and Old. By William Graham, M. A. D. Appleton & Co. New York, 1891.

A History of Socialism. By Thomas Kirkup. Adam & Charles Black. London and Edinburgh, 1892.

The Quintessence of Socialism, 1889 : and the Impossibility of Social Democracy, 1892. By Dr. A. Schäffle. Swan Sonnenschein & Co. London.

A Plea for Liberty. Introduction by Herbert Spencer and Essays by various writers. Edited by Thomas Mackay. D. Appleton & Co. New York, 1891.

Individualism, A System of Politics. By Wordsworth Donisthorpe. Macmillan & Co. London, 1889.

French and German Socialism in Modern Times. By Richard T. Ely, Ph. D. Harper & Brothers. New York, 1883.

Fabian Essays in Socialism. Edited by G. Bernard Shaw. Walter Scott. London, 1889.

The Coöperative Commonwealth. Revised and enlarged edition : and Our Destiny : The Influence of Nationalism on Morals and Religion. By Laurence Gronlund, M. A. Lee & Shepard. Boston, 1890.

Christian Socialism. By Rev. M. Kaufmann, M. A. Kegan Paul, Trench & Co. London, 1888.

Social Aspects of Christianity and other Essays. By Richard T. Ely, Ph. D. Thomas Y. Crowell & Co. New York, 1889.

Socialism from Genesis to Revelation. By F. M. Sprague. Lee & Shepard. Boston, 1893.

Christian Socialism : What and Why. By Philo W. Sprague. E. P. Dutton & Co. New York, 1891.

Principles of Economics. Volume I. Second edition : and Elements of the Economics of Industry. By Alfred Marshall. Macmillan & Co. London and New York, 1892.

Political Economy. Third edition, revised and enlarged, 1888 : and First Lessons in Political Economy, 1889. By Francis A. Walker. Henry Holt & Co. New York.

Capital and Interest : A Critical History of Economical Theory, 1890 : and The Positive Theory of Capital, 1891. By Eugen V. Böhm-Bawerk. Translated with Prefaces and Anályses by William Smart, M. A. Macmillan & Co. London.

Institutes of Economics. By Elisha Benjamin Andrews. Silver, Burdett & Co. Boston, 1889.

An Introduction to Political Economy. By Richard T. Ely. Chautauqua Press. New York, 1889.

The Scope and Method of Political Economy. By John Neville Keynes, M. A. Macmillan & Co. London, 1891.

Recent Economic Changes. By David A. Wells. D. Appleton & Co. New York, 1889.

The State : Elements of Historical and Practical Politics. By Woodrow Wilson. D. C. Heath & Co. Boston, 1889.

Social Statics, Abridged and Revised ; together with the Man *versus* The State. By Herbert Spencer. D. Appleton & Co. New York, 1892.

State Railroad Commissions. By F. C. Clark. American Economic Association. 1891.

Man and the State. Popular Lectures and Discussions before the Brooklyn Ethical Association. D. Appleton & Co. New York, 1892.

Der Moderne Socialismus in den Vereinigten Staaten von Amerika. By A. Sartorius Freiherrn von Waltershausen. Verlag von Hermann Bahr. Berlin, 1890.

The Labor Movement in America. By Richard T. Ely, Ph. D. New Edition, Revised and Enlarged. Thomas Y. Crowell & Co. New York, 1886.

Guide Pratique pour l'Application de la Participation aux

Bénéfices. Par Albert Trombert. Introduction par M. Charles Robert. Librairie Chaix. Paris, 1892.

Profit-Sharing Precedents. By Henry G. Rawson. Stevens & Sons. London, 1891.

The Distribution of the Produce. By James C. Smith. Kegan Paul, Trench, Trübner & Co. London, 1892.

Exposition de 1889 : Rapports du Jury International. Economie Sociale — Section II. Rapport de M. Charles Robert. Imprimerie Nationale. Paris, 1889.

Congrès International de la Participation aux Bénéfices. Compte Rendu. Librairie Chaix. Paris, 1890.

Report to the Board of Trade on Profit-Sharing. Eyre & Spottiswoode. London, 1891.

Report on the Social Economy Section of the Universal International Exhibition of 1889 at Paris. Prepared by Jules Helbronner. Brown Chamberlin. Ottawa, 1890.

Le Società Coöperative di Produzione. Di Ugo Rabbeno. Fratelli Dumolard. Milano, 1889.

How to Coöperate. By Herbert Myrick. Orange Judd Co. New York, 1891.

Coöperative Life : A Course of Lectures. By M. E. Sadler and others. Coöperative Printing Society. London, 1889.

The Coöperative Movement in Great Britain. By Beatrice Potter. Swan Sonnenschein & Co. London, 1891.

The Wages Question : A Treatise on Wages and the Wages Class. By Francis A. Walker. Henry Holt & Co. New York, 1891.

Methods of Industrial Remuneration. By David F. Schloss. G. P. Putnam's Sons. New York, 1892.

The Conflicts of Capital and Labour. By George Howell, M. P. Second Revised edition. Macmillan & Co. London, 1890.

The Eight Hours Day. By Sidney Webb, LL. B., and Harold Cox, B. A. Walter Scott. London.

The Modern Factory System. By R. Whately Cooke Taylor. Kegan Paul, Trench, Trübner & Co. London, 1891.

Public Finance. By C. F. Bastable, LL. D. Macmillan & Co. London, 1892.

Taxation in American States and Cities. By Richard T. Ely, Ph. D. Assisted by John H. Finley, A. B. Thomas Y. Crowell & Co. New York, 1888.

The Corporation Problem. By William W. Cook. G. P. Putnam's Sons. New York, 1891.

The Public Regulation of Railways. By W. D. Dabney. G. P. Putnam's Sons. New York, 1889.

Mon Utopie : Nouvelles Études Morales et Sociales. Par Charles Secrétan. Felix Alcan. Paris, 1892.

An Introduction to Social Philosophy. By John S. Mackenzie. Macmillan & Co. New York, 1890.

The Philosophy of Wealth. By John B. Clark. Ginn & Co. Boston, 1889.

State Education for the People. By Sir W. W. Hunter and others. Subjects of the Day, No. 1, May, 1890.

The Labour Problem. By D. F. Schloss. Fortnightly Review, October, 1889.

The Road to Social Peace. By D. F. Schloss. Fortnightly Review, February, 1891.

What "Nationalism" Means. By Edward Bellamy. The Contemporary Review, July, 1890.

Progress of Nationalism in the United States. By Edward Bellamy. North American Review, June, 1892.

Profit-Sharing. By Professor J. Shield Nicholson. Contemporary Review, January, 1890.

Profit Sharing in the United States. By N. P. Gilman. New England Magazine, September, 1892.

Profit Sharing and Coöperative Production. By L. L. Price. The Economic Journal, September, 1892.

Subjects of the Day : No. 2. Part X. Social Problems in the United States. By Rev. Washington Gladden. George Routledge & Sons. London, 1890.

Current periodicals of value to the student of social questions are the Economic Journal and the Economic Review of London; the Quarterly Journal of Economics of Boston ; the Journal of Political Economy of Chicago ; the Political Science Quarterly, of New York ; Employer and Employed (George H. Ellis, Boston), devoted to profit sharing ; the *Bulletin* of the French Participation Society, and *Der Arbeiterfreund*, of Berlin.

INDEX.

ADAMS, Henry, the American character, 50.

Adams, John, four corner-stones, 130 n.; despotism, 208 n.

Agriculture little affected by labor troubles, 33; and tariff reform, 34.

America "all of a piece," 186.

American idea, the, 63; Hosea Biglow on, 64.

American literature, its beginnings in Massachusetts and New York, 57.

American spirit, shows a middle path, 15; its humaneness, 15; its hospitality to new ideas, 16; and socialism, 49; six features of, 57 seq.; a lineal descendant of the English temper, 69; individualistic and socialistic qualities in, 88, 89; and individualism, 90; not characterized throughout by individualism, 118; in no fear of socialism, 164, 169; and Nationalism, 207; will give the answer to socialism, 323.

Americans, a humane and social people, 65; the Greeks of the modern world, 77 n.

Anarchism the antithesis of socialism, 10.

Anarchist, a sentimentalist of the future, 2.

Andrews, E. B., individual liberty, 91; trusts, 315.

"Animated moderation," the party of, 14.

Arbitration and conciliation, local and State boards, 167, 256; compulsory, not advisable, 257; for transportation companies, 258.

Aristotle, the aim of the State, 322.

Arnold, Matthew, the political problem in America, 51 n.; American intelligence, 143; American holds the future, 190; Jerusalem not yet, 357.

Association, voluntary, in America, 83.

Australian ballot system, 169.

Authority and liberty, 3.

Bagehot, W., American genius for politics and regard for law, 73.

Baker, Sir S. W., the struggle for existence, 19 n.

Bancroft, George, American conservatism, 75 n.

Bellamy, Edward, his journal, 184; pessimism, 187; founder of Nationalism, 191; sketch of, 192; as an author, 193; as a prophet, 200; and American optimism, 201 n.; social dream, 202; as a political economist, 203; confidence as a prophet, 205; an inexperienced reformer, 206; advantage over his critics, 209; lack of intellectual seriousness, 209.

Bemis, E. W., municipal gas-works, 312.

Berkeley, Sir W., free schools, 131.

Besant, Walter, 26; socialist dream, 36; the Good Samaritan, 41.

Bible, property and labor, 223.

Biglow, Hosea, 64, 142; on the millennium, 206 n.

Billon & Isaac, profit sharing in bad times, 293.

Bliss, Rev. W. D. P., 230.

Boutmy, E., English and American Constitutions, 66; political wisdom and growth in the United States, 72; United States a commercial society, 76 n.; optimism and theology, 86 n.; democracy and philosophical theory, 163 n.

Bradford, William, on experience, 49.

Brownell, W. C., "French Traits," 47.

Bryce, James, 49; American ideality, 60; conservatism in democratic countries, 66; American conservatism, 74, 75; American enterprise, 75 n., 76 n.; success in America, 79; philanthropic and reformatory agencies, 83 n.; manifest destiny, 86; the two grounds of laissez-faire, 112; Americans as an educated people, 137; the universities, 143; doctrinairism, 163 n.; table showing State regulation, 165; America all of a piece, 186.

Building and Loan Associations, 260.

Burke, Edmund, on State partnership, 322 n.

California experience in State textbooks, 149 seq.

Calvinism of nature and history, 348.

Carlyle, Thomas, the Cash Gospel, 284 n.; industrial partnership, 297; the foolish and the wise, 332.

181 ; literary character, 193 ; its ideal a bureaucracy, 209.
Lowell, James Russell, earth's biggest country, 50 n., 323 ; founding a library, 156 n. ; " the people's whim," 180 ; on the Fathers of the Republic, 189 ; equality, 296.

Mackenzie, J. S., unrealizable ideals, 41; the new gospel, 334.
Maine, Sir Henry, the success of American institutions, 74.
" Manifest destiny " of the United States, Bryce on, 86.
Marx, Karl, and American legislation, 116.
Massachusetts, her influence, 55 n., 56 ; library system, 154 ; commission system, 314.
Masses in America, 342.
Maurice, Frederick Denison, and Christian socialism, 222, 223, 226, 227.
McCarthy, Rev. Mr., American school policy, 136.
Michigan, the University of, 55, 139.
Mill, J. S., 148 ; despotism, 204 n. ; cooperative production, 272.
Monogamy and socialism, 363.
Montague, F. C., the selfish theory of life, 18, 19 ; the State, 108.
More, Sir Thomas, quoted or referred to, 351-353, 355, 356; and modern world, 359, 366.
Morris, William, American freedom, 184.
Morrison, W. D., material prosperity, 347 n.
Municipal coal-yard, the, 218, 219.
Municipal lighting legislation, 116 ; systems, 312.
Myrick, H. L., " How to Coöperate," 263 n.
Mythology in social discussion, 126.

Nationalism in the United States, 191 seq. ; taken too seriously, 216 ; its practical programme, 217 ; and municipal lighting, 218 ; a ferment, 195 ; indebtedness to Professor Ely, 196 ; clubs, 196 ; magazine, 198 ; agitators but not leaders, 219 ; out of touch with the American spirit, 220.
Nature, an aristocrat, 341.
Neale, E. Vansittart, Christian socialism, 222 ; the Coöperative Union, 225 ; profit sharing, 225.
Nelson, N. O., 265, 329 ; resolutions of employees, 300 n.
New England, intellectual and moral leadership, 54.
New Nation, the, 196 ; on the Homestead strike, 201 n.
New Testament, the ethics of the, 19 ; its letter not an authority in economics, 246, 247.
Newton, Mass., appropriation for schools in 1892, 135 n.

Noailles, Duc de, American conservatism, 70, 71 ; American superiority, 73 n.
Novel, the philanthropic, 26 ; its importance in social discussion, 43.

Ohio, Constitution of, on education, 132 ; State text-books, 151.
" One-man power " in America, 81, 82.
Opportunism, best name for American social temper, 162.
Opportunist, position of the, 15.
Opportunity, equality of, 361.
Optimism, American, 83, 184 ; M. Boutmy on, 86 n. ; and Mr. Bellamy, 201 n.
Owen, Robert, Emerson on, 44.

Parker, Theodore, definition of the American idea, 63 ; " a taste of knowledge," 138.
Patent system, American, 91.
Peabody, F. G., problem of rich men, 331.
Peace and order, the first duty of the immigrant, 32, 125, 126.
Pensions and socialism, 321.
People's Party, and nationalism, 201 ; its platform, 302 ; its future, 321.
Personal liberty, love of, a mark of the American spirit, 57.
Pessimism of the socialist, 3, 187.
Philosophy and progress, 28.
Pillsbury flour mills, profit sharing in bad times, 293.
Political bearings of industrial change, 308.
Politicians, distrust of, in America, 81 ; and the people, 188 n.
Postal service, national, 316.
Poverty, method of its abolition, 35.
Profit sharing, and the coöperative societies, 225 ; as a training for coöperative production, 273 ; its extension, 274 ; its meaning, 275, 276 ; loss sharing as an objection to, 276 seq. ; a conservative movement, 284 ; for the interest of employers, 285, 288 ; its justification, 286 ; in bad times, 293 ; not a social panacea, 295 ; Carlyle on, 297 ; reconciles aristocracy and democracy, 298 ; its claims on the employing class, 299 ; recent progress in, 300 ; American Association, 301 ; literature of, 301 ; number of cases at present, 306.
Progress, American faith in, 85 ; rate of, 364.
Property, natural right to, 61 n. ; its safety in America, 70; moral discipline of, 362.
Proudhon, definition of socialism, 223.
Psychology, national, its difficulties, 46, 47.
Public opinion, its virtual omnipotence in America, 255.
Public spirit, an American characteristic, 82.